William Forbes-Leith

Narratives of Scottish Catholics under Mary Stuart and James VI.

Now first printed from the original manuscripts in the secret archives of the Vatican

and other collections

William Forbes-Leith

Narratives of Scottish Catholics under Mary Stuart and James VI.
Now first printed from the original manuscripts in the secret archives of the Vatican and other collections

ISBN/EAN: 9783337230722

Printed in Europe, USA, Canada, Australia, Japan

Cover: Foto ©Lupo / pixelio.de

More available books at **www.hansebooks.com**

NARRATIVES OF
SCOTTISH CATHOLICS

UNDER

MARY STUART AND JAMES VI.

NOW FIRST PRINTED FROM THE ORIGINAL MANUSCRIPTS
IN THE SECRET ARCHIVES OF THE VATICAN
AND OTHER COLLECTIONS.

EDITED BY

WILLIAM FORBES-LEITH, S.J.

NEW EDITION.

LONDON:
THOMAS BAKER, SOHO SQUARE.
1889.

PREFACE.

MANY causes have hitherto restrained Scottish Catholics from publishing important documents which might have supplied the chief materials for a history of the Church in Scotland. Meanwhile, much that was valuable has suffered from the ravages of time, or has been irrevocably lost during the troubles of the French Revolution, when the libraries of the Scotch Colleges abroad were either dispersed or destroyed.

We can, at this date, scarcely hope for the discovery of any hidden store of records to put us in easy possession of the severed thread of our Catholic history. It is therefore perhaps best to make use of such documents as are still within reach, and, as far as can be, to bring our gleanings together.

In publishing these Narratives and Letters, my object has been to make the condition of Catholics in Scotland, after the Reformation period, more clearly and widely known.

Without professing to be a consecutive history, they will enable the reader to form his own judgment from the evidence of contemporary witnesses.

The writers of the various narratives were not only men of superior capacity, but in many cases of gentle blood, who in the very flower of their age despised both the ease and comforts offered them, and the prospects of inheriting their family possessions, that they might become in their own country the despised, hated, and persecuted priests of Jesus Christ.

Their correspondence bears witness to two great principles animating them—their love of country and their love for the Faith. Years of concealment in caves and secret places, rapid journeys, hair-breadth escapes, captivity, and even death under torture and the privations of a long confinement, are ample proof of their earnestness.

Some of the following narratives contain a few hard words. I should have been glad not to have any such to print, but if I had suppressed them, I should have failed in my attempt to produce the materials for an accurate idea of those times.

W. F. L.

CONTENTS.

PART I.

NARRATIVES OF SCOTTISH CATHOLICS UNDER MARY STUART.

PAGE

I.—SKETCH OF THE HISTORY OF SCOTLAND DURING THE MINORITY OF MARY STUART.
The Scottish Nobility—The Clergy—Eminent Churchmen — Scotch Scholars abroad — Abuses amongst the Clergy—Henry VIII. intrigues in Scotland—Marriage of James V.—Rise of Cardinal Beaton—Sadler's Mission to Scotland—Ecclesiastical Reforms—Invasion of Scotland—Death of James V.—The "English" Lords—Imprisonment of Cardinal Beaton—The Treaties repudiated by Scotland — Cardinal Beaton's escape from Blackness Castle — Vigorous action of Beaton—Henry VIII. proceeds to extremes—Scotland devastated by an English Army—Plots to assassinate Beaton—Offer of Blood-money—George Wishart—Death of Henry VIII.—Somerset invades Scotland—Battle of Pinkie—Cruelty of the Earl of Lennox—The Infant Queen of Scotland sent to France—Mary of Lorraine proclaimed Regent—John Knox—Schemes of the French Court—The First Covenant—The Lords of the Congregation—Spoliation of the Monasteries—Destruction of St Andrew's Cathedral—Appropriation of the Church Property—Landing of French Troops—Secret Aid of Money from Elizabeth—Arrival of the English Fleet—Relations with France and Spain—Disasters to the French Fleet—The Treaty of Edinburgh—Claims of the Lesser Barons—Catholics ejected from Parliament—How the Kirk was established by Law—Claims of Knox and his Colleagues—Death of Francis II. King of France—Devastation of the Churches—Queen Mary invited to return to Scotland—Treachery of D'Oysel—The Lord James—Queen Mary's hesitation . . 3-58

CONTENTS.

II.—RETURN OF MARY STUART TO SCOTLAND. NARRATIVE OF NICOLAS DE GOUDA'S EMBASSY TO SCOTLAND.
Mary Stuart and the Reformers—Religious Disturbances—Attack on the Royal Chapel—A Message from the Pope—Letter of the Pope's Legate—Letter of Edmund Hay, S.J.—The Lord James aspires to the Crown—The Division of Benefices—The Earl of Huntly at Stirling—The Lord James a Mortal Enemy of Huntly—The fall of Huntly 58-84

II.—BISHOP LESLIE'S NARRATIVE OF THE PROGRESS OF EVENTS IN SCOTLAND, 1562-1571 85-126

PART II.

I.—NARRATIVES AND LETTERS OF SCOTTISH CATHOLICS UNDER JAMES THE SIXTH.
Regency of Mar—Regency of Morton—Mary Stuart and the Countess of Lennox—Design for abducting the young King—Letters of Bishop Leslie—Letter of Fr. John Hay of Dalgaty—Fall of Morton—Letter of Fr. Robert Parsons—Letter of Cardinal Allen—State of Scotland in 1582—Mary Stuart urges that Catholic Priests be sent to Scotland—Arrival of William Crichton, S.J.—William Crichton despatched to Rome—The Raid of Ruthven—Letter of King James to his Mother—James VI. and the Duke of Guise—Letter of Lord Seton to the Pope—Letters of William Holt, S.J.—Letters of James Beaton, Archbishop of Glasgow—Letter of Edmund Hay, S.J.—Letter of James Beaton—Growth of the Catholic Religion in Scotland—Public discussion on matters of Faith—Christmas at Dumfries in 1585—Death of John Dury, S.J.—Letters of James Tyrie, S.J.—Return of the Banished Lords to Power—James becomes the Pensioner of Elizabeth—The Babington Plot—Negotiations for the Murder of Mary Stuart—Elizabeth Signs the Death-warrant—Execution of Mary Stuart—The Armada—Pension offered to King James—James urged to assail the Catholics—Marriage of King James VI.—Remarks of Tytler on the Persecution of Catholics—The Spanish Blanks—Proceedings against the Catholic Lords—The Pope's Legate at Aberdeen—James urged to severity against Catholics—Battle of Glenlivet—Huntly and Errol withdraw from Scotland—Letter of Robert Abercromby, S.J.—Huntly and Errol return to

Scotland — Domiciliary Intrusion — James' Letter to Huntly—Letters of James Gordon, S.J.—The Ministers remonstrate with the Queen — Letter of Robert Abercromby, S.J.—Catholics at Court—Letter of Alexander MacQuhirrie, S.J.—State of Scotland in 1601—James' Accession to the English Crown 128-274

II.—LETTERS AND MEMORIALS OF THE STATE AND PROGRESS OF EVENTS FROM 1603 TO 1625.
Letters of Alexander MacQuhirrie, James Seton, Robert Abercromby, William Crichton, S.J. — Persecution of Catholics in England—Persecution in Scotland—Letter of Robert Abercromby, S.J. — Missionary Excursions — Letter of James Gordon, S.J.—Letter of the Earl of Angus—Imprisonment, Trial, and Martyrdom of John Ogilvie, S.J.—Imprisonment of Patrick Anderson, S.J.—Trial for Heresy—Death of Patrick Anderson—Imprisonment of George Mortimer, S.J.—Letter of William Leslie, S.J.—The Spanish Match—Death of King James . 275-350

III.—NOTES AND ILLUSTRATIONS.
Account of the Present State of the Catholic Religion in the Realm of Scotland, in the Year of our Lord 1594, by Sir Walter Lindsay of Balgawies . . . 251-360
A List of Catholic Noblemen in Scotland in 1594. . 361

PART THE FIRST.

NARRATIVES AND LETTERS

ILLUSTRATING THE HISTORY OF SCOTCH CATHOLICS
UNDER MARY STUART.

I.

SKETCH OF THE HISTORY OF SCOTLAND DURING THE MINORITY OF MARY STUART.

THE condition of Scotland at the beginning of the sixteenth century was most critical, and of all countries in Europe, perhaps, not one was more exposed to the horrors of civil and religious war. During a long course of years there had been a frequent succession of tedious minorities in the Royal Family. This had naturally given rise to many factions among the nobility, whose contemptuous overriding of the laws produced much weakness in the Government. The kings from James I. to James V. were not only long under age, but all died in the flower of youth,[1] before they could either reform the abuses which had crept in during their minorities, or place their Governments on a steady footing.

After the death of James IV., in 1513, the nobles, during the minority of his son, James V., became so powerful, that the Regent Albany twice threw up the reins of Government in despair, and at length abandoned them altogether. The Douglases soon obtained possession of the person of the young king,[2] compelled Beaton,

---

[1] Of these monarchs no fewer than three perished—the victims of anarchy.

[2] It seems to have been a matter of great importance for rival factions to get a prince into their custody. Thus, in 1526, Sir Walter

Archbishop of St Andrews, to resign the office of chancellor, and filled every post with their adherents. In 1528, however, James, with the help of Archbishop Beaton, effected his escape from the hands of the Douglases, and took refuge in the Castle of Stirling. The reins of Government were now delivered over to the clergy, to whom the king owed his liberty, and who were his natural protectors.[1] His first act was to issue a proclamation that no lord or follower of the House of Douglas should dare to approach within twelve miles of the court, under pain of treason.[2] The Earl of Angus was driven out of Scotland, and his estates confiscated.[3] The Earl of Bothwell, the Lords Home and Maxwell, the two Kerrs, the Barons of Buccleugh, Johnston, and Polwarth were seized and thrown into prison.[4] But though

---

Scott of Buccleugh was anxious to take James V. from the Earl of Angus, and the young king inclined to a change of masters; but the Earl's brother, having in vain attempted to seduce him " by alluring words," resorted to a more convincing argument :—" Rather," said he, " as the enemies take you from us, we must keep one-half of your body with us." (Calderwood, " Historie of the Kirk," vol. i. p. 98) When, in 1543, the Earl of Arran endeavoured to get possession of the young Queen's person, " it was in hopes that he should not only have upon his side the shadow of her name, but also might dispose of her by marriage as he thought good, and either feed the English king with promises, or draw him to his partie." (Ibid., p. 164.) The repeated attempts to seize upon King James VI., the raid of Ruthven, Gowrie's conspiracy, need no comment.

[1] The Archbishop of St Andrews became his principal adviser, and the important post of Chancellor was conferred on the Archbishop of Glasgow (" State Papers of Henry VIII.," vol. iv. p. 501). The Abbot of Holyrood was made treasurer, and the Bishop of Dunkeld became Privy-Seal (" Diurnal of Occurrents," p. 11).

[2] " Diurnal of Occurrents," pp. 10, 12.

[3] Ibid., p. 11.

[4] " De Origine, Moribus et rebus gestis Scotorum," Authore Joanne Leslæo, Romæ, 1578, 4°, p. 411.

excluded from Government, the nobles preserved their social influence. The real foundation of their authority was unshaken because that authority was the result of a long train of circumstances, and was based on a community of blood and language between the vassal and his lord. Therefore it was that the nobles, even such as had been exiled and attainted, were able to conduct an arduous, but eventually successful, struggle against the Sovereign. Excluded from all state employment, their anger burst out into act the instant that the Reformation promised its gratification. The plunder of the English churches and monasteries enkindled their cupidity, and they descried in the downfall of bishoprics, abbeys, &c. great accession of territory and wealth to themselves. The desire of revenge also was fresh motive for their exertions, and gave rise to a deadly contest between the Scottish aristocracy and the Church, which lasted without interruption for thirty-two years, and was only concluded by the triumph of the Protestant nobles, who, in 1560, overthrew the Catholic Church in Scotland.[1]

Unlike the nobles, the clergy of Scotland were conspicuous for their loyalty; and we learn from Sir Ralph Sadler[2] that they alone were capable, from their habits and education, of rendering efficient aid to the king in the conduct of public affairs. Interest, as well as intellectual sympathy, therefore induced James to prefer them to the unruly and unlettered barons, whose power his ancestors had in vain attempted to break down.[3]

[1] Keith, "Affairs of Church and State in Scotland," Spottiswoode Society edit., vol. i. pp. 35, 36. Buckle, "History of Civilization in England," vol. ii. pp. 209, 210.

[2] Sadler's "State Papers and Letters," i. p. 47.

[3] James' reasons are stated by himself in a very curious letter which he wrote so late as 1541, to Henry VIII. "We persaif," writes James, "be zoure saidis writingis that ze ar informyt that thair suld be

On the eve of the Reformation, the Church of Scotland could glory in prelates who were distinguished equally for their talents and their virtues. Foremost among these were Robert Reid, Bishop of Orkney, and abbot of two northern monasteries, known as the founder of libraries, the introducer of foreign schoolmasters and gardeners, the restorer of the buildings as well as of the discipline of the cloister[1]—also Alexander Myln, Abbot of Cambuskenneth, and first president of the College of Justice instituted by James V. in imitation of the law courts of France, one who united in himself the man of business and man of letters, the lawyer and reformer of learning.[2] The bishopric of Ross was held successively by several men of eminent qualities. David Panter, consecrated in 1546, whom Bishop Keith pronounces "a person of most polite education and excellent parts," belonged to a family of statesmen and scholars.[3] Another Bishop of

sum thingis laitlie attemptat be our kirkmen to oure hurte and skaith, and contrar oure mynde and plesure. We can nocht understand, quhat suld move zou to belief the samyn, assuring zou *we have never fund bot faithfull and trew obedience of yame at all tymes*, nor thai seik nor attemptis nouthir jurisdictioun nor privilegiis, forthir nor thai have usit sen the first institutioun of the Kirk of Scotland, quhilk we may nocht apoun oure conscience alter nor change in the respect we have to the honour and faith of God and Hali Kirk, and douttis na inconvenient be thame to come to ws and our realme therthrou; for sen the Kirk wes first institute in our realme, the stait thairof hes nevir failzeit, bot *hes remanyt evir obedient to oure progenitouris*, and in oure tyme mair thankefull to ws, nor evir thai wer of before." ("State Papers of Henry VIII.," vol. v. pp. 188-190, 4to, 1836.)

[1] Tytler's "Life of Sir Thomas Craig," p. 51.
[2] Ibid., p. 46.
[3] "The Quarterly Review," vol. lxxxix, p. 40-46. Knox admits the public report of his learning, his honest life, and his fervency and uprightness in religion. "History of the Reformation," edited by D. Laing, p. 105.

Ross after a very short interval, was Henry Sinclair, "the reformer of the law, and the patron of the literature of his country."[1] He was succeeded by John Leslie, "whose character combined all that was pious and amiable in the prelate, sagacious, firm, and upright in the statesman, learned and elegant in the scholar and man of letters."[2] James Beaton, Archbishop of Glasgow, beloved by all who knew him, was ambassador at the French Court for forty-two years.

The inferior clergy could also pride itself on many learned and virtuous priests, who, after undergoing for several years the various trials of a severe persecution, were at last banished; and who, strangers though they were, acquired, in foreign universities, a high reputation for character, ability, and learning.[3]

Unfortunately the same sad causes, which elsewhere led to the relaxation of discipline and the multiplication of abuses, had operated in Scotland with still greater force. The Church was completely under the sway of the king and nobles. During a considerable period the

[1] Tytler's "Life of Sir Thomas Craig," p. 274.

[2] Tytler, Ibid.

[3] M'Crie says: "They were to be found in all the universities and colleges. In several of them they held the honourable situation of principal, and in others they amounted to a third of the professors." In Paris alone, we find John Fraser, the fourth son of Alexander Fraser of Philorth, elected in 1596 Rector of the University of Paris; (Crawford's "Lives of the Officers of State," p. 282; cf. Borghese MS., i. 931); Patrick Cockburn, who held a Professorship of Oriental Languages, James Tyrie (of Drumkilbo), John Hay of Dalgaty, lectured successively on philosophy and theology; Edmund Hay was Rector of the College of Clermont; John Bossevile, James Laing, John Bellenden, David Cranstoun, James Ballantyne, David and William Chamber, and many others, were Doctors of Sorbonne (Præmetiæ sive Calumniæ, &c., auctore G. Conæo, Scoto, Romæ, 1621).

posts of highest dignity had, with few exceptions, been held by either the illegitimate or younger sons of the most powerful families,[1] men who, without learning or morality themselves, paid little deference to the learning and morality of their inferiors. According to contemporary and Catholic historians,[2] the negligence of these in the discharge of their functions, and the rigour with which they exacted their dues, had become favourite subjects of popular censure. When the new preachers appeared, they dexterously availed themselves of a never failing theme for invective in the scandalous lives, ostentatious pomp, and occasional exactions of the unworthy

---

[1] "James," says Mr J. Gairdner, "provided for his natural children in a manner that was scandalous indeed. One of these, Alexander Stewart, he caused to be made Archbishop of St Andrews before he had passed the age of boyhood" (Keith, "Historical Catalogue of Scottish Bishops," ed. 1824, p. 34). "In Scotland, so far from the centre of ecclesiastical authority, abuses had been permitted that were unknown elsewhere. Numerous instances of bishops of one family succeeding each other in the same sees show the extraordinary prevalence of nepotism, while the names they bore indicate the influence to which it was due. . . . It was owing to the landed aristocracy. In one see there had been a succession of Stewarts, in another of Gordons, in another of Hepburns; and the Church, which in all other countries had broken the neck of feudalism, which, even in its worst days, was the asylum of true greatness, and made genius independent of birth, fell, like everything else in Scotland, completely under the sway of the king and nobles. During the fifteenth century in England, Cardinal Beaufort was the only bishop who came of the blood royal; but in Scotland during the same period were two sons and two grandsons of kings holding the see of St Andrews alone" ("Letters and Papers illustrative of the reigns of Richard III.," ed. by J. Gairdner, vol. ii. pp. 59-70). James V. provided for his illegitimate children by making them abbots and priors of Holyrood, Kelso, Melrose, Coldingham, and St Andrews (Keith, i. p. 59).

[2] G. Con., "De Duplici statu Religionis apud Scotos," Romæ, 1628, pp. 89, 90. Leslie, "De Origine, et rebus gestis Scotorum," lib. x. p. 504 *et seq.*

men who had been thus unlawfully foisted into bishoprics and abbacies.

Allured by the troubled state of Scotland after the battle of Flodden, Henry the Eighth endeavoured, either by open invasions or domestic treachery, to bring Scotland into subjection to England, and establish the Reformation in the North. With this view, and before the son of James IV. was old enough to assume the government of his kingdom, more than a hundred of the principal nobles and gentlemen of Scotland had been seduced from their allegiance by Henry's bribes and promises.[1]

As early as 1535, we find Henry labouring to convert his nephew of Scotland to his faith. With this view he made an earnest proposal for a marriage between James and his daughter the princess Mary, holding out to him the hope of succession to the English crown. He despatched his chaplain, Dr Barlow, to present to the young monarch a book recently published, called the "Doctrine of the Christian Man," and, if permission were granted, to preach to the Scottish Court. James submitted the treatise to theologians who pronounced it full of heresy, and Barlow, finding every pulpit closed against him, wrote to secretary Cromwell informing him that the king "was surrounded by the Pope's pestilent creatures and very limbs of the devil."

Barlow was succeeded by Lord William Howard, who was intrusted to propose a conference at York between his master and James; but though James at first consented to meet his uncle, he afterwards found pretexts for delay, and the conference never took place.

Following the traditional policy of Scotland, and

---

[1] Cf. Tytler, "History of Scotland," ed. 1842, vol. v. p. 210. State Paper Office, Letter from Otterburn to Cromwell, 18th October 1535.

encouraged by the cordial approval of his own people, James renewed the league with France, and, in order to cement more closely this time-honoured union, he hastened to Paris and became a suitor to the princess Magdalen, the only daughter of Francis I. Their nuptials were celebrated with great pomp in the Church of Notre Dame on New Year's Day of 1537. Refused a passage through England, the royal pair were compelled to return to Scotland by sea. When the young Queen landed at Leith she knelt down upon the beach, kissed the very sand, and solemnly thanked God for having brought her husband and herself safely through to the land of her adoption.[1] But the health of Magdalen, fragile from her childhood, could not endure the keen air of the North, and forty days after she landed at Leith, on the 10th of July, her brief hours of life and royalty were brought to a close.

The popularity which had attended James's wedlock with a royal daughter of France, disposed him to turn his thoughts to that realm for a second alliance, which might strengthen all the political advantages procured by his first marriage; and, before the days of his mourning were accomplished[2] he had sought and obtained the hand of Mary of Guise, the youthful sister of the Duke of Guise, and by her became the father of Mary Stuart, Queen of Scotland.

If the first marriage displeased Henry, the second wounded his jealousy to the quick. Henry himself had passionately coveted the hand of Mary,[3] but she had kept her fidelity to the Scottish King inviolate. If Henry was exasperated at the preference shown by Mary for his

---

[1] "Lindsay of Pitscottie," p. 159.
[2] According to a letter from Wharton to Cromwell, October 4, 1537.
[3] Carte's History, vol. iii. p. 152.

nephew, his conduct during the absence of James in France was little calculated to allay the feelings of irritation and resentment which already existed between them. Ralph Sadler had been sent to Scotland to gain some influence over the nobility, and to sound the inclinations of the people as to the adoption of the reformed religion, or a maintenance of the ancient faith.[1] Dissembling his wrath, Henry again endeavoured to induce his nephew to follow his example, and warned him "against the craft and deceipt of the Bishop of Rome." He urged upon him the wisdom of making himself independent by casting off the "usurped authority of the Pope," and of increasing his revenue by seizing the lands of the Churchmen. James was unmoved by Henry's arguments, and Sadler had to report that the Scottish King would not listen to the sacrilegious proposal.[2]

An event, which happened about this time, was attended with important consequences. James Beaton, Archbishop of St. Andrews, who had long exercised a great influence over the affairs of the kingdom, died in the autumn of the year 1539, and was succeeded in the primacy by his nephew, Cardinal Beaton, a man far superior in talent and devotedly attached to the interests of the Catholic Religion. So good an opinion did James form of his abilities in the management of State affairs that he soon selected him as his principal adviser.

Beaton's accession to the supreme ecclesiastical authority was marked by the most stringent measures against

[1] Meanwhile the Douglases were maintained with high favour and generous allowances in England; their spies penetrated into every quarter, followed the king to France, and gave information of his most private movements.

[2] "State Papers, Henry VIII.," vol v. p. 81-89.

the Reformers, and this may have led many of the persecuted to embrace the interests of the Douglases.

Meanwhile Henry received intelligence of a coalition between Francis I. and the Emperor Charles V. Alarmed lest James should be invited to join it, he once more despatched Sir Ralph Sadler to the Scottish Court to discover, if possible, James's real intentions. Sadler's letters and despatches have been preserved, and throw much light upon the state of parties in Scotland.

The private instructions of the envoy were to destroy, if possible, the credit of Cardinal Beaton, who openly advocated the alliance with France. He was to state that Henry had discovered among certain letters, which had accidentally fallen into his hands, a dangerous plot by which Beaton designed to usurp the whole government of Scotland, and to place it under the absolute control of the Pope. James was poor, and Henry knew it, and Sadler was instructed to persuade him to replenish his exchequer by seizing all the abbey lands and church property, to imitate Henry's rupture with Rome, and to make common cause with England against France. He was also to renew the proposal of an interview between the monarchs at York, and to flatter the hopes of James' succession to the English crown in the event of Prince Edward's death.[1]

James received Sadler with marks of distinction and kindness; but the reasoning of his uncle made but slight impression on his mind. He respected the talents and learning of his clergy, who alone of his subjects had the education necessary to assist his councils.[2] "I thank my uncle for his advice," said James, "but in good faith I cannot follow it, for methinks it against reason and

---

[1] Sadler's "State Papers," vol. i. p. 9, 10.

[2] *Ibid.*, i. p. 47.

God's laws to put down these abbeys and religious houses which have stood so long and maintained God's service; and what need have I to take of them to increase my livelihood, when I can have anything I can require of them? I am sure there is not an abbey in Scotland at this hour, but if we mister [1] any thing, we may have of them whatsoever we will desire that they have, and so what needs us to spoil them?" Sadler urged that the monks were an idle unprofitable kind of people, and withal very unchaste. "Oh," replied the king, "God forbid that if a few be not good, for them all the rest should be destroyed. Though some be not, there be a great many good, and the good may be suffered, and the evil must be reformed; as ye shall hear that I shall help to see it redressed in Scotland, by God's grace, if I brooke life." [2] Driven from this point, a meeting with Henry was warmly pressed by Sadler, and politely evaded by the Scottish King. The wily tempter reminded him that his uncle was "well stricken in years," and flattered the hopes of James succeeding to the English crown in the event of Prince Edward's death. James was unmoved by the suggestion, and Sir Ralph Sadler left the Scottish Court without attaining material success as regards any object of his mission.

In the parliament which assembled during the month of December 1540, James showed that he was not indisposed to a moderate reformation of the abuses which existed among the clergy. Severe statutes were passed against heresy, but James also exhorted the clergy to reform their lives, declaring that the negligence, the ignorance, and the scandalous example of some of the

---

[1] If we need.
[2] Sadler's "Papers," i. p. 30, 31.

clergy, were the causes why Church and churchmen were scorned and despised.[1]

These acts were hardly passed when a rupture took place between Francis I. and Charles V. Milan became once more a bone of contention, and the alliance for the invasion of England, if ever contemplated, was for the present abandoned.

It was this moment which Henry selected for another embassy of Sadler to the Scottish Court. He appears all along to have believed that by means of a personal interview he would succeed in persuading his nephew "to renounce his spiritual errors." James may have given a reluctant consent, but Cardinal Beaton and his Council did their utmost to prevent the meeting; and they advised wisely, for we have undoubted proof that Henry had formed the design of kidnapping his nephew, and of carrying him off prisoner into England.[2] James sent a courteous apology, but, thwarted in his intentions of making either a convert or a captive of the King of Scots, Henry conceived himself slighted and insulted, and now determined to accomplish by force what he had in vain attempted to do by artifice or persuasion.

In the autumn of 1542 the old Duke of Norfolk was sent to the border with twenty thousand men, and gave to the flames two towns and twenty villages; but the left wing of the invading force was defeated near Jedburgh by the Earl of Huntly, and partly from this cause, partly from want of supplies, Norfolk was soon compelled to retreat. It was in vain that James urged his nobles to follow him in a counter invasion; they refused to cross the border, asserting that they were not bound by their allegiance

---

[1] Act. Parl. Scot., vol. ii. p. 370.

[2] For Henry's plan and the remonstrance of his Council, see Burton's "History of Scotland," vol. ii. p. 367.

to leave their native country. They knew that the war in which they were desired to participate, had been encouraged by the clergy with the object of checking the introduction of heretical doctrines. This hope they resolved to frustrate, and, being assembled on the field, they declared with one voice that they would not invade England. Threats and persuasions were equally useless. James, stung with vexation, returned home, and ordered the troops to be disbanded. It was to no purpose that he afterwards with a smaller army attempted the invasion of Cumberland. At Solway Moss the soldiers not only refused to obey the leader he had appointed to command them, but, without striking a blow, laid down their arms to a small English force. Thousands of men, with twenty-four pieces of artillery, being the whole of the royal train, fell into the hands of the enemy. This last disaster broke James' gallant heart. A slow fever wasted his strength; he sank into a long stupor, and refusing all comfort, died in December 1542, leaving the crown to his infant daughter, the Mary Stuart of later history.

The king had in his will appointed Cardinal Beaton guardian of the infant Queen and Governor of the realm. The nobles, however, declared this will to have been forged; and, encouraged by the exiles, who had returned to Scotland upon hearing of James' death, they put in Beaton's place James Hamilton, Earl of Arran, a very feeble and changeable man, who claimed to be at once tutor of the young Queen and Governor of the realm of Scotland during her minority. The country, torn by factions, and with only a babe for Sovereign, seemed to lie at the feet of Henry, who now altered the oppressive tone he had assumed towards the Scotch nobles and gentlemen captured at Solway Moss. He invited them to a banquet on the 26th of December, and after sumptuously entertaining them and treating them with the most flattering demonstrations of regard, intimated his desire of uniting the two realms, by a marriage between their new-born queen and his only son, Prince Edward, the heir to the English crown. He pointed out how largely it would contribute to the advantage of both nations, asked them to join in this good work, and promised that, if they would act along with him, they should find he was neither ungrateful nor ungenerous. The Scottish nobles received the proposition favourably on the whole, and seven of them pledged themselves under oath to invest Henry with the government of Scotland during the minority of their sovereign, and to place in his hands the young Queen, Cardinal Beaton, and some other noblemen, and admit English garrisons into the principal fortresses of the realm. Having thus purchased their liberty they returned home, bound by the most solemn obligation to employ their strength in reducing their own country to the condition of a province of England.[1] But information of this act had preceded them. On their arrival in Edinburgh these "English lords," as they were contemptuously styled by their countrymen, cautiously abstained from revealing the full extent of their ignominious bond, and spoke in general terms upon the advantages to be derived from the alliance with England. All their efforts, however, could not prevent the Cardinal from becoming acquainted with their intrigues, and the use which he made of this knowledge in strengthening his party inspired them with a daring resolution. Beaton was known to correspond with France; his act was construed

---

[1] Keith, i. pp. 65, 66. Rymer's "Fœdera," vol. xiv. pp. 796, 797.

into treason, the cry of a French invasion was raised, and the Cardinal was hurriedly seized on the 26th January 1543, and committed as a prisoner to Blackness Castle. Hereupon all the priests of the diocese of St Andrews ceased to celebrate the Divine Mysteries.[1]

The Catholics loudly exclaimed against Arran and the "English Lords" for so daring an act of sacrilege and injustice, and the people began to identify the cause of Beaton with the independence of the country, exclaiming against the Douglases and the Scottish prisoners as the pensioners of England. The Earls of Huntly, Bothwell, and Moray, suspecting that more was concealed under the proposed marriage and alliance with England than the friends of Henry dared as yet avow, offered themselves as surety for the appearance of the Cardinal to answer the charges made against him, and insisted that he should be set at liberty. Their demands being refused, these three earls, together with Argyll, supported by a powerful body of the barons and landed gentry, and a numerous concourse of bishops and abbots, assembled at Perth, avowing their determination to resist the measures of the Governor and the Douglases. They despatched Reid, the Bishop of Orkney, a prelate of primitive simplicity and integrity, to their opponents, bearing certain proposals. Of these the first insisted that the cardinal should be set at liberty, and that the Scottish ambassadors who had been named by Henry should not be entrusted with the negotiations of the marriage, but others chosen in their stead; and they asserted their right to be consulted by the Governor in all affairs of importance. Their message met with a blunt and scornful refusal, and the Governor charged

[1] Keith, i. p. 27. "Diurnal of Occurrents," p. 26. Sadler's "State Papers," vol. ii. pp. 137, 138.

them, under pain of treason, to break up their convocation. As they had evidently miscalculated their strength, they deemed it prudent not to push matters to extremity, trusting by their own influence in Parliament to neutralise the influence of the English Lords, so as to ensure the independence of their country.[1]

The temper of the nation itself was shown in the answer made by the Scotch Parliament. If the estates agreed to the young queen's betrothal, they not only rejected the demands which accompanied the proposal, but insisted that in case of such union Mary should reside within her own kingdom until she was ten years of age, and that none of their fortresses should be entrusted to Henry. Scotland was to preserve her laws, her customs, her independence, and her royalty.[2]

Warned by his very partisans that the delivery of Mary was impossible, that if such a demand were pressed "there was not a little boy but he would hurl stones against it, the wives would handle their distaffs, and the commons would universally rather die than submit to it,"[3] Henry consented that the young queen should remain with her mother till the age of ten, and offered guarantees for the maintenance of Scottish independence. But a private agreement was formed between Henry and his partisans, Maxwell, Glencairn, Angus and the other Scotch peers and barons taken at the Solway, by which they once more tied themselves to his service, and promised, in the event of any commotion in Scotland "by practice of the Cardinal or

---

[1] R. O. Scot., Henry VIII., vol. vi., No. 10. Letter addressed by the Earl of Angus and his brother, Sir George Douglas, to Lord Lisle, 16th March 1543; Tytler, vol. v. pp. 267, 268.

[2] Act Parl. Scot. ii. p. 411.

[3] Sadler's "State Papers," i. p. 70.

kyrkmen," to adhere solely to the interest of the English monarch.[1]

Meanwhile Cardinal Beaton made his escape from Blackness Castle, having in all probability obtained information of the second combination of Henry and his Scottish prisoners against the independence of their country, and succeeded in consolidating a formidable opposition. He entered into a negotiation with France, in which it was arranged that a force of two thousand men, under the command of Montgomery, Sieur de Lorges, an officer of great reputation, should be sent to Scotland. A convention of the clergy was at the same time held at St Andrews, and in this the likelihood of a war with England was discussed. It resolved to levy a sum of ten thousand pounds by a tax upon all prelacies and benefices of the yearly value of not less than forty pounds "for the independence of the Catholic Church and of Scotland;"[2] and such was the spirit of the clergy, that rather than the war should languish they vowed they would melt down both their own plate and the plate of their churches; nay, if need were, would take the field in person.[3]

Henry's resentment against the Cardinal, with whose practices Sadler did not fail to acquaint him, now rose to a high pitch, and he repeatedly urged the governor and his abettors to seize and imprison the prelate. Such, however, were Beaton's vigilance and ability, that he not only escaped the snares but for a while defeated the utmost efforts of his enemies; and many of the nobles,

---

[1] "The Copie of the Secrete Devise," "R. O. Scotland," Henry VIII., vi. No. 38; cf. Tytler, "History of Scotland," vol. v. p. 281.

[2] "Pro manutentione libertatis ecclesiasticæ et republica regni præservanda," (Robertson, Concilia Scotica i. p. cxlii.)

[3] Sadler's "State Papers," vol. i. p. 204, 211.

made aware of the plots which were in agitation for the subjugation of Scotland, eagerly joined his party, and prepared by arms to assert their freedom. With this object the Cardinal and the Earl of Huntly concentrated their forces in the north, Argyll and Lennox in the west, whilst Bothwell, Home, and the Laird of Buccleugh mustered their feudal array upon the borders.[1] They declared that they were compelled to adopt these measures for the protection of the Catholic faith, and the defence of the independence of the realm, which had been sold to Henry by Arran whom they stigmatized as a heretic and an Englishman.[2] Sadler informs us that Arran, in the event of the Cardinal becoming too powerful for him, had proposed that an English army should be sent to invade the country, with which he and his friends might effectually co-operate, alleging that, by this means, although forsaken by their countrymen, he doubted not that the whole realm might be forcibly brought under subjection to England.[3]

During these transactions the young queen was strictly guarded in the Palace of Linlithgow by the Governor and the Hamiltons. Aware of the dangerous intrigues of the "English Lords" for the subjection of the realm, Beaton exerted every effort to obtain possession of the royal child, and whether by the connivance of her immediate guardians, or from some relaxation in the vigilance of Arran, the Cardinal at last succeeded. To his party this was an important accession of strength, and having so far weakened his adversaries, Beaton now laboured to detach the Governor from England.

In the early part of September 1543 the Earl of

[1] Sadler's "State Papers," i. p. 236.
[2] Ibid., i. pp. 233, 234.
[3] Ibid., i. pp. 253, 256, 257.

Arran rode to Callander and met the Cardinal, all causes of animosity were removed, and a complete reconciliation took place. Beaton proceeded with Arran to Stirling, where in the Church of the Franciscan Convent the Governor received absolution for his having wandered from the Catholic faith.[1] Arran renounced the treaties with England, delivered his eldest son to the Cardinal as a pledge of his sincerity, and consented to a union with Beaton, whom he never afterwards deserted.[2] The young Queen was crowned at Stirling, a new council was appointed, and the vigour of its measures soon showed that Beaton and not Arran was its real head.

Henry's wrath at this overthrow of his hopes declared itself in a brutal act of vengeance. The resources furnished by the dissolution of the abbeys in England had been devoted in part to the building of ships of war. And then, while Scotland was guarding herself against an expected attack across the border from the army that had been gathered together by Lord Hertford, the Earl's forces were quietly put on board and appeared suddenly in the Firth of Forth. So great a surprise made resistance impossible. Leith was seized and sacked; Edinburgh was given up to the flames, and continued burning for three days and three nights, while Lord Hertford's commands were to put all to fire and sword.

"Do what you can," wrote Henry, "out of hand and without long tarrying, to beat down and overthrow the Castle; sack Holyrood House, and as many towns and villages about Edinburgh as ye conveniently can; sack Leith, and burn and subvert it, and all the rest, putting

---

[1] MS. Letter of Lord William Parr to the Duke of Norfolk, Sept. 13, 1543, quoted in Chalmers's "Life of Mary," vol. ii. p. 404.

[2] Sadler's "State Papers," i. pp. 282, 283.

man, woman, and child to fire and sword, without exception, when any resistance shall be made against you. And this done, pass over to Fife land, and extend like extremities and destructions in all towns and villages whereunto ye may reach conveniently, not forgetting among the rest, so to spoil and turn upside down the Cardinal's town of St Andrews, as the upper stone may be the nether, and not one stick stand by another, sparing no creature alive within the same, especially such as either in friendship or blood be allied to the Cardinal."[1] Sir Ralph Evers was remarkable for his cruelty " by spoiling and burning in divers places, not sparing to burn wives and bairns in their houses without any mercy."[2] As many as "192 towns, parish churches, castel-houses, and 243 villages were cast down or burnt, and the country was reduced almost to a desert."[3] The Lords of the English Privy Council laud these proceedings as "wise, manly, and discreet." They add that Henry took these doings of theirs in very thankful part, and gave them his most hearty thanks for the same.[4]

If Henry aimed at the conquest of Scotland, he gained nothing by these brutal raids; if the marriage he had proposed was still in his view, such a rough courtship disgusted the whole nation; for, exasperated by so many indignities, the Scots were never at any period more attached to France or more alienated from England.

Mortified at this disappointment, Henry became more

---

[1] Despatch of the Privy Council to the Earl of Hertford, 10th of April. Notes and extracts in the Hamilton Papers, 93, 94. Tytler, vol. v. p. 379.

[2] Leslie, "History of Scotland," p. 187.

[3] Haynes State Papers, 43 and 52, July-November 1544. Cf. Tytler, vol. v. p. 310, footnote.

[4] Ibid., p. 33.

vehement than before. In the autumn of the following year (1545) Hertford crossed the Border with a large force, and encamped before Kelso. The town, which was an open one, he occupied with ease; but the abbey held out, and the Spanish mercenaries who assaulted it were repulsed by the garrison, composed partly of monks.[1] Hertford brought up his ordnance, and a breach being effected, the church was carried, the steeple stormed, and its defenders put to the sword. The abbeys of Melrose, Dryburgh, and Jedburgh shared the same fate. There is preserved among the Cecil Papers a full list of all the " fortresses, abbeys, friar houses, market towns, . . . burnt, rased, and cast down by the Earl of Hertford, between the 8th of September and the 23d of the same, 1545. It chronicles the destruction of 7 monasteries, 16 castles, 5 market towns, 243 villages, 13 mills, and 3 hospitals."[2]

All this misery so wantonly inflicted did not yet satisfy Henry's anger. He regarded with intense hostility the man who from the first had detected and who finally defeated his policy in Scotland. For several years he had expressed an earnest desire to secure Beaton's person;[3] now he could not conceal an earnest desire for the Cardinal's destruction. On the 17th of April 1544, the Earl of Hertford transmitted to him a letter from Crichton of Brunston, containing a proposal on the part of the Master of Rothes and Kirkaldy of Grange, " to apprehend or slay the Cardinal at some time when he shall pass through the Fife-land, as he doth sundry times, to St Andrews."[4] This proposal met with Henry's

[1] " R. O. Scotland," Henry VIII., vol. viii. No. 79, 11th Sept. 1545.
[2] " R. O. Scotland," Henry VIII., vol. viii. No. 86.
[3] Sadler's " State Papers," i. 103, 106, 107, 249, 311.
[4] " State Papers," Henry VIII., vol. v. p. 377. The answer from the Privy Council is printed by Haynes, p. 32.

approval. The removal of the Cardinal would be "acceptable service to God." But he would not give the traitors a written warrant by which to pledge himself to pay the blood-money. The conspiracy now slept for a year, when we find it again agitated by the Earl of Cassillis, the friend and coadjutor of Brunston. There is still in existence a letter from the English Privy Council[1] to the Earl of Hertford, dated May 30, 1545, which refers to a letter from the Earl of Cassillis to Mr Ralph Sadler, "containing an offer for the killing of the Cardinal, if his Majesty would have it done, and would promise when it were done a reward." Hertford is informed by the Privy Council that "To the first point His Highness . . . reputing the fact not mete to be set forward expressly by His Majestie, . . . will not seem to have to do in it; and yet not misliking the offer thinkyth good that Mr Sadleyr . . . should write to the Earl . . . what he thinkyth of the matter, [he shall say] that if he wer in the Earl of Cassillis place, and were as able to do His Majesty good service there, as he knowyth him to be, and thynkyth a right good will in him to do it, he would surely do what he could for the execution of it, believing verily to do thereby not only acceptable service to the King's Majesty, but also a special benefit to the realm of Scotland, and would trust verily the King's Majesty would consider his service in the same; as you doubt not, of his accustomed goodness to them which serve him, but he would do the same to him . . ."

Again the conspiracy slept, for the blood-money could not be stipulated. But the plan was not given up, and Henry evinced the continuance of his mortal enmity against Beaton, by recommending the Earl of Hertford to advise the French deserters that they should show

[1] It is printed in "State Papers," Henry VIII., vol. v. p. 449.

their desire to be of service by trapping or killing either the Cardinal or the Governor.[1] This was on the 9th of September 1545, and on the 6th of October, about a month after, the Laird of Brunston is once more in communication with the English Government, "hoping to God that the Cardinal's proposed journey will be cut short,"[2] but insisting in a letter to the Earl of Hertford that "his Majesty must be plain with them, both what his Majesty would have them to do, and in like manner what they shall lippen to[3] of his Majesty."[4] After this the correspondence appears to cease, or at least is not preserved.[5]

Of the existence of the plots against his life Beaton was most likely aware;[6] and, looking on George Wishart, not only as a disseminator of forbidden doctrines, but the friend of his most mortal enemies, he earnestly laboured to apprehend him. Having heard that he was living under the protection of Brunston, waiting for the arrival of Cassillis, and about to hold a meeting at Edinburgh with those hostile to himself, Beaton determined on his instant arrest; and when arguments and threats had

[1] "R. O. Scotland," Henry VIII., vol. viii. No. 75.

[2] Letter from the Laird of Brunston to Henry VIII., quoted by Tytler, vol. v. p. 386.

[3] Trust.

[4] "State Papers," Henry VIII., vol. v. p. 550.

[5] This strange mystery is traced by Tytler, both in the text and in valuable notes appended to the fifth volume of his "History of Scotland."

[6] Such was the perilous position of the Scottish Church, that Card. Beaton, although thrice summoned by Pope Paul the Third to share the deliberations of the Vatican (in 1541, in 1542, and 1544), had not ventured to quit Scotland. (Theiner, *Vetera Monumenta*, pp. 613, 614. Raynald. Annal. Eccles. ann. 1544, sec. 32 vol. xiv. p. 85.)

proved alike unavailing to induce him to renounce his errors, he was led to the stake on the 28th of March 1546.

The death of Wishart produced a great sensation all over Scotland. Some praised the Cardinal for his seasonable severity; others muttered threats of revenge, and the Cardinal's enemies declared that there must be life for life. And so it was. On the 29th of May 1546, Cardinal Beaton fell a victim to the dagger of the assassin; and his mangled body, treated with every indignity, was suspended from the window of the Castle of St Andrews. In the language of Sadler the bloody deed was done "to please God" and "for Christian zeal" as well as for a "small sum of money."[1] Thus the mainstay of religion in Scotland, and the master mind of national independence, received the martyr's crown.

The conspirators who accomplished the bloody deed were immediately joined by a number of other adherents, among whom were John Knox and Henry Balnaves, amounting in all to about one hundred and fifty persons. They held the castle for fourteen months, setting at defiance all the Regent's efforts to retake it. With the help of the French the rebels were at last obliged to yield, and were sent to the French galleys.

A few months after the murder of Beaton, on the 28th January 1547, Henry was summoned to his great account. During the last four years he had wasted and destroyed the fairest part of Scotland with most wanton barbarity; "not so much harm having been done, these hundred years."[2] He had pulled down churches and

---

[1] "State Papers," Henry VIII., vol. v. p. 470. The principal assassins were rewarded with pensions. The master of Rothes got £250, Kirkaldy of Grange, £200, and others of less note got smaller sums. (Privy Council Records, February 6th 1547; *cf.* Froude's "History of England," vol. v. p. 31.)

[2] "R. O. Scotland," Henry VIII., vol. viii. No. 81.

monasteries, and murdered the leader of the Catholic party. He had organised and paid to carry out his work of destruction, a numerous party of nobles who had pledged themselves to unite their banners to his for the conquest of their native land, and, as they said, "to make the Protestant religion be taught in their territories, the Bible being the foundation of all truth and honour.[1] It is a matter of justice to remember how and by whom the ruin of the Catholic Church was effected, and Henry's share in it appears so great, that he may well be considered as the Father of the Reformation in Scotland.

The Duke of Somerset who now ruled England in the name of the young King Edward VI., inherited Henry's undying hatred towards Scotland. The English Monarch had bequeathed to his successor the resolve to subdue that country under the cloak of a marriage with its infant Queen. After an ineffectual attempt at negotiation, Somerset invaded Scotland with twenty thousand men. At this crisis, Arran was completely stunned by discovering, among the papers of Balnaves in the Castle of St Andrews, a document containing the signatures of two hundred noblemen and gentlemen who had secretly sold themselves to England, had undertaken to assist Somerset in the marriage project, and were bent on the entire subjugation of the kingdom.[2]

Notwithstanding these discouragements, the military array of the kingdom was quickly mustered. The fiery cross was despatched through Scotland; thirty thousand

---

[1] "State Papers," Henry VIII., vol. v. p. 387.
[2] "R. O. Scotland," Edward VI., vol. i. No. 49. Rymer's "Fœdera," (Syllabus), vol. ii. pp. 785, 786, 787. Tytler, vol. vi., Froude, vol. v. pp. 32-46. Burnet, "History of the Reformation," vol. i. p. 322; *cf.* Keith edit. 1844, book I. ch. iii. p. 87. "R. O. Scotland," Edward VI., vol. i. Nos. 5, 6, 40.

men obeyed its summons and collected in great force near Musselburgh. A large number of priests and monks, seeing that the hour had come for facing a deadly struggle in defence of the Catholic faith and their national independence, accompanied the Scottish army. Without armour or weapon they marched under a white banner, on which was painted a crucifix, with this motto embroidered beneath it, "*Afflictæ Ecclesiæ ne obliviscaris.*"[1] When the English came upon them, the Scots occupied a position of great strength on the west bank of the little river Esk. To their left was the sea, toward the right an impassable morass, while in front a river ran in a deep bed, which could be crossed by cavalry at one bridge only. Strong in numbers, the Scots believed that the English would refuse to fight and would try to escape them. To prevent this they deserted their unassailable position. Somerset's advance from the hills of Falside and Carberry, where he had been encamped, towards Inveresk Church, which partially commanded the Scotch position, seems to have been mistaken for an attempt to reach the fleet, anchored outside Musselburgh. The Scots crossed the river by Musselburgh bridge, passed to the west of Inveresk Church, and occupied the back of the hill, between which and the sloping terraces of Falside there was a depression. They also advanced southward, as though to attempt to occupy the end of the ridge which the English were leaving, and thus enclose the English army between themselves and the river. This movement hastened on the battle. The charge of the English cavalry upon the advancing right wing of the Scotch was repelled by the pikemen. But they were unable to

[1] W. Patten, "The Expedicion into Scotlãde," Dalyell's edition, Edinburgh, 1798, p. 73.

follow up their success, and covering his movement with his artillery, Somerset brought the whole of his army upon the Scotch, somewhat disordered by their change of position, and shaken by the discharge of arrows, musketry, and artillery. Their broken troops were attacked by the English cavalry, and the battle became a rout. But little quarter was given, the slaughter was enormous, and it was recorded by an eye-witness that "little pity was shown to the priests," multitudes of whom were slain and found mangled amongst the dead bodies of the common soldiers, whilst their sacred banner lay trampled under foot and soiled with blood.[1] Admiral Wyndham, who commanded the English fleet, vied with Somerset in the work of destruction. He had pledged himself—"not to leave one town nor village, nor fisher boat unburned from Fifeness to Combe's Inch.[2] Balmerino Abbey was destroyed; near Perth a nunnery was burnt, and the Admiral brought away all the nuns and many gentlemen's daughters." Dundee was taken and the Church destroyed, Dryfe's Dale was laid waste, above five hundred Scots were taken, slain, or drowned in the Nith; the prisoners, priests and friars, were dragged along with halters round their necks, amid threats of being tied up to the nearest trees.[3] The Earl of

[1] "Among them lay thear, many prestes and kirkmen as thei call them, of whom it was bruted among us, that their was a whole band of iii. or iiii. M. (thousand) but we wear after enfourmed, it was not altogyther so."—W. Patten, p. 72. According to Patten, one of the war cries of the Scottish army was "*Death to the heretical English*," which proves that the common people in Scotland were still true to the ancient faith.—Cf. Patten, p. 60.

[2] "R. O. Scotland," Edward VI., vol. ii. No. 57, Dec. 18, fol. 592.

[3] The Warden of the Grey Friars was executed. MS. letter from Lennox and Wharton to the Earl of Somerset, 25th Feb. 1547-8.— "R. O. Scotland," Edward VI., vol. iii. No. 53, 25th Feb. 1548, fol. 939.

Lennox, who was in command of some of the English forces, drew upon himself the execration of all humanity, not only as a ruthless soldier in the field, but as the perpetrator of a deed of blood that "whispered despair to his own soul whensoever it communed with itself."[1] In the last of Lennox's inroads, a body of Scottish horsemen, which he had forced into his service by getting their children under his power, deserted him at a critical moment. Twelve of these youths were confined in prison, as hostages or pledges, at Carlisle.[2] When the Earl of Lennox returned defeated[3] along with Lord Wharton to that city, he clamoured for the execution of these unhappy victims, and eleven of the boys were hanged by his orders.[4]

Had Somerset prosecuted his advantages, he might have imposed his own terms on the Scottish nation; but he was impatient to return to England, where he heard that some of the councillors, and even his own brother, Lord Seymour, were caballing against him. As most of the strongholds were now in the hands of the English, it was thought best to send the infant Queen of Scotland to France that she might be out of harm's way. Within a short time the marriage question was settled once for all, by Queen Mary being solemnly contracted to the

[1] Letter of Margaret Countess of Lennox, quoted by Miss Strickland, "Lives of the Queens of Scotland," vol. ii. p. 332.

[2] Ridpath's "Border History," p. 563.

[3] "R. O. Scotland," Edward VI, vol. iii. No. 57. Letter of Lord Grey, Feb. 27.

[4] Holinshed. The heir of Maxwell was one of the devoted number. The rope had been placed round his neck, but he was so very young and boyish that one of the English soldiers who had to do the work turned sick with horror, and could not pull the rope to destroy him, and so the poor child's life was saved ("Herries' Memoirs"). Maxwell of Herries lived to be one of the most manly protectors of Mary Queen of Scots.

Dauphin, afterwards Francis II., and a war of nine years was brought to a close by the proclamation of peace at Edinburgh in the month of April 1550.

From that period of frightful devastation, civil tumult, lawless ambition, and reckless deeds of ferocious passion, may be dated the decline of the true faith in Scotland, the progress of the English Protestant party, and the continued growth of the different sects.[1] The Scotch bishops were not unmindful of the evil. They assembled in convocation at Linlithgow under the presidency of John Hamilton, Archbishop of St Andrews, and drew up several canons, the object of which was to regulate the morals of the clergy, to enforce the duty of religious instruction, and to repress abuses in the collection of clerical dues.[2] They bound themselves by a common declaration to remain faithful to the Roman Pontiff and to the Sacred Council of Trent which was then holding its sessions, and swore that they would approve or reject whatever that assembly should receive or condemn. Arran had, in two successive parliaments, revived the old statutes against the teachers of heretical doctrines, but the transfer of the Regency to the queen-mother allowed the reformers time to breathe. By the advice of her brothers, the Dukes of Guise, Mary of Lorraine had formed the bold design of supplanting Arran in the possession of the supreme power. To dispossess him by violence would have been madness, she therefore quietly bided her time, employing every artifice to draw the "English Lords" to her party; she kept regal state at Stirling, till at last Arran, finding the tide running strongly against him, consented to resign, and the Queen-Dowager

---

[1] Father James Tyrie's Report to the Pope on the state of Scotland. (Blairs College MS.)

[2] Wilkin's Conc., iv. pp. 46, 47, 69, 72, 78.

was proclaimed regent. Arran's good will was immediately rewarded with the Duchy of Chatellerault. Being indebted mainly to the Protestant Lords for her elevation to the Regency, Mary of Lorraine was especially bound to prove her gratitude for the service they had rendered her. The favour she manifested to them, and the toleration tacitly extended by her to their ministers, and to the preachers who fled from the persecution in England, combined with the return of John Knox from Geneva in giving a new impulse to their zeal.[1] The enthusiasm of this new apostle, together with his rude and commanding eloquence, soon raised him to a high pre-eminence above his fellows.

During the winter of 1555-6 Knox was indefatigable in preaching, not only in the capital but in the provinces. Repairing to Kyle and Cunningham, where his friend the Earl of Glencairn was omnipotent, he proclaimed the doctrines of the Reformation. Under the shield of Erskine of Dun he preached in the County of Angus. The proselytes, inflamed by the lessons of their teacher, and by scriptural denunciations against idolatry, abolished, wherever they had power, the Catholic worship by law established, expelled the clergy, dissolved the monasteries, and gave the ornaments of the churches, often the churches themselves, to the flames.[2] A

[1] In the unpublished "*Narrative of the State of Scotland*" by young Maitland of Lethington, "Mary of Lorraine is censured for the liberality of her conduct with regard to the Reformers."—Miss Strickland, "The Queens of Scotland," vol. ii. p. 795.

[2] Lingard and Tytler remark, "it is not true to say that the burning of churches was begun by Knox at Perth. These excesses are mentioned thrice in the proceedings of the Council held at Edinburgh, which was dissolved before the arrival of Knox in Scotland" (Wilk. Conc., iv. pp. 208, 209, 211), and in the Acts of Parliament of Scotland (vol. ii. p. 470).

summons was issued for his arrest, but, having been warned by his friends of some imminent danger, Knox had again sought refuge in Geneva.

It was with pain that the Queen-Regent viewed these revolutionary proceedings, but she dared not oppose or punish them at a time when the approaching marriage of her daughter to the Dauphin of France induced her to win by condescension, rather than alienate by severity. Her efforts were successful; both parties joined in gratifying her wishes, and the Estates, not only consented to the marriage, but named a deputation to assist at the ceremony, which took place in April 1558. Unfortunately, three days before the wedding, the young queen had been advised to convey her kingdom away by deed to the House of Valois. The deed was kept secret, but Mary's act in demanding the crown for her husband as consort aroused suspicions. It was known that the government of Scotland was discussed at the French Council-board, and whispers came of a suggestion that the kingdom should be turned into an appanage for a younger son of the French king. Meanwhile French money was sent to Mary of Lorraine, a body of French troops served as her body-guard, and on the advance of the "English Lords" in arms, the French Court promised her the support of a large army. These were not the only schemes of the French Court. The Duke of Guise persuaded Mary Stuart and her husband to assume, on the accession of Elizabeth, the arms of England in addition to those of Scotland and France. This clearly meant that the Queen of England was a bastard, and that the Queen of Scots was the heiress of Mary Tudor. To this circumstance we may trace the beginning of that rivalry between the two queens which led to consequences so serious to both.

C

Alarmed at the growing power of France in Scotland, and perceiving that the union of Mary with the heir-apparent of the French monarchy would yield a considerable advantage to the Catholics, the Reformers entered into a religious covenant (3 December 1557). The subscribers, with the Earls of Argyll, Morton, and Glencairn at their head, assuming the title of the *Congregation of the Lord*, bound themselves to stand by each other at the hazard of their lives,[1] to forsake the "Congregation of Satan" (the Catholic church), and to declare themselves manifest enemies to it, its abominations, and its idolatry.[2] They now took the name of Lords of the Congregation, and sent forth their agents to secure the subscriptions of those who wished for a reformation of the church.

This covenant was considered by the Catholic party as a declaration of war. The Archbishop of St Andrews replied to the challenge by urging the laws against heresy, which since the death of Beaton had been abandoned. The attempt hurried on matters to a crisis. Walter Mill, an apostate friar, was seized and executed for heresy, and the Protestant party was roused to fury. All the efforts of the Regent to pacify and conciliate the two parties proved ineffectual.

---

[1] It had long been the received practice in Scotland that those who were about to embark in any dangerous enterprise should sign a "band" or bond to stand by each other, at the hazard of their lives. Mathew Paris says that it was a custom of the men of Galloway (a district which in his day included nearly the whole of the south-west of Scotland from the Solway to the Clyde), and one derived from the remotest times, before engaging in any dangerous enterprise, to pledge themselves in blood drawn from their own veins, to stand by each other to the death.—M. Paris, London, 1640, fol. p. 430, No. 20.

[2] Keith, "Affairs of Church and State in Scotland," vol. i., 154 (Edinburgh, 1845).

With the appearance of the Lords of the Congregation as an avowed league in the heart of the land, under resolve to enforce a change of religion, the attitude of the Regent suddenly changed. Smooth as were her words she expressed her determination to oppose the Reformation with all her power. The Lords demanded that bishops should be elected by the nobles and gentry, and parish priests by the votes of the parishioners, and that divine service should be henceforth conducted in the vulgar tongue.[1] These demands were rejected by the bishops, and the Lords resolved to defy both the temporal and spiritual power by openly celebrating the Protestant form of service at Perth. The preachers who had thus violated the law were summoned to appear before the Regent and her Council at Stirling. As they did not appear they were outlawed.[2] This sentence was a signal for open strife. The Lords wrote to Knox, whose style of preaching would, they thought, be useful in stirring up the people to rebellion. Knox was then in Geneva; he obeyed the summons, and arrived at Leith on the 2d of May 1559.[3] Two nights were spent in Edinburgh arranging plans for future action, that done he hastened on to Dundee, the head-quarters of the conspirators. It was on the 11th of May, the day after the leading "Lords of the Congregation" had been denounced as rebels, that Knox publicly entered the pulpit of St. John's Church at Perth, and thundered against idolatry. The indignation which glowed in his breast was soon communicated to his hearers. The

---

[1] Spottiswood, p. 120.

[2] Probably they offered to appear, but with so large a multitude behind them that the Regent refused to see them.

[3] Knox, "History of the Reformation," edited by D. Laing, vol. i. p. 318.

sermon being ended the crowd dispersed, and only a few loiterers remained in the church. The clergy, overwhelmed with grief at the exhibition they had witnessed, and the sentiments they had heard uttered by the innovator, gathered around the altar to expiate his offence, and to offer prayers to God. The altar was surmounted by an exquisitely carved crucifix, which was held in great veneration by the faithful, and behind it stood a rich painting of the martyrdom of St Bartholomew, at that moment uncovered. No sooner, however, were the tapers lighted around the altar, and the prayers of the Church intoned, than the hired agents of the "Congregation," who had come from Dundee well instructed and prepared for every emergency, cried out "Away with this idolatry." A stone flung at the painting of St. Bartholomew was the signal for a general attack. The followers of Knox rushed to the altar, assailed the priests, tore off their sacred vestments, and broke the crucifix to pieces. In a few minutes every chapel was ransacked, and all the costly furniture of the church scattered in fragments on the floor. Immediately the whole city heard of what had been done, and a mob, still under the excitement of the sermon, began to assemble. Tradition has ascribed to Knox the party cry, "Down with the crows' nests, or the crows will build in them again," which shows a far-reaching policy. The usual tactics of war are to destroy everything that shelters the enemy, and the Reformation was a war to the death against monasteries.[1] The cry was raised, "To the monasteries," and after hearing a prayer from Knox, who was again among them,[2] all

---

[1] J. Cunningham, "The Church History of Scotland," vol. i. p. 260.

[2] "Lindsay of Pitscottie," folio edit., p. 203.

the chapels of Perth were wrecked, the houses of the Franciscans, Dominicans, and Carmelites were plundered and reduced to ruin. Voices next cried out, "To the Charter House," and, rushing on to the noble edifice, the mob burst open the massive gates with a large wooden cross, which they pulled out of the ground near the walls, and in a few hours the monastery was razed to the ground.[1]

On the 9th of June Knox passed into Fife, accompanied by the Lords of the Congregation and his *rascal multitude*, as he himself lovingly styled them. He preached first at Crail. Here the sermon on idolatry was repeated and was followed by the same results.[2] On the morrow Knox marched along the Fife coast, westward to the burgh of Anstruther, which was also adorned with a church. It was *reformed*, and the rows of broken arches long attested how well the work was done. Cupar had already followed the example set by Perth.

The Archbishop of St Andrews, finding that the storm was approaching, and having only 100 men at his

---

[1] Keith's "History, &c.," vol. i., pp. 191, 192; cf. "Sketches of Scenes in Scotland," by Lieut.-Colonel Murray; Spottiswood, p. 122.

[2] Knox's own letters, quoted by M'Crie (Life of Knox, Edinburgh, 1846, p. 487). In a letter, of June 23, 1559, he thus describes the manner in which he *reformed* (such is his phrase) *the Abbey of Lindores:* "Their altars overthrew we, their idols, vestments of idolatry, and Mass-books we burned in their presence, and commanded them to cast away their monkish habits." Kirkaldy, who was an active agent in the work, wrote on the 1st of July 1559, to Sir Henry Percy: "The manner of proceeding is this: they pull down all manner of friars' houses, and some abbeys which willingly receive not the reformation; as to parish churches they cleanse them of images, etc., and command that no Masses be said in them."—Record Office, "Scotland, Eliz.," vol. i. No. 48. W. Kyrkcaldy to Sir Henry Percy, 1st July 1559.

command, fled from the city on the morning of Sunday, the 11th of June. That day Knox marched to the cathedral of St Andrews, and mounting the pulpit, repeated his denunciations against idolatry, comparing his own mission to that of our Divine Lord, who drove the buyers and sellers out of the temple. For three days he kept up, with unabated energy, a series of these inflammatory harangues. The result is easily told. "The fine cathedral, the building of which occupied 160 years —the metropolitan Church of Scotland, in which prelates, nobles, and illustrious individuals had been interred—was gutted and reduced to a melancholy ruin. Not only did the mob spoil the Cathedral church, but every church in the city, levelling the priory and the monasteries of the Black and Grey Friars."[1]

In alarm at the scenes of riot which had accompanied such fearful sacrilege, the royal troops were ordered to take the field for the maintenance of public order, and the defence of the lives of peaceable subjects. They marched to Cupar Moor, but there they were met by the army of the "Congregation," which now numbered three thousand fighting men, and was commanded by Lord James Stuart, the most skilful general in Scotland. The Queen Regent feared to risk a battle, and it was arranged that Commissioners should be appointed to enquire into all matters of dispute between the "Congregation" and the Crown.

In the meantime the fine abbey of Scone was devoted to destruction. Situated about three miles west from Perth, where now stands the Castle of the Earls of Mansfield, this abbey was venerable in the eyes of every Scotchman, as the place where the kings of Scotland

[1] Spottiswood, p. 124.

had from time immemorial been crowned. The torch was applied, and soon the beautiful house, in which our fathers had worshipped and our monarchs had been crowned, was burned down by fire.[1]

Only a day after this the noble churches of Stirling, and the abbeys, even to the very gardens, were destroyed by the mob in the presence and by the order of Argyll and Lord James.[2] The citizens, however, guarded the Franciscan Church, and it alone was saved. Proceeding to the magnificent abbey of Cambuskenneth, which lifted up its lofty walls amid the windings of the Forth, they reduced it to a mass of ruins. Flushed with these victories over the monuments of architecture, the Congregation marched upon Edinburgh, " for reformation to be made there likewise," as Knox himself assures us. Half-way they halted at Linlithgow, to renew their work of desolation. The Queen Regent fled in terror from Edinburgh, and the mob sacked all the monasteries within the city. " We arrived the 29th of June," says Knox, but such devastation was made, that " we were the less troubled in putting order to such places." A contemporary record assures us that Edinburgh presented one vast scene of riot and plunder. " All kirkmen's goods and gear were spoiled and reft from them, in every place where the same could be apprehended; for every man, for the most part, that could get anything pertaining to any kirkmen, thought the same as well won gear."[3] Even the Chapel Royal was involved in the common ruin. Its paintings and costly ornaments were torn down and cast into the fire, whilst its superb

---

[1] Cf. Knox, " History," book ii. ; Spottiswood, p. 125.
[2] Teulet, *Papiers d'Etat*, vol. i. p. 321, 4to edition.
[3] " Diurnal of Occurrents," p. 269.

altar vessels were seized for the private family use of the plunderers.[1]

Such were the first scenes enacted in the name of the Reformation in Scotland. One who a few years later was driven from the country by the same storm, has vividly described the use to which the plundered monasteries were now converted. "They made stables in Holyrood House, sheep-houses of St Anthony's and St Leonard's chapels, tolbooths of St Giles, &c., which this day may be seen, to the great grief and sorrow of all good Christians."[2] The example was infectious, and spread fast and far. The abbeys of Paisley, Kilwinning, and Dunfermline were attacked, and all their "popish stuff" burned.[3] With the monasteries of Scotland were destroyed the noble libraries, and the collections of manuscripts that had been gathered with so much industry, and so long faithfully guarded within these asylums, both of science and of religion.

All this was done in seven weeks time from the breaking out of the first riot. Yet these many deeds of violence and plunder perpetrated by the lawless mob, who finally carried away the bullion from the mint, gradually awakened the alarm of the citizens. So that the ranks of the insurgents began to grow thinner whilst the strength of the royalists increased; and, when at

---

[1] A few days sufficed to overturn to the very foundations Our Lady's Kirk in the Fields, the Monastery of the Greyfriars, and the other monuments of ancient piety which adorned the capital and its environs.

[2] "True Information," &c., by Rev. A. Baillie. Wurzburg, 1628.

[3] Sadler's "State Papers," vol. i. p. 468. "All the monasteries are everywhere levelled with the ground, the theatrical dresses, the sacrilegious chalices, the idols and the altars are consigned to the flames, not a vestige of ancient superstition and idolatry is left." (London, 1st August 1559). Zurich Letters, Parker Society.

length the troops of the Regent approached the city, "the saints," as Knox pitifully records, "quailed before the congregation of Satan;" a capitulation was signed, and Edinburgh was again occupied by the Royalists.

Towards the end of August two thousand French soldiers landed at Leith, and strongly entrenched themselves. It was in vain that the Lords of the Congregation appeared in the field and demanded the withdrawal of the foreigners. They were ordered to disperse as traitors, were beaten off from the fortifications of Leith, and attacked by the French troops in Fife itself. For their own safety these Lords were obliged to seek the help of Elizabeth.

Sir James Croft, Governor of Berwick, had already been in confidential correspondence with the leading men of the Scottish Reformation. On the 3d of August Knox was at Berwick and suggested that Stirling Castle should be seized and strongly garrisoned; that Broughty Castle should, in like manner, be occupied; that in order to do this, money to pay the troops must be furnished by England, ships of war must be ready to give assistance in case of need, and pensions allowed to some of the reforming barons."[1] Shortly afterwards Sadler and Croftes received a visit from Balnaves. When talking to friends Balnaves had no hesitation in unfolding the real design of the Congregation, and he openly declared that the principal mark they shot at was an alteration of the State and of authority, so that they might enter into open treaty with Elizabeth. They meant to throw off their obedience to their Queen, and bestow it upon the

---

[1] "R. O. Scotland," Eliz., vol. i. No. 80. Croft to Cecil, 3d Aug. 1559. Sadler's "State Papers I.," p. 456. "Scotland," Eliz., vol. i. No. 97.

Duke of Châtellerault; or, if he refused it, upon his son, who would be rather more meet for the purpose. In furtherance of this plan the Reformers expected they should receive some secret aid of money from England. Sadler and Crofts were delighted no less with the candour of Balnaves than with the designs of the party which he represented. They granted him £2000 forthwith, and gave him to understand that if Queen Elizabeth saw this sum so employed as to advance their cause she would show herself more liberal. It was money, in fact, that the Lords of the Congregation chiefly wanted; money to pay their mercenaries, and money to support their own state as feudal barons. Elizabeth was parsimonious and did not like to part with her wealth; but, overcome by the urgency of the case, she repeatedly sent considerable sums to "the Reformers,"[1] and the discovery by the Queen Regent of the source whence the money came only tended to make the English Council less heedful of concealment.[2] The Queen Regent determined, as Noailles expressed it, "to hammer the iron while it was hot," boldly charged Elizabeth with assisting "the disobedient and rebellious Scots," and informed her that in consequence it had become necessary to obtain further aid from France.

D'Oysel, who commanded the French forces, believed that he could easily hold Leith until the arrival of

[1] In October 1559, £3000, which Elizabeth had recently sent for their aid, reached Berwick in safety. Of this sum £1000 was by Sadler entrusted to the Laird of Ormeston. He had a further sum of 200 crowns for his own relief. "R. O. Foreign," Elizabeth, No. 153, 162, 163, 177, 211, 212, 215. In December Sadler sends to Arran and the Prior of St Andrews £2000 for the furtherance of the common cause. "R. O. Scotland," Eliz., vol. i. 155, iii.. Dec. 6, 1559.

[2] The Queen Dowager of Scotland to Queen Elizabeth, Nov. 13, 1559. "R. O. Scotland," Elizabeth, vol. i. No. 134.

succours from France, and so assured was he of the issue of the struggle in which he was engaged for his Sovereign, Mary of France and Scotland, that he professed himself ready to march against the insurgents who had retired to Stirling.

It was by no means, however, the policy of the Lords to risk the success of their enterprise upon the uncertain issue of a battle, "although proclamation had been made by the drum for listing more men of war, yet partly for lack of money, and partly because men had no will to hazard themselves, the Reformers could make no number."[1] When intelligence reached Stirling that D'Oysel was on his march thither, the Lords hastily abandoned that position, and commissioned Secretary Maitland to proceed to London for the purpose of obtaining immediate help from the queen.[2] Elizabeth had long been unwilling to give public countenance to rebels who claimed for subjects the right of sitting in judgment upon the title, the opinions, and the actions of their rulers. The peculiar delicacy of her position at this time, arising from her questionable legitimacy, made her specially sensitive of any discussion as to her right to the English throne. On the other hand, the treaty of *Câteau Cambresis*, so recently and solemnly executed, was supposed to have secured a long period of tranquillity for Europe. By virtue of that treaty England was at peace with France and Scotland, and no cause for the renewal of hostilities had occurred. Yet, under these circumstances she ordered the Duke of Norfolk to march into Scotland at the head of a powerful army; whilst a numerous fleet of English ships of war under the com-

[1] Knox to Croftes, Oct. 25, 1559. "R. O. Foreign Papers," Elizabeth, No. 138, sec. 2.
[2] "R. O. Foreign Papers," Elizabeth, No. 320.

mand of Admiral Winter, was cruising in Scotch waters. In doing this Elizabeth had a twofold object in view. Having undertaken to assist some Scottish nobles in their attempt to depose the Queen Regent, she now sought to prevent the arrival of troops sent from France.

This step had been urged upon her by Cecil as a matter of simple necessity, on the acceptance or rejection of which depended her own personal safety and the independence of the realm of England. Let the French but secure a firm footing in Scotland, it was said, and they will soon find their way across the border. The moment they pass the Tweed they will be joined by the English Catholics, who will rise in a body, and Mary Stuart will be proclaimed Queen of England. It is therefore wiser and cheaper to anticipate this movement by helping the Scotch Lords to drive every Frenchman out of Scotland. As soon as her preparations were complete Elizabeth threw off the disguise and formally intimated to the Queen Regent that, unless she sent home the French troops which were at that time garrisoned in Scotland, it would become the duty of England to expel them by force.

France lost no time in invoking the aid of Spain. Philip had watched Elizabeth's proceedings with increased jealousy and dislike, for he knew that the growing discontent of his subjects in the Low Countries was encouraged by her direct interference. There existed, however, a conflicting interest by which his wish to interfere was balanced and controlled. Should he prevent England from interposing between France and Scotland he might possibly thereby give the preponderance to a rival even more dangerous than Elizabeth herself. As the Duchess of Parma declared, the ascendency of the

French in England would be a crushing disaster for Spain.[1] The finances of Spain were so crippled that they could not bear the expense of a war,[2] and before Philip II. had time to come to a decision, his navy sustained a crushing defeat at Gerbes, from which he did not recover for many years. He there lost thirty-eight galleys and twenty-seven large ships, containing 5000 or 6000 men. Elizabeth had no need to fear the King of Spain. Her preparations were continued with greater activity, and she declared more firmly and loudly than ever that she would drive the whole of those foreigners out of Scotland.

It was no fault of Mary of Lorraine if this sudden declaration of the English Court found her unprepared for the conflict thus forced upon her. The troops at her disposal consisted only of a small body of French,[3] but they were highly disciplined and admirably equipped, and thought themselves a match for the entire force which Scotland could bring into the field against them. They had but to entrench themselves within the walls of Leith, and there await the arrival of the reinforcements which they daily expected from France.

The first object of the English Privy Council was, of course, to prevent the arrival of additional troops from France; and with this design, on the 22nd of January 1560, Admiral Winter took up a position in the Firth of Forth which effectually commanded the approach to Leith from the shore. The French garrison viewed with alarm the advent of this powerful fleet, but they soon

---

[1] Teulet, i. 463, 469.

[2] Correspondence of Cardinal de Granvelle, vi. 27, 40, 41.

[3] According to Maitland of Lethington, the whole number of the French in Scotland immediately after the arrival of the English did not exceed 2200 men. Cecil's calculation was a little higher.

drew fresh courage from the conviction that, within a few days, they would witness the arrival of their own gallant fleet under the command of the Marquis of Elbeuf.

In these anticipations they were doomed to disappointment, for the French squadron was signally unfortunate at a juncture when delay was ruin. Early in December four men-of-war, laden with stores and provisions for Scotland, were driven upon the sandbanks by which Zealand is surrounded, and at least 1000 soldiers were drowned. Still it was not too late, the loss might yet be supplied; accordingly, another fleet was manned and despatched from France; again a storm caught the second squadron, which had sailed about a month after the former one, and six or seven vessels, carrying about 2000 men, perished upon the Danish coast. Thus deprived of ships, troops, and stores, the French Court was compelled for a time to abandon the hope of reinforcing their scanty army in Scotland; and D'Oysel was given to understand that he must hold out for the next six months as best he could.[1] He had now no alternative but to shut himself up in Leith, and there await the attack which he knew to be impending on the arrival of the troops under the Duke of Norfolk.

In the early days of April the English army, consisting of 6000 foot and 1250 light horsemen, encamped on the fields to the south and south-east of Leith, and opened fire on the town. Here, however, the Regent's army made an easy stand against the Protestant attacks. The crippled state of France now induced Elizabeth to send a reinforcement of 8000 men, as she retained little fear of French interference. The Reformation was

[1] Calendar of State Papers, Foreign Series, 1560-1561, Preface, p. xx.

fighting in her interests on both sides of the channel. The English ambassador, Throckmorton, had orders to press the Huguenots to take up arms; Southern and Western France was on the verge of revolt; the House of Bourbon had adopted the Reformed faith, and put itself at the head of the Protestant movement.[1] In the face of such dangers as these, the Guises could send to Leith neither money nor men. Elizabeth therefore remained immovable, while famine did its work on the town. At the critical point of the siege, the death of Mary of Guise threw the direct rule into the hands of Francis the Second and Mary Stuart, and the extreme exhaustion to which the garrison was reduced, forced the two sovereigns to purchase its liberation by a pacification, known as the treaty of Edinburgh.[2]

By this treaty the French army was to be withdrawn from Scotland, the government during the young queen's absence was committed to the hands of a Council of the Lords, and the obnoxious coat-of-arms was no longer to be used. A special article of the Convention guaranteed the restoration of the ecclesiastical lands and revenues which the Protestants had everywhere seized, and it was stipulated that in the month of August next a parliament should be held, duly authorized by a commission sent by the king and queen. It was scarcely to be expected that Queen Mary should have ratified this treaty; but the death of the Queen-Regent had left the state without

---

[1] From the struggle for ascendency which sprang up between the Houses of Guise and Bourbon during the successive minorities of Francis the Second and Charles the Ninth—a struggle which was fed and fanned by the English ambassador in France—ultimately arose the so-called wars of religion, by which that kingdom was devastated during the remainder of the century.

[2] July 6, 1560.

a head, and the departure of the French troops had awakened the distrust and timidity of the royalists. The whole power of administration was thus virtually consigned to the Protestant Lords, and the treaty was acted upon as if it were good in every respect.

The article which permitted the Scotch to hold a Parliament, gave them the opportunity of effecting a reformation in the Church, if it were found that a majority of the representatives of the nation desired it. The estates assembled on the 1st of August, without any royal commission; the Parliament House was unusually full, and a scrutiny of the faces showed there were many who had never sat in Parliament before.[1] In ancient times the lesser barons had the privilege to sit in Parliament, but their number was afterwards restricted to one or two elected in a county, and none of them could have a seat but by a special writ.[2] Now, upwards of a hundred of these appeared and claimed their seats,—"a plain indication," says Bishop Keith, "that the faction have made it their business to convene their friends and adherents from all parts of the Kingdom, in order to terrify their Sovereign with the sight of such a splendid appearance, and thereby to force out of her hands a ratification of all the Acts voted by them in that numerous Assembly; and though it might be true that that great convention of gentlemen was *without all armour*, yet their arms and armour might be near enough, though not by their sides and on their bodies; and they, together with their dependents, could trample upon the rights of the queen at their own will and pleasure."[3] After some ineffectual opposi-

---

[1] Keith gives the parliamentary roll. The Reformers far outnumbered all the others. (Book i., chap. xii. p. 311.)

[2] *Ibid.*, i. p. 316.

[3] Keith, book i., chap. xii. p. 317.

tion, the claim of the lesser barons was allowed, and an overwhelming majority was thus secured in favour of the Reformation. On the other hand, all that refused to subscribe to the new creed were ejected from Parliament, and while the ministers from the pulpit urged the nobility to slay every Catholic priest and prelate[1] who stood out against a change of religion, it was suggested to call for those who, in conformity with the treaty of Edinburgh, claimed restitution of their possessions. As had been foreseen, when summoned, they were found to be absent. Forming a considerable part of the ejected members, they were unable to appear; and, although it was well known that "they had made their claim, and solicited an answer during thirty-three days,"[2] they were declared to have forfeited their rights.[3] The Protestants retained what they had seized, and were enabled by their newly acquired influence, and by English aid,[4] to prove more

[1] "All thir new precheris perswadis opinly the Nobilitie, in the pulpit, to putt violent handis, and slay all Kirkmen that will not concurr and tak thir opinion; and openly reprochis my Lord Duk that he will nocht begin first, (cf. Leslie) and oder to cause me do as thai do, or els to use the rigour on me be slauchter, sword, or at the leist, perpetuall prison: And with tyme, gif thai be thollit, na man may haif lyf bot without thai grant thair Artickilis; quhilk I will nocht. Thairfor provide remeid.

All the poor priests that will not recant are banished the town of Glasgow." Letter from John Hamilton, Archbishop of St Andrews, to the Archbishop of Glasgow. (Keith, vol. iii. p. 6.)

[2] Letter of Thomas Archibald to the Archbishop of Glasgow, at Paris, 28th August 1560, quoted by Keith, iii. p. 8.

[3] Keith, i. p. 325.

[4] "So completely were the English interests predominant in the assembly of the Estates, that Lethington and Moray in all important measures received the advice of Elizabeth and her ministers; and so far was this carried that Cecil drew up and transmitted to them the scroll of the Act which was to be passed in their assembly." (Tytler, vol. vi. p. 192.)

than a match for the adherents of the crown and of the ancient faith.

In the same Parliament an Act was passed to abolish the papal jurisdiction in Scotland, and to inflict punishment on any who should presume to submit themselves to it. The administration of baptism after the Catholic rite, and the celebration of mass in public or private, were prohibited under the penalty, both to the minister who should officiate, and to the persons who should be present, of forfeiture for the first offence, of banishment for the second, and of death for the third.

A confession of faith, framed by Knox and his associates after the Genevan model, was approved, and every statute which had ever been enacted in favour of the Catholic Church was at once repealed.[1]

According to Spottiswood, the Earls of Athole, Cassillis, Caithness,[2] and the Lords Somerville and Borthwick alone dissented, saying, "they would believe as their fathers before them had believed. The Popish prelates were silent."[3] But how many of them were present? Had they not been previously ejected? And, if any were present, is it not a question, as Keith remarks,[4] whether they were allowed to speak? The Duke of Chatellerault threatened with death his brother, the Archbishop of St Andrews, "if he attempted to speak a word at this time," and no doubt the same intimation was made to other prelates.[5] A protestation was however issued by Arch-

[1] Acts of the Parliaments of Scotland, 1814, folio, vol. ii. p. 535, 24th August 1560.

[2] Randolph to Cecil, 19th August 1560, R. O. Scotland, Elizabeth, vol. v. No. 11.

[3] Spottiswood, p. 327. Keith, p. 321, 322.

[4] Keith, i. p. 322.

[5] From the example of what had happened to his immediate predecessor in the See of St Andrews, Cardinal Beaton, Archbishop

bishop Hamilton, "in the name of the whole clergy and kirkmen of Scotland."[1]

The Lords of the Congregation had at last carried the point. The hierarchy was overthrown and stripped of its wealth. They had slain the enemy and thought they were to divide the spoil.[2] This, however, did not suit the views of the Reforming ministers, who held that it was right, indeed, for the lords to plunder the Church; as for themselves, they took for granted that they were simply to remove the old Catholic incumbents, and then take possession of their benefices. With this intent, Knox and his colleagues presented a petition to Parliament, calling on the nobles to restore the Church property, of which they had unjustly possessed themselves;[3] but to this request those powerful chiefs did not even vouchsafe a reply.[4] Hence, as we shall presently see, the Presbyterian clergy, smarting under the injustice with which they were treated, displayed that hatred of the upper classes, and that peculiar detestation of monarchical government, upon which they acted whenever they dared.[5]

Hamilton had too much reason to dread personal violence from the Reformers, and his own final fate amply corroborated the fears he may have entertained. He also ran a very narrow risk of his life about this time, at the destruction of the Abbey of Paisley, of which he was Abbot.

[1] Keith, vol. iii. p. 372.

[2] "In all this time all Kirkmennis goodis and geir were spoulzeit and reft fra thame, in everie place quhair the samyne culd be apprehendit." (Diurnal of Occurrents, p. 269.)

[3] M'Crie, Life of Knox, p. 179. Cf. Knox's "History of the Reformation," Edinburgh, 1848, vol. ii. pp. 89-92.

[4] Spottiswood's "History of the Church of Scotland," vol. i. p. 327. Keith's "Affairs of Church and State," vol. i. p. 321.

[5] Buckle, "History of Civilisation in England," vol. ii. p. 235, 236. In December 1561, the nobles declared that one third of the

The Convention of States, improperly called a Parliament, after abolishing the ancient religion and establishing a new form of worship in its stead, separated on the 27th of August 1560. Sir James Sandilands, a Knight of Malta, proceeded to the French Court with an account of its proceedings, but Francis and Mary refused to sanction the Acts which it had passed, as it had assembled without any lawful authority. The two sovereigns were deterred by the troubles in France from demanding immediate redress; and, in less than a month, all chance of taking action against the Lords of the Congregation was cut off by the young king's death on the 6th of December.

This event was hailed with exultation by the leaders of the Congregation. The government of Scotland was now entirely in the hands of the Protestant nobility, and the course of the Reformation proceeded without interruption. Nearly two years had elapsed since war had been declared against the monastic houses in the midland counties of Scotland; but throughout the other districts of the country, north, south, and west, numbers of religious houses still remained. An Act was now passed for their total destruction, and it was obeyed to the letter. "The work of destruction was superintended

Church revenues should be divided into two parts; one part for the Government, and another part for the preachers. The remaining two thirds were assigned to the Catholic priesthood, who, at that very moment, were liable, by Act of Parliament, to the penalty of death, if they performed the rites of their religion. 'Men, whose lives were in the hands of the Government, were not likely to quarrel with the Government about money matters, and the result was, that nearly everything fell into the possession of the nobles.'"

Even the small stipends, which were allotted to the ministers, were not regularly paid, but were mostly employed for other purposes. (Acts of the General Assemblies, 1839, 4to, vol. i. p. 53.)

in the north by the Lord James, Prior of St Andrews; in the west by the Earls of Arran, Argyll, and Glencairn; and in other parts by some barons that were held most zealous."[1]

"Thereupon," says Spottiswood, "ensued a pitiful devastation of churches and church buildings throughout all parts of the kingdom, for every one made bold to put their hands, the meaner sort imitating the example of the greater. No difference was made, but all churches either defaced or pulled to the ground.[2] The holy

---

[1] "The Lordis of Secreit Counsall maid ane act, that all places and monuments of ydolatrie suld be destroyit. And for that purpose wes directed to the West, the Erle of Arrane, having joyned with him the Erlis of Argyle and Glencarne, togidder with the Protestants of the West; quha burnt Paislay, the Bishope [of Sanctandrois, quha was Abbot thareof] narrowlie eschapit, kest doun Failfurd, Kylwynning, and a part of Corsraguell. The Lord James wes appointed to the North. . . ." (Knox, vol. ii. p. 167, D. Laing's edition.)

[2] "In the year 1560, the reformers of our religion, in the vehemence of their zeal, after having accomplished the destruction of some of the monasteries of Aberdeen, proceeded in a body to the old town; and, being disappointed of the spoil of the jewels and sacred ornaments belonging to the Cathedral, the greatest part of which had been previously secured by the Earl of Huntly and the Canons, they wreaked the fury of their vengeance upon this venerable edifice by stripping it of its roof, and carrying off the lead as their booty, along with the three valuable bells which had been presented to it by Bishop Elphinston. At the same time they demolished the choir and chancel on the east end, which was furnished with stalls for the accommodation of the priests in the celebration of mass. The further progress of the work of destruction was fortunately prevented by the timely interference of Huntly, who through his exertions saved the building from being completely destroyed. The lead of the church, along with the three bells was, however, carried off by these sacrilegious people, and shipped at Aberdeen for the purpose of being sold in Holland; but their avaricious views were disappointed, for the vessel, with the whole plunder, had scarcely left the harbour, when she sank, within half a mile of it, near the Girdleness." (Kennedy, "Annals," vol. ii. p. 342.)

vessels, and whatsoever else men could make gain of, as timber, lead, and bells, were put to sale ; the very sepulchres of the dead were not spared," and, among others, those of all our kings and queens since King Malcolm III., at Dunfermline, and elsewhere, as at Scone, Arbroath, Melrose, the Charter House of Perth, etc., insomuch that of all our kings and queens there is not so much as one monument left entire within Scotland.

"In a word, all was ruined ; and what had escaped the first tumult did now undergo the common calamity, which was so much the worse, that the violences committed at this time were coloured with the warrant of public authority."[1]

In the midst of these dismal scenes, the leading members of the two jarring parties which divided Scotland—the adherents of the old faith and the supporters of the Reformation—had each sent a deputy to invite Mary Stuart to return to Scotland. The Catholic party sent for this purpose John Leslie, afterwards the celebrated bishop of Ross ; the Protestants were represented by Lord James Stuart, the natural brother of the queen. Leslie tells us that he warned the queen not to allow herself to be ensnared by the artifices of her brother, who would probably advise her to bring with her no French forces into Scotland, and would strive to insinuate himself so far into her good graces, as to obtain under her the chief management of affairs, and use his power to crush the Catholic Religion, wrest the sceptre out of her hand, and set the crown upon his own head. In the name of the Catholic nobility Leslie entreated Mary either to retain her brother in France, until she

---

[1] Spottiswood, p. 175. Cf. Innes' Essay on the ancient inhabitants of Scotland in "The Historians of Scotland," vol. vii. p. 307, Edinburgh, 1870.

had arrived in Scotland, and had settled her affairs at home, or at least to come supported by a military force from France. The Catholic nobles promised, if she decided on landing at Aberdeen, where every one was of her own religion, they would meet her with twenty thousand men, and enable her to repeal, with a high hand, all the statutes that had been passed by the illegal Parliament, and to re-establish both Church and State on the old footing.¹ But the much-abused French counsellors of her mother, the unfortunate Queen-Regent, and d'Oysel especially, in whom Mary Stuart placed such confidence, although he was untrue to her,² convinced her of the impolicy of attempting to put down the reformed party by force, and suggested the expediency of her conciliating those who had hitherto been formidable opposers of her Government by taking them into office. They recommended her to bestow her favour on the Lord James, Prior of St Andrews, and the Earl of Argyll, who had married her illegitimate sister, the Lady Jane, and by all means to secure the services of the Lords of Lethington and Grange.³

James Stuart had been brought up with the young Mary, who placed full confidence in the playmate and friend of her happy, childish days. James was received with extreme cordiality as well by his sister as by her uncles. Mary not only treated him with as much favour and distinction as if he had been a legitimate scion of the royal house of Scotland, but consulted him on her most

¹ Leslie, "De Rebus Gestis Scotorum," Romæ, 1675, p. 531.

² d'Oysel at this time acted in the interest of Elizabeth. "This," says Tytler, "is quite apparent from the secret correspondence of Throckmorton and Cecil in the State Paper Office."

³ F. James Tyrie's MS. Memorial on the State of Scotland (Blairs College Library). Sir James Melvill's "Memoirs," folio, London, 1683, p. 26.

private affairs, and was disposed to grant him a commission to govern her realm till her proposed return in August. Had Mary been aware that the man in whom she was about to confide was already the pensioned spy of Elizabeth, and had recommended Cecil to intercept her on her voyage to Scotland,[1] she would have hesitated before she entrusted herself to the guidance of one so certain to play her false. But of this her open and unsuspicious disposition left her in ignorance; and one of the most fatal defects in her character was the facility with which she allowed her affections to be engaged, and her confidence to be won by all towards whom she felt drawn.

If Mary adopted externally her brother's policy of accepting the religious changes in Scotland, she was at heart resolved to remain firmly attached to the Catholic faith. Throckmorton had no doubt been instructed to sound her real sentiments upon this important point. But she stopped him at once by a frank avowal of the truth; "I will be plain with you, the religion which I profess I take to be the most acceptable to God, and indeed, neither do I know, nor desire to know, any other. I have been brought up in this religion, and who might credit me in anything if I might show myself light in this case." She concluded: "You may perceive that I am none of those that will change my religion every year; and as I told you in the beginning, I mean to constrain none of my subjects, but would wish they were all as I am; and I trust they shall have no support to constrain me."[2]

[1] Tytler ed. 1842, vol. vi. p. 222-5; Hardwicke, "State Papers," i. 157; Keith, vol., ii. p. 57, 58, edit. 1850; Chalmers's "History of Mary Queen of Scots," i. p. 63.

[2] Throckmorton to Elizabeth, 23d June. Keith ed. 1850, vol. ii. p. 33.

Mary was only nineteen. She had neither troops nor money, nor any other means of making head against her rebellious subjects. The Princes of Lorraine, apprehensive that she might possibly be driven out of her own realm, at last came to the following arrangement. The Earls of Huntly and Arran were the two most powerful nobles of the kingdom, and were mutually united by kindred and friendship; moreover the realm of Scotland descended to them by hereditary right after the Queen. There was, therefore, grave cause for fear lest these two families should coalesce, and either make the Queen prisoner or expel her from the throne. The wisest plan, in the opinion of the Princes of Lorraine, was for the Queen to follow the advice of the Earl of Moray, who was not only her brother, but also a man of considerable influence among the nobility, and (this being the principal consideration) accounted by them as free from any ambitious aspirations after royal power.[1] It was under the influence of such ill-starred instructions as these that Mary returned to Scotland.

[1] Father Tyrie's Report upon the state of Scotland during the reign of Queen Mary, written in A.D. 1594 and sent to Pope Clement VIII. (Blairs College MSS.). The report is entitled: "Quo tempore Scotia Religionem Christianam susceperit, a quibus gradibus in heresim sit delapsa, deque præsente illius statu in iis quæ ad Religionem spectant, brevissima narratio." It was written in the year 1595 by Father James Tyrie, S.J., who was born at Drumkilbo in 1543, and entered the Society of Jesus at Rome on the 19th of August 1563. He published the first part of the Report in 1594, and entitled it: "De Antiquitate Christianæ religionis apud Scotos," 4°, Romæ, 1594. A translation of the second part was published for the first time by the Rev. F. J. Stevenson, S.J., in his "Memorials of the Reign of Mary Stuart," Edinburgh, 1883. F. Tyrie died on the 20th of March 1597.

II.

RETURN OF MARY STUART TO SCOTLAND—NARRATIVE OF NICOLAS DE GOUDA'S EMBASSY TO SCOTLAND.

ROBERTSON pictures Scotland as being "in a state of pure anarchy when the government fell into the hands of a young queen, not nineteen years of age, unacquainted with the manners and laws of her country, a stranger to her subjects, without experience, without allies, and without a friend." The Catholic nobles, the Catholic clergy,—her best friends, excluded from all State employment, expelled from their houses, and spoiled of all their property, were now outlaws and exiles.[1]

The insubordination of the Scotch aristocracy was of itself sufficient to render any royal rule a task of great difficulty. Unfortunately for the young Queen, two other causes combined with it to make this government impossible. They were, first, the jealous enmity of Queen Elizabeth, who, with men, money, spies, and plots, never ceased to weary and trouble her; and, secondly, the most potent and dangerous religious hatred of many of her subjects. "The preachers of the Word of God," wrote Randolph to Cecil, "will make the place too hot for the woman when she comes."

With a heavy heart Mary bade farewell to the receding shores of France, and on the 20th of August landed at Leith. Her reception seemed to chide her forebodings.

[1] Leslie, lib. x. p. 527.

She had landed a fortnight before she was expected, yet the whole population poured out to meet her. Hearty greetings, enthusiastic cheers from all classes,— noble, burgher, and peasant,—at once dispelled her fears; she thought she had wronged her native land, and she entered the palace of her fathers with bright anticipations.

That very night she was serenaded by the psalm-singing of a mob of Reformers. "There came under her windows," says an eye-witness, " six hundred ragamuffins, who gave her a concert of the vilest fiddles and little rebecs, which are as bad as they can be in that country, and accompanied them with singing psalms, but so wretchedly out of tune and concord that nothing could be worse. Ah, what melody it was, what a lullaby for the night."[1] These solemn serenaders were the minstrels and musicians of the congregation. To close her eyes during the first three nights of her abode in her own palace, was impossible in consequence of the diligent zeal with which the unwearied psalmodists continued their nocturnal chorus. A few days after, one of her chaplains narrowly escaped being immolated as "a priest of Baal."

Nothing further was settled about religion than that it should be permitted to remain as it stood at the date of her return home until the meeting of Parliament, at which period the Queen and the Princes of Lorraine imagined that the Catholic faith would be restored to its former condition. The leading Reformers, however, contrived to prevent any such meeting from being held,[2] and construed the concession made to be an establishment of their doctrines and worship, and an abolition of the religion of the State.

"The Queen having protested that of the two she

[1] Brantôme in Jebb's Collection, vol. ii., p. 485.
[2] Father Tyrie's "Report."

would rather lose her crown than the exercise of her religion, an exception was made in her favour. She was allowed to have solemn High Mass daily in her chapel, and might then cause Divine service to be celebrated according to the form of the Catholic Church, with permission that such of her subjects might assist thereat as had not made a profession of faith to the contrary. Leave was also granted for the Canons of the Chapel Royal of Stirling to celebrate Mass in the Queen's absence."[1]

Notwithstanding this agreement passed in Council, the celebration of Mass in the Chapel Royal on the following Sunday, 24th of August 1561, occasioned a tumult which was with difficulty appeased. The more intolerant of the Reformers had resolved to resist by force every attempt to raise up the "Idol," as they termed the Mass, once more in the land. When the Divine service was about to begin, Patrick, Lord Lindsay, clad in full armour, and followed by a party of zealots, rushed into the Chapel brandishing his sword, and shouting aloud, " The idolater priest shall die the death." The Lord James, however, opposed the violence, and placing himself at the door of the chapel, overawed the multitude, and preserved the lives of the chaplains who officiated, " and then," says Knox, " the godly departed with grief of heart."[2]

In spite of Mary's efforts to conciliate the Reformers these seemed to take every possible opportunity of insulting her religion. On the 2d of September she was entertained at a banquet in Edinburgh Castle, and after the repast it was intended to have burnt a priest in effigy, but the interference of the Earl of Huntly

---

[1] Father Tyrie's "Report."

[2] Knox, "History of the Reformation," book iv., p. 270, David Laing's edition. Cf. Randolph to Cecil, 24th September 1561; "Keith," vol. ii., p. 85.

prevented this fresh outrage.[1] A few days after Mary proceeded to Stirling Castle. On the Sunday morning during the Mass which she had ordered to be said in her private chapel, "the Earl of Argyll and the Lord James so disturbed the choir that some, both priests and clerks, left their places with broken heads and bloody ears." "It was," observes Randolph, "sport alone for some that were there to behold it. Others there were," continues he, in allusion to the young Queen and her ladies, "that shed a tear or two and made no more of the matter."[2] A similar outrage was repeated a few weeks after. On All-hallow day during Mass one of Mary's priests was set upon by a servant of the Lord Robert.[3] Scarcely had the Queen returned to her metropolis when Knox and some of the preachers threatened the nation with the vengeance of Heaven if idolatry was suffered to remain. We learn further from Randolph that the question began to be mooted whether the princess, being an idolater, was to be obeyed even in civil matters. Mary, however, gradually succeeded in softening the asperity which many had felt towards her because of her religion. Her beauty, her grace, her affable and winning manners, charmed all who were admitted into her presence. There was in her some enchantment by which men were bewitched.[4] Within two months after her arrival she felt herself strong enough to take a step in defence of Catholics. On two occasions the magistrates of Edinburgh had published a proclamation requiring all priests, monks, friars, and

---

[1] "Randolph to Cecil, 7th September 1561" (given in "Keith," vol. ii., p. 82).

[2] "Keith," vol. ii. p. 86; "Randolph to Cecil, 24th September 1561."

[3] Nov. 4, Wright's "Eliz.," i. 85.

[4] Knox's "History," book iv., p. 276.

nuns to leave the city within eighteen hours, under pain of being carted through the town and burned upon the cheek. The Queen instantly issued a counter-proclamation, commanding the Town Council to meet and deprive the provost and bailies of their offices. The Council obeyed, and elected others in their stead.[1] Convinced, however, that from France, distracted as it was by civil and religious dissension, she could derive no support, Mary steadily carried out the advice of her uncles to subdue by conciliation the hostility of her opponents. She appointed a council of twelve, of whom seven were reformers,[2] and she continued to follow the advice of her brother, the Lord James, on all important subjects.[3]

Mary, having settled her Cabinet and Council, and made the necessary diplomatic appointments, was desirous of showing herself to her people, and acquainting herself with the condition of her realm, by undertaking a progress through the central counties. She was making preparations for her departure when she learnt that a Jesuit had arrived in Scotland with a secret message from the Pope.[4] So violent at this time was the repugnance of the reformers to any intercourse with Rome that Mary did not dare to receive him openly; but, whilst the Protestant nobles were at the sermon, he was

---

[1] Keith's "History," book ii., chap. ii.

[2] "Spottiswood," p. 179.

[3] "R. O. Scot. Eliz.," vol. vi., No. 84; "Lord James to Cecil, 8th Nov. 1561." By a special Act, which Mary ordered to be inserted in the Book of Privy Council, it was declared: "Whatever the Lord James, by the advice of the most part of the Lords of the Privy Council, happens to do, . . . the same shall be held as lawfully done, as if special commission were given to him, upon every point and particle thereof, in the most ample form under the great seal ("Keith," ii., p. 107).

[4] Letter of Randolph to Cecil, 7th Dec. 1561 ("Keith," ii., p. 114).

conveyed by stealth into the Queen's closet. The Pope's legate was Nicolas de Gouda, who in the following letter has left us a most interesting account of his interview with Mary:

Nicolas de Gouda, of the Society of Jesus, to James Laynez, General of the Society of Jesus.

"VERY REVEREND FATHER IN CHRIST,—PAX CHRISTI. —Being in Holland at Easter, I received on Tuesday in Holy Week a letter from the Reverend Father Everard, the Provincial, calling me to Lorraine. I went, and he showed me a letter from the Rev. Father Salmeron, Vicar-General, along with an apostolic brief and a letter from the most Reverend Cardinal Armelius, directing me to proceed to Scotland to deliver the apostolic brief to the queen, the bishops, and some of the ministers of state.

"I did not set off at once, but waited till June, for reasons already explained in my letters, and in those of the Rev. Father Provincial, addressed to the Cardinal and to the Vicar-General, which I need not here repeat. I will only relate the particulars of my mission, and what occurred on my arrival, and introduction to the persons to whom I was accredited; with a few words about their situation and that of the kingdom generally.

"Your Reverence will easily gather why I did not write to report my proceedings sooner to the Cardinal and to your Reverence.

"By the singular favour of God, who sweetly disposes all things, I was just starting from Lorraine when I perceived a wonderful increase in my strength, beyond any expectation of myself or others. This was not all, for a

Scottish priest, named Edmund Hay,[1] a Bachelor of Theology, came and offered to go to Scotland with me. He not only did this, but with extraordinary charity remained with me all the time I was there, and but for his aid I hardly think I could have accomplished what I came for. Guided by this good man, as by an angel Raphael, I reached Antwerp on the 10th of June, where through God's goodness and providence I found a Scottish vessel on the point of sailing, so that the Scottish heretics on shore and on board, whose suspicions were somewhat aroused, had no time to ask questions or try to stop us. They would certainly have done so, had they but known on what errand we were going. We went on board, Christ accompanying us, and sailed out to sea that day, June 10th, with a favourable wind. Next day a great storm rose, and we were in imminent danger of being sunk, but the Lord Jesus delivered us through His goodness, the prayers of your Reverence, and those of the Society. We reached Scotland safely in nine days. Before we left the ship the heretical Scots, who were many in number, and who now very strongly suspected us, began to question Mr Edmund Hay about me; who I was, and why I had come? He answered rather stiffly that he had nothing to do with me, and that I was old enough to speak for myself, and so I passed undiscovered.

"Reaching the harbour, Mr Hay took me privately

---

[1] Edmund Hay, belonging to the family of the Earl of Errol, entered the Society in 1562. His zeal and courage in serving the cause of Mary Queen of Scots merited for him the honourable commendation of St Pius V. He reconciled Francis, Earl of Errol, to the Catholic Church; was appointed Rector of the College of Clermont, first Rector of the new Scotch College at Pont-à-Mousson, and Assistant both for Germany and France to Father General Aquaviva. He died at Rome, November 4, 1594.

to the house of a relative of his own. Here, almost immediately, and very opportunely, the Lord Jesus sent us a servant of the Queen, Mr Stephen,[1] a Scotchman, who told her Majesty of our arrival, and enquired where I could see her, and in what dress, whether as a cleric or an ordinary traveller. I had to wait a whole month for a definite answer, the Queen being engaged in various matters of business. The delay, however, was providential for me, as I had time to recover from severe pain in my feet of some days' standing, and an injury to one of my legs received on board ship. I wrote to the Queen often, and sent word by Mr Hay, asking for an audience. On seeing him she arranged to receive me, but could not allow the Pontiff's letter to be read, or any message delivered publicly and before the officers of State, who are all heretics and deadly enemies of the Apostolic See.

"I had therefore to be received privately, and the queen desired Mr Hay and Mr Stephen [Wilson] to bring me secretly to Edinburgh, her capital, which she expected to reach in a few days. The arrival of a Nuncio from the Supreme Pontiff had meanwhile been rumoured all over the kingdom, throwing the heretics and their adherents into the wildest confusion and alarm. Their leader and most famous preacher in Edinburgh, John Knox, a Scot by birth, raged against the Pope as antichrist, and stigmatized me as a Nuncio of Baal and Beelzebub, and an agent of the devil, in all his harangues, urging the nobility and people, who used to crowd to his sermons, that they should take up violent measures, not against me only, but against the Queen as well, for admitting into her realm, and receiving messages from men who were bent on corrupting the pure Gospel, now at length made known to his hearers. We were conse-

[1] Stephen Wilson.

quently often threatened with stripes or death, and could not venture out. On this account Mr Hay took us to his parents' house, who welcomed us most kindly, and kept us concealed for two months. When at last we were summoned to the Queen, they sent three horsemen to attend us to Edinburgh, lest we should be attacked on the road, as there was some reason to fear. But we arrived in safety, and dismissing our guards, proceeded under the guidance of Mr Stephen, not without danger, across the fields and along the town walls, to the residence of the royal almoner. He had refused to see us before, for fear of the heretics, but he now admitted us out of respect for the Queen and the Supreme Pontiff, and announced our arrival to her Majesty. She sent us word to present ourselves at the palace next day, July 24, the Vigil of St James. We were ushered along with the almoner into a private room, at an hour when the courtiers were attending the great preacher's sermon, and could not therefore know of our interview. I was admitted first, by myself, and having respectfully saluted the Queen in the name of the Pope, briefly stated the object of my mission, and delivered his Holiness's letter. She said she understood my Latin, but could not well reply in that language. I asked if I might call in my colleague, Mr John Rinaldus, who was a Frenchman, and Mr Hay, a Scot, who were outside, and who would interpret faithfully. She agreed, and they came in, when the Queen turned at once to Mr Hay, as a subject of her own, whom she had not met before, and spoke in the Scottish language. She began by excusing herself for receiving the Pope's Nuncio with so little ceremony, which she said was owing to the disturbed state of the kingdom. Having read the apostolic brief, she hoped the Supreme Pontiff would have regard to her ready will rather than to anything she had actually done since her return, and much wished that his Holiness could have seen the condition in which she found her kingdom. She herself, and the other adherents of the orthodox religion had been obliged to do many things which they did not like, in order to preserve the last traces of the Catholic faith and worship in the country. The Pope exhorted her in defending the faith to follow the example of Queen Mary of England, now departed in Christ; but her position, and that of her kingdom, and of the nobility, was unhappily very different from that of the English Queen. To the request that Scottish prelates should be sent to the Council of Trent, her reply was that she would consult the bishops as to the means of accomplishing this, but greatly feared it would be found impracticable. For herself, she would rather forfeit her life than abandon her faith. Such was the substance of her reply to my message, and to the Pope's brief, and there was no time to add more for fear the courtiers should come back from the sermon. I then asked what I should do with the letters from the Pope addressed to the bishops, and how these could be delivered. Would she send for the bishops and give the letters to them herself, or should I convey them? She said it was out of the question my delivering them, adding, after a moment, that the attempt would cause a great tumult, and the heretics would stop at no violence in order to prevent it. I said my orders were to deliver them, but she again replied that it was impossible, except perhaps in the case of one bishop. She alluded to the Bishop of Ross, the president of the Council, or of the Parliament, who was then in town, and to whom she sent her secretary the same day, requesting him to see me; but all this may be more conveniently related further on. I then asked her whether she

would like me to speak to her brother, the Earl of
Moray (who is a natural son of the late king, and
the first man in Scotland), and to explain the object
of my embassy, lest he should suspect me of any
designs against himself or any of the great nobles.
She said she would inquire whether he would see me,
but I heard no more of it, and learnt afterwards that it
would never have done for me to have gone near him,
since every one is so prejudiced and embittered against
the Pontiff. I then asked for a safe conduct, or security
of some sort, while I remained in the kingdom, but was
assured by her that no one would attack me publicly.
Were I in danger of being privately murdered she could
not prevent it, and did not suppose she could punish it
by a legal sentence, but I should be in greater peril than
ever if she gave me a safe conduct, because this would
indicate under what character I had come, whereas I
was safe in my present concealment. She warned me to
keep my room, and never to venture out. In concluding
our interview, I remarked that I had been anxious to
consult her, had time allowed, on the best means of
succouring her people, so miserably led astray by heretics;
but as it did not permit (for it was necessary she should
dismiss us before the return of her brother and the
other heretics from the church), I would only say that
the best thing to do was what had been done by the
Emperor and most of the Catholic princes, including her
uncle, the most Reverend Cardinal of Lorraine, namely,
to establish a college where she could always have pious
and learned priests at hand, and where the young men, on
whom the hopes of the country depended, could be
trained in the Catholic religion. She replied, in one
word, that this might come in time, but was impracticable just then, and immediately dismissed us. Later

in the same day she sent her secretary to me to ask what further I wished to treat of with her; I mentioned two points, which I stated to the secretary, and expressed afterwards more fully in a letter to the Queen. One was, that I had intended, before I came to Scotland, to try and confirm her in the orthodox religion, by examples and testimonies taken from the Scriptures; but I had since heard so much, and on such good authority, of her piety and constancy in the faith, that I thought this superfluous. I only begged her to reflect on the great benefit her perseverance would occasion to the country, to return thanks to God for the grace given her, and to continue as she had begun. For the other matter, I should like to have dwelt upon the benevolent feelings of Pope Pius towards her, his good will and hearty affection both for her and her kingdom, as well as his endeavour to promote its peace, tranquillity, and happiness, as he did that of all Christendom, and as became a true pastor of the Church, who is also the Supreme Vicar of Christ on earth.

"Once more she sent the secretary to ask for the letters to the bishops, promising to have them duly delivered. I gave them up on condition she should inform the Pope, in her reply, that she had taken charge of these letters, and that I could not possibly have delivered them myself. This she willingly promised, and sent me her letter to the Pontiff open, and when it had been read by Mr Hay and Mr John, my colleague, she signed and closed it. This, Reverend Father, is the history of my dealings with the Queen. I will next relate briefly what occurred in my negociations with the bishops, and with some officers of the State.

"The Queen, as I have narrated, sent her secretary to

the Bishop of Ross,[1] requesting him to confer with me, and received for answer that he would speak to the Queen herself on the subject. He went to her directly after dinner, but told her he could not possibly venture upon seeing me. At any time, in any place, in whatever dress, my visiting him would bring about the sacking and plundering of his house within twenty-four hours, and would involve himself and all his household in the peril of their lives. Such was the bishop's message brought me by the Queen's almoner. I endeavoured to open a correspondence with him by letter, explained my business, and pressed for a reply, or still better, that he should himself write to the Pope. Receiving no answer, I wrote again, and sent my second letter by the hand of a Carthusian friar, a good and learned man who was living at Edinburgh, in the hope of obtaining from the Queen some portion of the property of his monastery, which the heretics had plundered and burnt. He gave my letter to the bishop, whose answer was, 'I do not like it at all.' When the prior told him he ought to acknowledge the letter, or else write to the Pope, he owned he did not dare do either. No one would convey such a letter, and it must eventually fall into the hands of the heretics, for the Nuncio would never get away from the country without his letters being opened and read. So he desired the Prior to offer his excuses, alleging that the administration of justice or some other occupation took up all his time, and he could not find leisure to write to me. So much for his Lordship. There was another Prelate in Edinburgh at that time, the Bishop of Dunblane,[2] a

[1] "Henry Sinclair, a son of the house of Roslin, a person of eminent parts."—Keith's "Scottish Bishops," p. 194. He was president of the Court of Session.

[2] William Chisholm, "one of the chief pillars of the Papisticall Kirk."—Knox's "History," edited by D. Laing, vol. ii. p. 88.

kinsman of whose, named William Chisholm, wished to join our Society at Rome. I had not yet seen this prelate, but about eight days afterwards he left for his Episcopal city, and thinking there could be no danger in his seeing me there, I asked one of his relatives to take me, as it was less than a day's journey. None would have suspected me of being the Pope's Nuncio, for I was disguised as one of the Bishop's servants. He was, however, afraid to see me, for the same reasons as the Bishop of Ross. Considering that it was from these two Bishops, more than anyone else, I had looked for some result of my efforts, I foresaw how far I was likely to succeed with the others. I had of course given up all idea of delivering the Apostolic Brief, from what the Queen had told me, and many others since; but I thought I might have been able to see the Bishops and talk over the objects of my mission; this, however, I must now abandon as equally hopeless. I then tried writing letters, and addressed them to the Bishops though not quite to all, seeing that two of them are heretics, and that two sees, Galloway and Brechin, are vacant, Bishops having been only designated to them. Two out of the number replied[1]—the Archbishop of St Andrews, who wrote to me, and the Bishop of Dunkeld,[2] who directed

[1] Fr. de Gouda in a subsequent letter to Fr. General acknowledges that the Bishop of Aberdeen replied a little later. "I send his letter to your Reverence that you may see his good disposition to the faith. Most of the Bishops think as he does, but dare not do anything owing to the tyranny of the heretics, against which even the Queen herself is powerless. He says he will write to the Supreme Pontiff as soon as he receives the Apostolic Brief. I sent him a copy of it by Mr Hay, but left the original in the hands of the Queen, who would not let me attempt to deliver it myself as being too perilous an undertaking. She therefore took charge of it, and promised it should be delivered some day."

[2] Robert Crichton, who succeeded John Hamilton in Dunkeld, and continued Bishop until ousted by the Reformers.

his answer to the Pope. Both these letters I send enclosed to your Paternity. The Bishop of Dunkeld was the only prelate I was admitted to speak to in Scotland; and he insisted that I should pass myself off as a banker's clerk come to receive payment of a debt. He hoped thus to prevent his servants finding out who I was, though, as he resides in an island somewhere, with no other human habitation near, the danger of discovery did not seem very great. His Lordship entertained me at dinner, but on condition that we talked of nothing except money matters all dinner time. Your Reverence will be at no loss to gather from these particulars, how far the cause of religion is likely to be advanced by negotiation with these good men. So much then for the Bishops.

"As regards the Queen's Councillors and officers of State, your Reverence is no doubt aware that she has not a single Catholic adviser. Nearly all public business is transacted by heretics, both at court and throughout the kingdom. Many nobles and Earls are Catholics, but the heretics take care to keep them away from Court, and from any share in the administration. I asked to whom I might forward the Apostolic Briefs, and I then sent them to three men of rank by a safe hand, not being allowed to go myself. I enclosed, at the same time, letters which I had written, expressing the kind wishes of the Supreme Pontiff towards them and to the whole realm of Scotland, and I now await the answers which Mr Hay is to bring.

"The above is a brief narrative of my negotiations with the Queen, the Bishops, and some of the nobility. I will add a few words as to their position at present, and that of the kingdom in general, especially as regards religion. The aspect of things from this point of view is miserable enough. The monasteries are nearly all in ruins, some completely destroyed; churches, altars, sanctuaries are overthrown and profaned, the images of Christ and of the Saints broken and lying in the dust. No religious rite is celebrated in any part of the kingdom, no Mass ever said in public, except in the Queen's chapel, and none of the sacraments are publicly administered with Catholic ceremonial. Children can be baptized only after the heretical form, and that on Sundays only, so that many infants die unbaptized. The ministers, as they call them, are either apostate monks, or laymen of low rank, and are quite unlearned, being cobblers, shoemakers, tanners, or the like, while their ministrations consist merely of declamation against the Supreme Pontiff, and the holy sacrifice of the altar, the idolatry of the mass, worship of images, and invocation of Saints. These and other impieties they are continually shouting into the ears of the credulous multitude, who know no better. They are so insane as not only to have destroyed the images of the saints, but also burnt the writings of the holy Fathers of the Church, thus repudiating the authority of General Councils and Apostolic tradition. They reverence nothing but Holy Scripture, and this they interpret in a sense as opposite as possible to the doctrines of the Church. They have superintendents, who diligently visit the churches, drive out by force the legitimate pastors wherever they find any, and not only confirm the wretched people in their errors, but draw away Catholics, and sometimes even priests, from the true religion. One day, close to the place where I lodged, three priests publicly abjured the Catholic faith; and another time, while I was there, one of the principal superintendents, a doctor of theology and a monk, then about seventy years of age, was openly married. This was done to enforce practically, as he had often done verbally, their doctrine of the unlawfulness of the vow of chastity, which they are perpetually proclaiming from the pulpit. They use every possible device to lead the wretched people astray. Whenever any one comes into a court of law, the magistrates always enquire first if they are "Papists" or belong to their congregation. Should they be Papists they can get very little, if any, attention paid to their cause. The men in power acknowledge the Queen's title, but prevent her exercising any of the rights of sovereignty; whenever her opinion does not agree with theirs, they oppose her at once. Not only so, but they deceive her as well, and frighten her with threats of an English invasion, especially when she is meditating any step in support of her faith, reminding her that the English did really invade Scotland three years ago, at the time when her mother, of pious memory, endeavoured to shake off her heretical tyrants with the aid of the French. What can this good young princess[1] effect, brought up amid the splendour and luxury of the French court, scarcely twenty years old, and destitute of all human support and counsel? Her very confessor abandoned her just before I came away, and returned to France with some of her Catholic attendants, leaving her alone among heretics, whom, notwithstanding, she continues to resist and counteract to the best of her power. There is no mistaking the imminent peril of her situation. Meanwhile the great men take unfair advantage of her gentleness, do what they like, and take care to keep every one from her presence unless they know the errand on which he comes, so that she is obliged to receive her visitors in secret, as she did us. The bishops see all this, yet make no effort, Catholics though they be for the most part; but in truth things have now gone so

[1] Pia domina juvencula.

far that they can do nothing against the heretics, however much they may desire it. The Bishop of Dunkeld is a case in point. He meant last Easter to administer the sacraments with the Catholic rite, and sent for an able Catholic preacher to teach his people. Thereupon he was impeached before the Queen for acting in contravention of the orders of the government, and was compelled to desist by the Queen's command; for it seems that when she first came to Scotland the Lords cunningly extorted from her a pledge to allow no change in matters of religion until the assembling of Parliament, and that till then all was to remain as before her arrival. The bishops therefore keep quietly at home, and in truth are for the most part destitute of all personal qualifications requisite for taking any lead in such stormy times. The only exception is the coadjutor Bishop of Dunblane, whom I have already mentioned. Though holding but a secondary position during the lifetime of his superior, he has already made his influence felt, both in public and in private, having succeeded in confirming a great many people in the faith, and being justly held in high esteem and regard by all good men. There are some Catholic preachers of note, but they are few in number, and seldom venture to attack controverted points, being indeed unequal to the task of handling them with effect. Only a few Religious are left, and most of these have no fixed residence, but go about from place to place, or wear the secular habit and live among their friends. The Priests, of whom but few remain, are not distinguishable from laymen in dress or appearance. The nobles and wealthy Catholics hear mass occasionally with the greatest secrecy, and in their own houses. Indeed any public profession of the orthodox religion would expose them and their whole families to immediate danger. A large number of the common people are still Catholics, but they are so trampled in the dust by the tyranny of their opponents, that they can only sigh and groan, waiting for the deliverance of Israel. Yet they continue to hope for freedom, encouraged by their Sovereign's firmness in the Catholic faith, and zeal for religion. Those of the common people who have been led astray by the heretics are beginning to see how miserably they have been cajoled, and to feel the hollowness of the promises of liberty held out to them. It would be an easy matter to bring them all back to the Catholic faith. I will explain shortly how I think this might be done, but must first indicate in brief to what the best and most sensible of the Catholics attribute all these misfortunes. They consider them as owing to the suspension of the ordinary mode of election to abbacies and other high dignities. These preferments are conferred upon children, or other incapable persons, without any care for God's honour and the service of the Church, and very often one such person holds several offices in the same church. For instance, a son of one of the Bishops has been appointed to the archdeaconry and two canonries in his father's cathedral. Besides which, the lives of priests and clerics are not unfrequently such as to cause grave scandal; an evil increased by the supine indifference and negligence of the Bishops themselves. Though we can hardly wonder at this, as they are so miserably oppressed that they cannot venture to discharge their duty, however much they may desire it, on account of the fury and audacity of the heretics. I will not describe the way in which these prelates live, the example they set, or the sort of men they nominate as their successors; only, it is hardly surprising if God's flock is eaten up by wolves, while such shepherds as these have charge of it.

"Leaving this subject, let me explain the steps which, in the estimation of those whom I have consulted, should be taken for the relief of the Kingdom and the restoration of the old Religion.

"First, it is absolutely necessary that the Queen should marry a Catholic prince—one powerful enough to put a restraint on the excesses of the enemies of the faith, who have shown themselves very sensitive to a stringent line of argument.

"Next, she must have good Catholic councillors and ministers of state. Then the Church in Scotland must be supplied with faithful Bishops and prelates, who will do their work, and labour for the welfare of the people. To accomplish this the Holy See should send legates invested with sufficient authority to examine into the lives and conduct of the prelates, and remove them from office if necessary. A college also should be established where good and learned Priests would be ready when wanted, and where pious and Catholic instruction could be given to the people, especially to the rising generation, for on these the future hopes of the Commonwealth depend.

"Lastly, King Philip of Spain must be induced to promise his protection to the Queen of Scotland, in case of invasion from England; for it is by hurling this threat in her face that her Councillors, and the more violent heretics, always frighten her from acting in opposition to their designs, or taking any steps in favour of her Religion. She is anxious to do all she can, but her absolutely isolated and helpless position renders her best wishes ineffectual, and deprives her of all power. If she could only be aided in the way I have pointed out, I have no doubt whatever of the reconversion of this Kingdom to the orthodox faith.

"There are still large numbers of Catholics among the people, and even amongst the nobility; whereas the heretics are inferior both in numbers and influence. They are scared at the idea of having a powerful Catholic prince in Scotland, while they cannot but feel, and are fain to acknowledge, that the present lawless sway of madness and impiety, if it continues, will soon put an end to their own tenure of authority.

"The trouble undergone on our account by Mr Hay's parents, and the history of our return to Flanders, must be briefly noticed, and then I will conclude.

"Such bitter threats were uttered against Mr Hay for bringing us to Scotland, and against his parents for receiving us into their house, that I thought it well to write to the Queen, entreating her not to give credence to any lies or calumnies which might reach her. The measures taken against ourselves need not be recorded in detail,[1] but I understood that all the ports were watched and guarded, to prevent our getting away with our letters, and it was only by the extraordinary courage and ingenuity of Mr Hay himself, and his relative, Mr William Crichton (who have both since joined the Society), that we succeeded in escaping unharmed. They dressed me as a sailor, and hired a boat to take us to the sailing vessel when she was some miles out at sea, and so parting from Mr Hay, we went on board. He returned, to make sure we had got clear off, and were not followed,

---

[1] Father de Gouda was diligently sought for to be put to death. On one occasion the constables apprehended a French merchant proceeding from the town of Aberdeen to Stonehaven, and mistaking him for the apostolic nuncio in disguise, beat him nearly to death, though he continued vehemently to assert that he was not the person they took him for. They would certainly have killed him, had he not succeeded in getting back to the town, where he was recognised as a merchant. (M. Tanner, "Societas Jesu apostolorum imitatrix," p. 104, Pragæ, 1694, in fol.)

and also to bring with him a band of young men whom he had collected together to be educated by us as Catholics[1]—no contemptible result of our foray into Scotland. Mr William Crichton, however, accompanied us as our guide, showing us throughout a degree of charity and kindness which I cannot easily describe. We left Scotland, under Divine guidance, in a Flemish vessel, on the 3d of September, and reached Antwerp, safe and sound, by God's mercy, on the 13th of the same month. We went on to Louvain the same day, and not finding the Father Provincial there, proceeded to Cologne, and thence to Mayence, where we met Father Natalis, and the Father Provincial, to our great contentment.

"So much for our expedition to Scotland and return thence. Other particulars will be more easily communicated by word of mouth. Mr Hay and Mr Crichton, whom we daily expect, will give full information. For the rest, I pray Christ to complete the work He has undertaken through His Supreme Vicar on earth, for the relief and consolation of the Queen and Kingdom of the Scots, by the hands of the same holy Pontiff, to the honour of His holy name, and the salvation of His people. And may the same most kind and loving Jesus long preserve your Reverend Paternity to us and the Church. Farewell,

    "Your Reverend Paternity's
     "Unworthy Son,
      "NICOLAS DE GOUDA.

"MAYENCE, *September* 30, 1562."[2]

[1] These all joined the Society of Jesus, and some of them became famous in after years. Their names were James Tyrie, William Crichton, John Hay, Robert Abercromby, and William Murdoch.

[2] Latin MS. Archives S.J. Recently discovered and printed in "Stimmen aus Maria-Laach."

How far Father de Gouda's letter faithfully expressed the state of Scotland may be ascertained from a letter of Fr. Edmund Hay who had accompanied him to Scotland. He writes : " Father de Gouda has described in great part, what no letter could describe fully, the miseries with which Scotland is afflicted (the particulars of which he has collected with great diligence, and recorded with great accuracy), as well as the causes which produced these evils, and the best way of remedying them. On these heads I have nothing to add, unless I were to describe still more in detail the tyranny exercised towards the Catholics by the heretical party now in power, under pretence of carrying out the laws, of which the effect is exactly that of a sword placed in the hands of a madman. But what I want most particularly to impress upon your Paternity, is that all the plans hitherto suggested, and all that may be suggested, however wise perhaps, and however pious and prudent their authors, will be premature, not to say absolutely useless, as long as the Queen's illegitimate brother, the Lord James, is alive, or at any rate, as long as he continues to govern the kingdom, which he has done ever since the Queen's return. He holds all the heretics, except the Earl of Hamilton, so completely under control by interest, and all the Catholics, who are fewer in number, by fear and by the use of the royal authority, which is scarcely, even nominally, in possession of the Queen, that no one ventures to oppose his will. Many of them are even compelled by force, or the dread of force, to join the private feuds and seditions which he carries on for his own interests. He always pretends that he is acting in support of the Queen's title and hereditary right, but no one in Scotland who has a gleam of sense, and is not blinded by prejudice, can

entertain the smallest doubt what his real purpose is."[1]
Mary herself wrote to the Pope to thank him for his
kindness, and to express her regret that, owing to the
state of things in Scotland, she could not send any
bishops to the Council of Trent. At the same time she
assured him that she was defending the holy faith with
all her strength, and was ready to suffer the greatest
calamities, and even death itself, in defence of it."[2]

The Lord James, however, retained his power, and
although he had defeated the Nuncio's designs, Mary as
usual left everything in his hands. "Her brother," says
Leslie, "perceiving that his influence prevailed so far
that it was no use for any one to speak to the Queen
about any matter, without consulting him first, began to
entertain still more ambitious views, and, not content
with the administration of the kingdom, aspired to the
crown itself.[3] There were, however, four things which
he considered necessary in order to attain his end. First,
he must take the management of public affairs entirely
out of the hands of the Queen, who was totally ignorant
of Scottish politics, and must secure it in his own; next, all
public offices must be filled with his adherents; thirdly,
the revenues of the clergy must be reduced by every
means possible, because he foresaw their influence would
be used against himself; and lastly, knowing that the
ablest and most powerful of the nobles were opposed to
him, he determined that they should be put out of the
way or thrown into prison. All this he successfully carried
out by fair means or foul, as we shall see in the sequel."[4]

[1] Letter of Fr. E. Hay to Father Laynez, General of the Society of
Jesus, dated 2d January 1563. (Archives of the Society. Latin MS.)

[2] Labanoff, "Lettres de Marie Stuart," vol. i. p. 177.

[3] This is not only related by Leslie, but was also observed by
Randolph, the English resident. See "Keith," vol. ii. pp. 79, 80.

[4] "Secret Archives of the Vatican: Politicorum Variorum," vol.

Soon after the Reformation the Protestant preachers had claimed as their due inheritance the lands and tithes of the Catholic Church. Many of them were in abject poverty, and they were clamorous against the Government, as hungry men always are. Under these circumstances "Lord James held a meeting in Edinburgh, at which the prelates who were present, the Archbishop of St Andrews, the Bishops of Dunkeld, Moray, and Ross, the Abbot of Cupar, and some others, were consulted on a proposal to set apart a third portion of the Church revenues for the wants of the Queen and the support of the preachers of the new gospel; and many controversies were held on this subject between the churchmen and James and his adherents. The latter insisted on claiming the Church property entrusted to the bishops, while the bishops refused to decide the question without consulting the Roman Pontiff, or to impose such a burden on the clergy without their consent. At length the prelates who were present agreed to give a fourth part of their revenues for one year to the Queen as a voluntary offering. James determined to obtain by force and violence what he had been unable to extort either by chicanery or by terror. He sent commissioners, supported by armed soldiers, all over the kingdom, without consulting the other nobles, to collect a third part of the ecclesiastical revenues, in spite of the opposition of the prelates; and this act of spoliation was so cruelly executed that not even the goods belonging to poor Religious and inmates of collegiate houses, nor alms contributed for the benefit of the departed, were exempted. The third part which they nominally demanded was much more than

---

xvi., 297. "Paralipomena ad historiam. . . . Scotiæ, Joannis Leslæi, Episcopi Rossensis, eodem auctore."

the two thirds they professed to leave, and this injustice was continued for many years."¹

It was not to be expected that the bishops and the Catholic nobles should bear the Lord James' proceedings with equanimity; they protested against his conduct and respectfully remonstrated with Mary respecting a policy so injurious to the interests of the Church. "During the Queen's stay at Stirling the Earl of Huntly conferred with her as to the means of restoring the Catholic religion to its former condition, and used many arguments to induce her to undertake it. He also persuaded her secretary, a Frenchman, whom he knew to have great influence with her on account of his knowledge of business, and also to be in the confidence of the Cardinal of Lorraine and the Duke of Guise, to exert his efforts in the same direction. The secretary did so very earnestly, and represented to her at some length the extent to which the affections of many noblemen were being alienated from her, owing to the suppression of the Catholic religion; and that, if she wished to reconcile them to her cause, she must permit the Earl of Huntly to take measures for the restoration of religion. He would readily undertake the commission on condition of the removal from office of the men who were so diligently using their authority to overthrow the foundations of the Constitution. This advice was given to the Queen very secretly, but by some means not known it came to the ears of the Lord James.² He was furious, and, considering the Earl of Huntly as his principal enemy, determined to set no terms to his hostility till he

¹ Leslie's "Paralipomena."
² Randolph to Cecil, 24th September 1561. "It is said that the Earl of Huntly and Lord James greatly discord. Some alleged that the cause of the quarrel was a boast of Huntly that, if the queen commanded him he could set up the Mass in three shires; to which

had accomplished his death; while Huntly, informed of this threat, withdrew from Court to his own residence in order to escape his anger."[1]

So great, however, were Huntly's power and influence that, as long as he survived, Lord James could not make any progress either towards obtaining the crown to which he aspired, or towards establishing the Protestant religion in Scotland. He therefore employed every means to rouse the Queen's suspicions against Huntly's overgrown power. On the occasion of his marriage with the Lady Agnes Keith he obtained an inchoate grant of the earldom of Moray and of the lands of Abernethy; but the lands appertaining to the title were in Huntly's possession, and James made up his mind to have them. Huntly refused to part with them, and he was in consequence destined for ruin.

Moray, by which name we shall henceforward designate James, advised the Queen to visit the north of Scotland, in order that he might receive his earldom from Huntly in her Majesty's presence. But his real object, as the event proved, was to secure either the murder of Huntly, or, at any rate, the means of weakening his authority, and so rendering that nobleman powerless to conduct any serious opposition to his own plans. An incident occurred at that time which singularly favoured Moray's designs. A sort of skirmish took place in the streets of Edinburgh between John Gordon, son of the Earl of Huntly, and the Lord Ogilvie. The latter was wounded by John Gordon, who in consequence was apprehended by the citizens and committed to the public prison.

The incidents which follow are given in Bishop Leslie's own words.

Moray answered that it was past his power to do so, and so he should find the first moment he attempted it." ("Keith," vol. ii. p. 86.)

[1] Leslie's "Paralipomena."

III.

BISHOP LESLIE'S NARRATIVE OF THE PROGRESS OF EVENTS IN SCOTLAND.—1562-1571.

" . . . GORDON, after a few days imprisonment, being given to understand that he would not be liberated on bail, took an opportunity of withdrawing secretly from prison, and went to join his father in the North. Moray considered that this gave him a means of annoying the Earl of Huntly, and by public proclamation summoned John Gordon to trial at Aberdeen on the 3rd of September. The Queen meanwhile arrived at that city, and was splendidly greeted both by the students and members of the University and by the bishop and clergy. Huntly, who always showed the utmost respect for the royal authority, brought his son John Gordon to Aberdeen on the appointed day, to submit to whatever commands the Queen might impose. She, by Moray's advice, ordered him to be shut up in Stirling Castle until she should have completed her progress through the north, and arrive there herself. But having been warned by his friends that he would be in extreme danger if he allowed himself to be once more incarcerated, and being aided by the advice and assistance of some young men who took his part, he thought fit to disobey the Queen's injunctions, and meditated avenging the injury he had received from Moray. He therefore secretly prepared an armed force, and would unquestionably have taken Moray's life at Inverness, had not the latter received information of the attempt late at night, so as to make arrangements to protect himself by doubling his guards. The next day Moray sent orders in the Queen's name to the garrison within the Castle of Inverness to surrender the fortress to him without delay. Some of them resisted this order until they should hear from George Gordon, the eldest son of the Earl of Huntly, who was their chief; and these, together with Alexander Gordon, were put to death by hanging. The Queen remained some days at Inverness, and on her return to Aberdeen gained intelligence that another ambuscade was prepared for Moray by the Gordons at Strathspey. She accordingly summoned the chiefs of the clans, and the other inhabitants of the neighbouring country, and assembling a powerful force, returned by another route to Aberdeen. On this route is the strong castle of Findlater, whither Moray sent the Queen's heralds to require them to surrender. The garrison absolutely refused to do so without orders from John Gordon, who was the lord of the place. Accordingly John Stuart, the commander of the Queen's guard, was left with three hundred men to keep them from breaking out. But, a few days afterwards, they managed to receive reinforcements, made a sally, attacked John Stuart's soldiers while asleep, took away their arms, money, and everything else they possessed, and compelled them to quit the neighbourhood, John Stuart remaining a prisoner in the hands of the victors.

"While the Queen thus remained at Aberdeen messengers were sent out to call upon all men of noble birth in Fife, Loudoun, Mearns, and other districts in the vicinity, to protect her Majesty, or rather Moray, from the attempts of Huntly. The Earl was then summoned to defend his cause before the Council at Aberdeen; but he sent Master Thomas Keir, his secretary, to make his excuses to her Majesty and the Council for not appearing in Court, on the ground that he could not do so in safety, the whole proceedings being carried on according to Moray's directions, and in his interest. Lest, however, he should seem to be avoiding his trial through consciousness of guilt, he offered to surrender himself prisoner at Edinburgh, Stirling, or any other fortified place, on condition that no capital sentence should be pronounced against him, except with the consent of the whole nobility of Scotland. Moray prevented this message being carried to the Queen, threw the messenger into prison, and compelled him by threat of torture to give evidence against his master and his master's children; he also took from him the great seal which Huntly, who was the Chancellor of Scotland, had entrusted to him.

"On learning this, Huntly sent another messenger, Alexander Keir, the brother of the former, with the same message to the Queen, and from him also Moray violently extorted evidence against Huntly and his sons. Meanwhile John the Prior of Coldingham, another natural brother of the Queen, left Aberdeen, and hastened by night, with fifty men lightly armed, to the castle of Strathbogie, twenty-four miles distant, in the hope of surprising the Earl of Huntly and his sons, and making them prisoners; but they had information of the attempt, and eluded it by escaping to the mountains. Coldingham, nevertheless, entered the castle at the head of his men, where the Countess received them with external marks of friendship, and hospitably entertained them. Being a very clever woman, she took the opportunity of strenuously asserting, before Coldingham and the noblemen who accompanied him, her husband's innocence and loyalty towards the Queen, and earnestly entreated their advocacy with her Majesty on his behalf. They returned to Aberdeen, and Huntly, convinced that he would not be safe within the walls of any castle, assembled a force of twelve hundred brave and trustworthy men from among his relatives, clansmen, and followers, by whose means he occupied all the neighbouring hill country. He further sent Lady Gordon to the Queen with the same message which he had before endeavoured to send; but when she arrived within two miles of Aberdeen, she was met by a royal messenger commanding her to return as quickly as possible to her own castle. This order came from Moray; for the Queen was in reality very desirous to see her, and Moray was perfectly aware that, if he allowed anyone to explain to Mary the truth regarding Huntly's innocence and his own plots, she would probably take the Earl into favour, and place very little confidence for the future in himself. Huntly, then, having failed in all his efforts to obtain access to her Majesty so far, drew nearer to Aberdeen, and being very anxious to make his peace with her, sent a Calvinist preacher, named Strachan, with the same message that he had attempted to send previously, desiring him if hindered from conveying it, at any rate to assure the nobles and the common people, in public and private discourse, of his innocence. This man was imprisoned like the rest, and got only bonds as the result of his embassy.

"Moray, learning that Huntly's forces were not far off, hastened to collect some troops, and ordered them to be in readiness for instantly marching against the enemy. All being prepared, he set out, and having come in sight of the foe [at Corrichie],[1] he sent a herald to name a time within which they might lay down their arms and depart unmolested, with the exception of Huntly himself,

---

[1] About four miles north from Banchory. A small fountain near the spot is still called Queen Mary's Well.

of his sons, and some of his principal friends. This had the effect of detaching from Huntly a good many of his supporters, particularly among the common people. Perceiving that a large number of his followers were deserting, and that the enemy were beginning to surround him and render escape impossible, Huntly resolved to give battle, as the course most natural to his own courageous spirit, and one justified by his suspicions that many of his opponents were more strongly attached to his cause than to the side of Moray.

"Before giving the signal for battle he addressed such words to his companions as the time allowed of, in order to animate and encourage them. 'If we were about to fight on equal terms,' he said, 'or if we had the alternative of either fighting or retiring, and chose to engage in battle without the necessity which now compels us, I should exhort you to acquit yourselves well in the field. As it is, we are surrounded by an enemy who is advancing upon us, so that our only hope lies in displaying courage and fortitude; it needs not that I say more. To yield would be disgraceful, and death against the odds opposed to you were most glorious. When I look round and see you all so full of strength and courage, many words are uncalled for. Meet boldly the enemy's attack, and doubt not God will give us strength. It is His cause, and the cause of justice, which we defend against the oppressor of our country and of the true Faith. We are few, but God can preserve the lives of His servants, whether they be many or few. I hope some of those who now appear in arms against us will prove our friends. But should they all continue to oppose us, we have one friend a match for all—the justice of the cause for which we fight, and are ready to die, and if this suffers defeat, nothing will be left worth living for.'

The soldiers, encouraged by Huntly's words, stood the enemy's attack with such spirit, that they drove back the first line, and put to flight many that followed. But the men from Fife armed with long lances now coming up, and the light cavalry under Coldingham charging on the left wing, with the musketeers on the right, they were overwhelmed, after long and fierce contest, by the number of their enemies and the variety of weapons used against them, and at length turned and fled, though in truth but few of them were by that time left alive. The Earl himself was taken prisoner, and put to death by Moray's order, with a firelock discharged, as it was said, close into his ear. His son the laird of Findlater, and many others, were made prisoners of war, and about a hundred and forty noblemen fell in this battle, many being kinsmen of the chief. The body of Huntly was conveyed to Aberdeen along with the prisoners.

"The Queen had strictly enjoined Moray, when he was leaving Aberdeen, to preserve the life of the Earl of Huntly, and she received the intelligence of his death with tears. Her grief was much heightened, and was shared in by all the nobility, when Moray proceeded to condemn Findlater to a like fate. This sentence was carried out, and many of his servants and followers were hanged, after which Moray remained in undisputed possession of absolute power, for none of the nobles ventured even to open their mouths against him, and he could safely crush the most powerful amongst them against the Queen's wishes, and often without her knowledge.

"The dead body of the Earl of Huntly was exposed unburied in the royal palace at Aberdeen, and some months later in the Parliament House at Edinburgh; ostensibly because judgment could not be passed on one deceased except in the presence of his dead body, but really because Moray's hatred of all good men prompted him to insult even their remains. In the parliament sentence of death was also pronounced upon Huntly's eldest son, who had been apprehended by the Duke of Chatelherault and delivered up to Moray, and he would have been executed, but that the queen's earnest and repeated solicitation in favour of this nobleman was not to be resisted, and so he was rescued from Moray's cruelty.[1]

[1] Huntly's eldest son was Lord George Gordon. He remained in ward for several years. "Moray having noticed that the queen bore a kindly feeling towards Gordon, and being apprehensive lest she might liberate him at some time or other (a step which Moray saw would be very injurious to his projects), despatched a letter stamped with the queen's seal to the keeper of the castle, ordering him to cut off the head of the Earl of Huntly without delay, yet assigning no motive for the act. At the time of the delivery of this letter, Huntly was playing at dice with the keeper himself. When the latter suddenly grew pale on reading it, Huntly, seeing how matters stood, told him to be of good heart, and as no blame was due to him, he himself would willingly pardon him. The other, however, being a prudent man—although he could doubt neither the queen's seal nor Mary's signature attached, and knew well the danger in which he would place his own life by delay—thought it safest to make some inquiries. After letting Huntly know what he had been ordered to do, and how urgent and imperative the letter was which he had received, he decided upon visiting the Queen at his own risk. Posting off to the Court with all speed, he prayed her Majesty to pardon him for not having at once obeyed her commands. When Mary heard reference made to 'her letter,' she was much surprised, and told him that she had not sent any to him on the subject, and had no intention of so doing. As soon as he produced the letter she saw through Moray's fraud; and in order to protect Huntly from the recurrence of any such danger, she ordered that he should at once be set at liberty. At the next meeting of parliament, the entire family was restored to its former dignity and honour." (Fr. Tyrie's MS.)

The same story is told by Crawford, in his "Lives of the Officers of the Crown and State in Scotland" (p. 91), on the authority of Gordon of Straloch.

"In the following year, 1563, the parliament was held at Edinburgh. Moray's intention was to proscribe the late Earl of Huntly and his sons, John Earl of Sutherland, together with all the remaining Gordons, and deprive them of their ancestral privileges and estates. Fearing that the Archbishop of St Andrews might oppose, and perhaps hinder, this arbitrary measure, he imprisoned him, together with Hew Kennedy of Blairquhynneqhuy, uncle of the Earl of Cassilis, and many other persons of rank, on the ground that the archbishop had celebrated mass at Easter, and administered the Eucharist to many persons according to the Catholic rite, and contrary to the statutes of the realm.[1] They were not set free until the conclusion of parliament, by which time Huntly's heirs were unjustly deprived of their inheritance by an act of parliament, and the whole family of Gordon branded with perpetual ignominy as traitors. The Queen after this went to Argyllshire for relaxation, and spent all the summer in hunting and other royal diversions.

"Elizabeth was very apprehensive that the Queen of Scotland might marry a Catholic prince, a step which would endanger the tranquillity of England. She accordingly sent an embassy to her, demanding that, in case she should contemplate a second marriage, she must not choose a foreign in preference to an English husband, and promising, in the event of the Queen of Scotland following her advice in the choice of a husband, she would always regard her as a daughter and acknowledged heiress to the Crown. The Queen, having consulted Moray and Lethington, her secretary, replied that she had not yet got over the grief she experienced at the death of the late illustrious prince, her husband, and that she never

---

[1] Cf. Pitcairn's "Criminal Trials," part x. p. 427.

thought of happiness or marriage; but should she contemplate the step, she would do nothing in a matter of so much importance without consulting the Queen of England, who of all princes was nearest to her both in blood and in affection. Elizabeth was not satisfied with this reply, and wrote secretly to Moray and Lethington, using many artifices to gain them over to her side. All those who were aware that the Queen of England's assistance might materially further their designs likewise took her part, and they at length obtained from Mary the answer, that she was willing to accept the husband proposed to her by the Queen of England, on condition the estates of that realm should be summoned together, and should formally recognise her as heir to the crown, on the failure of legitimate issue of the Queen of England, who always shrank from naming her successor, for fear the successor thus designated should obtain more respect and attention than herself. During these negotiations the following noblemen were proposed to our Queen, that she might choose a husband from among them: the Duke of Norfolk; Robert Dudley, Earl of Leicester; Henry Stuart, Lord Darnley, son of the Earl of Lennox; and the Earl of Warwick. But the Queen of England seems to have preferred Robert, Earl of Leicester to any of the others.

"About this time ambassadors arrived from several Christian princes to visit Mary as Queen of Scotland, and tender their assurances of friendship and offers of service. One of these, Count Moret, who represented the Duke of Savoy, when about to return, after accomplishing the object of his mission, left with the queen a Piedmontese and a very able man of business named David, whom he much commended for his talents and good qualities. This Piedmontese was attached to the royal household, and as in a few days his value evidently more than justified the Count's praises, he was appointed to write the Queen's private letters in French, Italian, and Latin, and in this capacity rendered great services to her Majesty herself and to many of the nobles. The Queen soon afterwards returned from Argyll to Stirling, and Moray, in order to acquire some reputation as a dealer out of justice among his countrymen, went to the borders and scattered a numerous band of robbers, whom he not undeservedly caused to be hanged, and thus delivered the country from similar depredations in future.[1]

"Meanwhile the Queen of England, much alarmed lest the Scots should take up arms on behalf of the French, against whom she had sent an expedition into Normandy, and perceiving that the match she had proposed between the Queen and Dudley was not likely to come off, resolved to try and establish peace between her own country and Scotland. She therefore by envoys and by letters, pressed Mary to enter into a treaty of friendship

---

[1] This year died William Chisholm, Bishop of Dunblane. His successor was his nephew of the same name, who was afterwards driven into exile for his constancy in the Catholic faith, and plundered of all his goods, and was on this account appointed by the Supreme Pontiff, Pius V., to administer the bishopric of Vaison.

There died also this year Malcolm Fleming, Prior of Galloway, an earnest follower of the true religion. Shortly after, at the beginning of the following year, Henry Sinclair, Bishop of Ross, died at Paris, a man of remarkable wisdom and learning. He was descended from an illustrious family, and held the office of President of the Council of Scotland. His successor in the see was John Leslie, who was descended from another ancient and noble family, that of the Leslies. He had previously discharged several public offices with success, and the daring and strenuous efforts he made in favour of the religion of his forefathers, and the defence of his sovereign, and the banishment he underwent in consequence, will be sufficiently set forth in the sequel.

with her, engaging that each should support the other, to the utmost of their power, against any foreign enemies or revolt at home. These conditions of treaty Mary accepted; and in token of their confirmation rings of great value were mutually exchanged, besides other ornaments of beautiful workmanship, especially characteristic of the two royal donors. Directly after the conclusion of the treaty, Matthew Stuart, Earl of Lennox, arrived in Scotland, furnished with letters of recommendation from the Queen of England, and with a petition for the restitution of his ancestral property, honours, fame, and dignity; of which he had been deprived twenty years before by the Duke of Chatellerault, then at the head of the government, and by an order from the parliament; and for the restoration of which he now appealed to the generosity and clemency of the Queen. Her Majesty, always inclined to mercy, obtained this concession for him from the estates of the kingdom, having previously effected a reconciliation between him and the duke; each side agreeing to abandon their former animosities.

"This restoration of the house of Stuart gave some uneasiness to Moray, who being aware that several of the most powerful princes of Europe were united with the uncles of the Queen in proposing a French marriage for her, and reasonably fearing lest power might thus be transferred from his hands to those of her future husband, began to talk to her, at first in guarded language, of the great advantages of celibacy. Afterwards growing bolder, with his accustomed craft he took advantage of familiar intercourse to address her in these terms, 'I cannot omit taking this occasion, most gracious Queen, to lay before you thoughts that have been night and day on my mind, and are prompted simply out of regard for your honour and service, which I have all my life had more at heart than any other object I might desire. I know very well the high value you set upon womanly modesty, your great regard for your own honour, and the generosity which always prompts you to consider the public welfare before your own interest or inclination. Neither am I ignorant of your anxiety for the dignity and advancement of your own family. My long habit of allegiance will lead me to acquiesce in whatever you determine. Do I advise you to marry again? That undoubtedly is the most direct means of preserving to our family the succession of the crown of Scotland; but there are also others not less safe. Shall I advise you against it? I have, I acknowledge, a strong impression that your remaining single is the only way to secure the honour and tranquillity of your realm. Your own personal dignity, as you have no doubt considered, would be lowered by a marriage with any man of rank inferior to your late princely husband; yet where will you find on the earth a consort so illustrious in birth and descent as he? There are only three nations among whom you could find a fitting partner—France, Spain, and Italy. I leave out of consideration Sweden, Denmark, and foreign countries like these, as being barbarous and unbefitting your manners and mode of life. But even as regards the three I have named, great inconvenience would result from your taking a partner from any of them. In the first place, their princes are Papists, and bitter enemies of our religion. They agree with you personally in religious faith, but are far from sharing your equity and clemency. You retain your own religion, but you leave the same freedom of opinion to others, and by this means have secured the peace and tranquillity of your kingdom. If you were to place over us some one of these, who are as conceited as they are confident in the efficacy of their mass and religious rites, you would reduce one side or the other to the alternative of forfeiting either their life or their religion; for pride leads each to insist on his own particular judgment being followed. Our nation has always been zealous for liberty in every thing, and especially in religion; so much so, that often a mere handful of men has stood out against the royal authority, supported by a strong military force, in defence of their freedom and their faith. To take each foreign power in turn, you know how the houses of Spain and Austria have made themselves hated among the nations of Europe for their pride and ambition, and how calculated their governments are to provoke insurrection. England is witness of this, for the reign of King Philip, in conjunction with Mary, a woman otherwise of gentle character, occasioned the violent death and utter ruin of many citizens and persons of the highest rank. And unless I am misinformed, we shall soon have another very remarkable illustration of the like truth in Flanders. You remember the tragic events which your marriage with the French king occasioned in Scotland, when almost the whole kingdom was filled with war and conflagration. You also know, and France has bitter reason to remember for ever, the bloodshed and disturbance caused in it, when the crown of that country was by royal marriage placed on the head of an Italian princess; how would it be if ours was conferred on an Italian prince? Again, if you marry a French prince, you will incur the hostility of the Spaniards, and if you marry a Spaniard, you will make the French your enemies, instead of being your friends as now. Should you marry an Italian, you will encounter the resentment of both. Suppose you give your hand to any one of the three, you will only be introducing war, sedition, and tumult into your own kingdom. You will yourself see the course you ought to pursue; I think I have now said all that affection and duty would prompt. If any other step pleases you better than what I propose, my assistance shall not be wanting towards carrying it out.'

"The Queen replied that the life she had led for the last five years was that which was most agreeable to her, and which was best suited to the welfare of her kingdom and her own honour. One thing alone gave her anxiety, fear lest the inheritance of her house should devolve upon the family of Hamilton, who were anything but friendly to the Stuarts. Upon this Moray, firing the shot which he had all the time held in preparation, advised, and vehemently urged her to call together the estates of the realm, and get them to pass a law forbidding the accession of any but a Stuart to the crown of Scotland. He boldly requested for himself and his children the next place in the succession after the Queen, that after him should come the Earl of Lennox and his issue, and then the Earl of Athole, followed by his brother, the Prior of Coldinghame; with further remainder to Methven, Innermeath, and the rest in due course.[1] The Queen, shocked at such arrogance and presumption, could not restrain her tears; then repressing her grief, with a generous desire to soothe the storm of ambitious hope that seemed to rage in her brother's breast, she exclaimed, 'Is it possible, dearest brother,' for so she often addressed him, in spite of his illegitimacy, out of respect for his rank

---

[1] "Moray cherchait de se faire légitimer sous main, et feignant m'aimer, ne me laissait d'un pas, et voulait pourvoir à tout le gouvernement du royaume, et s'était si bien fortifié qu'il me tenait en tutelle; et enfin on proposa bailler une couronne à lui et à Argyle, et me défaire des Hamilton, comme j'avais fait de Huntly."—("Memoir of Mary on her Second Marriage," Labanoff, vol. i. pp. 268-275.)

and character, and from the affection with which she regarded him, 'that you are so ambitious of royal rank as to ask my consent to a measure which, not to speak of other objections, must be repugnant to my own feelings and to the laws and customs of the country? What has the house of Hamilton done either against us or the laws of Scotland, that they should be deprived of their just claim to their inheritance? Had such a law existed as that which you have described, the royal authority would probably never have devolved upon our family at all. No one living, and I least of all, ought to entertain any such idea. You know the antiquity of the house of Hamilton, its nobility, its influence, and abundance of followers; how is it likely they would stand such an affront? Depend upon it, they would rouse the whole kingdom against me, to my utter ruin. Lay aside, I entreat you, brother, this wild design. He who is not content with moderate fortune is often reduced to poverty, and to obscurity, while aiming at too high a destiny. Let me warn you henceforward not to breathe a word of the plan you have now unfolded, either to me or any of the nobles. Should it reach the ears of the Hamiltons, they may easily raise a storm, too formidable for us to be able to appease.'

"This repulse effectually destroyed all Moray's hopes of obtaining the crown of Scotland; he still, however, determined to retain the administration of public affairs in his own hands, and with this view directed his efforts to the arrangement of a marriage between the Queen and Henry Stuart, Lord Darnley, the son of the Earl of Lennox, as being the only means of securing to the house of Stuart its possession of the Scottish crown. He highly commended to the Queen the young prince's handsome appearance and corresponding qualities of mind; but

Darnley's principal recommendation in the eyes of Moray was his youth, which promised to leave him at the helm of government for some time to come. The Queen refused to do anything in the matter until she had seen the young man whom she was asked to wed; whereupon Moray at once made full proposals to the Earl of Lennox. Henry readily obtained from Elizabeth leave of absence for six months, hastened to Scotland, found the Queen at Wemyss Castle, and was presented to her by Moray. She received him graciously, and asked many questions respecting the Queen of England and the state of English politics. After this she frequently conversed familiarly with him, and gave him many signs of her affection and regard, so that in a short time their marriage was commonly talked about as probable. When this report reached the ears of Elizabeth, she greatly regretted that she had given Darnley permission to go to Scotland, and wrote to Moray, whom she knew to be entirely dependent upon her, desiring him to prevent the match, and demanding to have her subject restored to her hands again. She wrote also to Darnley, threatening him with her vengeance if he married the Queen. She put his mother in prison, and in fact omitted no means of throwing obstacles in the way of such a step. Mary sent her secretary, Lethington, to soothe the anger of Elizabeth, and obtain the release of the Countess of Lennox.

"Though Lethington had been always hitherto in high favour with Elizabeth, on account of his partisanship throughout Moray's treasonable correspondence with her, he obtained admission to her presence with great difficulty and after long delay; and even then could only obtain for answer that she was about to send an ambassador of her own to Scotland, who would fully explain her views. Meanwhile an assembly of the nobles had been held in Stirling, at which the Queen made known her intention of giving her hand to Darnley. Her design was approved by all present, and the transaction entered in the public records. The principal noblemen who attached their names to this report were the Duke of Châtellerault, the Earls of Argyll, Moray, Lennox, Athole, Morton, Glencairn, Marishal, Rothes, Montrose, and many other nobles, lords, and barons. Darnley was first made a knight, then a baron, and lastly, amid great applause, Earl of Ross, by commission from the queen; and, to add greater splendour to the ceremony, he himself conferred the honour of knighthood upon twelve barons. These public acts were followed by a banquet and ball, and other Court entertainments, conducted with the utmost decorum and magnificence. In the midst of the royal festivities Throckmorton, the English ambassador, arrived. He repaired at once to Stirling, but instead of waiting according to custom till summoned from the lodging assigned him, which had been fitted up on this occasion with extraordinary splendour, he went of his own accord to the castle gate, knocked loudly, and peremptorily demanded admission to the Queen's presence. Sir John Bellenden and other nobles met him, and explaining that the Queen was then engaged with other business, re-conducted him honourably to his own apartments. He was very angry, being afraid that the whole affair would be concluded before he had delivered his message; and complained that the Queen of England's envoy was disrespectfully and injuriously prevented from appearing at Court; but he gradually recovered his temper and returned to his lodgings. Soon after, when he had dined, the Queen sent for him, and listened to a long address from him. First he set forth at length the earnest desire of the Queen of England for her welfare and the proofs of love and goodwill which she had so often shown; and then exhorted and entreated her Majesty not to make any contract of marriage without consulting Elizabeth. To enforce this request he inveighed against Darnley in severe and insulting language; declaring that the Queen could not possibly long endure his dissolute behaviour, his insolence, vanity, and pride.

"Queen Mary endeavoured to take all this advice in as good part as she could, but finding it of no avail, began to threaten in her turn, very much as though she were already at war across the border. Her manner soon brought him to reason, when asserting that she had never done anything to the injury of the Queen or realm of England, she showed how the proceeding of which he complained, so far from being injurious, was an advantage and honour to England, since she had chosen for her husband a nobleman of that country, not particularly illustrious for rank or wealth, in preference to the most powerful princes of Christendom, many of whom had sought her hand. If all this was to be misrepresented and made an occasion of war, she could find among these princes an alliance and support that would repel every attack, especially as she had much more to fear from plots and machinations among her own subjects than from any external violence. Thus dismissed by the Queen, Throckmorton went to Darnley and the Earl of Lennox, and commanded them to return to England. They answered that the term allowed them by the royal license was not yet expired; meanwhile they would consider what to do, and let the Queen of England know their decision. Upon this Throckmorton had recourse to other measures. He first consulted Moray, and receiving promise of his assistance, assembled a great many of the nobles, including the Duke of Châtellerault, the Earls of

Argyll, Glencairn, the Lords Boyd and Ochiltree, and others, and not only privately but also publicly urged them to take up arms against the Queen and Darnley. There was no difficulty in persuading the Duke of Châtellerault to this course, for only a year before he had been in open enmity with Lennox, and greatly disliked the increase of influence which he now seemed on the point of obtaining; the others were instigated chiefly by their zeal for the maintenance of the Calvinist heresy, having heard that Darnley was a Catholic. Besides this, they were the more ready to appeal to arms, taking it ill that a young man of private station, not distinguished, as they considered, by any particular achievement, should be thus placed over their heads. Finding them inclined to acquiesce in his proposals, Throckmorton in the name of the Queen of England promised them money and aid, and every assistance they might require. He then besought and obtained leave to depart, and returned to England with many presents from the Queen. When he had left, John Hay was once more sent with letters to Queen Elizabeth, but after some length of stay in London, finding that she would neither see him nor receive a message from him, he made his way back to Scotland.

"The Duke of Châtellerault and the other rebel Lords now quitted the Court and proceeded to their own homes. Moray, who had hitherto managed all the affairs of government, remained at St Andrews, and though often summoned by the Queen, refused to attend Court. The Queen, thus deprived of her usual councillors, was compelled to choose new ones, and committed all public business to the hands of Lennox, Athole, and the Lord Ruthven. She also summoned to the palace from the High Court of Justice John Leslie and James Balfour, men of approved political wisdom and knowledge of public business. She liberated Huntly from his prison at Dunbar, and sent for Bothwell from France, that she might replace both in their former honours and dignities. The Bishop of Dunblane went, about the same time, on a mission to the Supreme Pontiff to obtain a dispensation because of Darnley's consanguinity with the Queen, and in this he was successful. The conspirators, Moray, Arran, and others resolved to seize the persons of the Queen and Darnley on their way from Perth to Edinburgh, intending to put Darnley to death, and confine the Queen in Lochleven Castle. While they were assembling in force, the Queen received notice of their intention. She left Perth suddenly late at night, and reached Edinburgh in safety. The very man who most strenuously exerted himself to obtain this information for the Queen, Lord Lindsay, a kinsman of Darnley, now deserted her cause and went over to the enemy. All was still in confusion when on the last day of July the Queen created Darnley Duke of Albany, and on the following day, the 1st of August,[1] the marriage was celebrated by the most Reverend Lord John Sinclair, Bishop of Brechin. It must be said that after the marriage-rites had been celebrated outside the chapel doors, Darnley, not further to irritate the Protestants who were already on the point of breaking into open violence on his account, would not enter the chapel to hear Mass with the Queen. On the same day, in compliance with the royal command he was publicly and with great ceremony proclaimed King by the heralds in the market place.

"The conspirators had meanwhile gathered their forces

[1] Mary was married to Lord Darnley in the chapel of Holyrood on Sunday the 29th of July 1565.

together. The Duke of Châtellerault, the Earls of Argyll, Moray, Rothes, the Lords Boyd and Ochiltree, and many other nobles and barons, though called to defend themselves before the Queen and the Council, had paid no attention to the summons. They were condemned for high treason and their goods declared confiscate to the treasury. It was stated that the confidential envoy of the Queen of England, who had come to entreat Mary to proceed no further in her projected marriage with Darnley, had sent a large sum of money to St. Andrews by James Johnson and James Molson for the purpose of hiring armed men from the towns; a great part of this sum had actually been sent to Perth and Dundee to pay the soldiers whose services were engaged by the rebel Lords. The Queen put herself at the head of an army and took the field in person against them. On reaching Glasgow she perceived the opposing force marching in the direction of the town, and gave orders for her troops to draw up in order of battle, but moved by the tender appeal of Lord Maxwell, she decided to refrain from shedding the blood of her own subjects. The conspirators then proceeded to Edinburgh, where they were very kindly received by the citizens. The Queen followed, and issued orders to the commandant of the castle at Edinburgh to fire on them with his cannon and drive them out. The commandant gave them due warning to withdraw, but seeing that they did not obey, he opened fire upon them and compelled them to quit the town. After they had dispersed and wandered about in search of refuge, the Lord Herries at Dumfries, close to the English border, gave them asylum in his castle. The merchants of Edinburgh having freely supplied them with funds, the Queen imposed a heavy fine on the city, and proceeding to Perth and Dundee did the same with those who had received money from England. Many of these, however, had fled beyond recall. From St Andrews she banished to the north of Scotland several barons who had favoured the conspirators. Returning to Edinburgh, Mary assembled a fresh army, and along with Darnley, at the head of many of the nobles of the kingdom, and a very large force, set out for Dumfries. When she drew near that town, Maxwell came to throw himself at her feet and ask for pardon. The Earl of Argyll and Lord Boyd fled to Argyll; the Duke of Châtellerault and the others escaped to England, with the exception of a very few who begged to be forgiven.

"Four months after celebrating her marriage, Mary, who was now with child, sent David Chalmers, one of the judges, to apprise the Queen of England and the French King of that fact. He was to request Elizabeth not to give assistance to her subjects in arms against her, but oblige them to leave English territory. The first of these demands the Queen promised to comply with, but as regarded the second, she constituted herself intercessor on behalf of the exiles. Chalmers went on to France, found the king at Angers, and begged assistance from him against the rebels. The Queen-mother, then acting as regent, made great promises of sending an embassy on the subject to the Queen of England, and of contributing money and troops. But she kept putting off, while everything in Scotland remained in a state of confusion. Moray, accompanied by Gavin Hamilton, the Commendator of Kilwinning, left the other conspirators at Newcastle, went to the Queen of England and urgently implored assistance. In private he pressed for the fulfilment of the promises made him at various times by Randolph, Throckmorton, and other agents of the Queen in Scotland. Elizabeth, in order to free herself from suspicion, required Moray, before any answer could be returned, to declare in the presence of the whole Council that she herself had no knowledge of, or share in, the proceedings of the rebel lords. This he did, and then renewed his request. At length the Queen, concluding from private information which had reached her that matters in Scotland were ripe for a revolution, and that she could now help towards hastening it, sent an embassy to Mary Queen of Scots entreating her to deal gently with the rebels; and meanwhile contributed a small sum of money for their daily expenses. The Duke of Châtellerault, at length perceiving that he was duped, sent messengers to Scotland, through whom, and through the Earl of Errol and his own brother, the Archbishop of St Andrews, he handed over himself and his possessions to the Queen's mercy, and sued for the pardon of his fault. Being ordered by her to go over to France and abide there in exile for four years, he took leave of Elizabeth and obeyed his mistress's command. The other conspirators were by the Queen judged deserving of severer punishment, since they had repaid the long series of favours shown them, and the many benefits conferred upon them, by a cruel and treacherous attempt to take her life; and by order of the Parliament they were called to take their trial before the Lords on the 10th of March. Seeing absolute ruin hanging over them, the rebels resolved to tempt the ambition of Darnley, whose imagination was capable of being dazzled by the offer of new honours and dignities. . They succeeded in persuading him to enter into agreement with them on the following terms. He was to pardon their treason, secure them in the possession of their estates and of the public offices they formerly held, abolish the Catholic religion of his forefathers, and establish Calvinism throughout the kingdom. In return they promised to do all in their power to transfer the government into his hands; the crown being made hereditary in his family, even if he should have no children by the Queen, and the claim of the Hamiltons being entirely set aside. Her Majesty was to be declared incapable, as a female, of administering the government of the kingdom, and was to be advised to give her attention to pursuits more befitting her sex. The terms of this compact being thus arranged, the king concealed his share in it, and appeared to enter heartily into all the measures taken for the restoration of the Catholic religion, and for restraining the audacity of the rebel party. The parliament was opened and two measures submitted for discussion, one allowing the bishops and rectors of churches the full exercise of their ancient religion, and the other punishing the leaders of the conspiracy, who had more than once broken their faith and had taken up arms against the Queen. This punishment was to be adjudged by the votes of the whole assembly, so as to cut off all excuse for complaining that they were unjustly treated. But on the day preceding that appointed for the commencement of the debates the action of the parliament was interrupted by the violent and atrocious outrage now to be related.

"While the Queen was taking supper in her palace of Holyrood, near Edinburgh, her sister the Countess of Argyll sat at table with her, and many nobles of high rank stood by. In the middle of supper the King broke into the room, armed, and followed by Lord Ruthven, George Douglas, first chamberlain to the king, Andrew Ker of Fawdonside, and many others, armed with helmets, swords, and loaded pistols. Seizing upon David

the Piedmontese, who had been left in the Queen's
service by the envoy of the Duke of Savoy, and was a
man of fifty years of age, they dragged him with great
violence into the adjoining bed-chamber, the Queen
earnestly interceding for him and entreating them to do
him no injury. There he was cruelly butchered by the
Earl of Morton, who had but recently received that title
together with the office of Chancellor of Scotland from
the Queen, by Lord Lindsay, and many others, who
inflicted a great number of wounds upon him. It is
said that while in their hands he repeatedly called out,
'Justitia, justitia!' as though to condemn their cruelty
and assert his own innocence, since he had done
nothing to deserve this fate. The motive of the conspirators for their particular animosity against Rizzio
was the constancy and firmness with which he had acted
throughout these transactions in support of the ancient
religion [1] and the Queen's authority, and the great ability
and acquaintance with Scottish politics which enabled
him ever to suggest fresh means of defeating their
machinations. The murder being accomplished, and
those present reduced to terrified silence, the bitterest
threats were uttered against the Queen; and worse still,
after reproaches, extortionate demands, and many other
indignities, she was thrust, pale with the terror she had
undergone, and in disregard of the critical state of her
health, into her own chamber, and there imprisoned.
Eighty soldiers were posted outside the door, with orders
to prevent any of her servants or maidens from attending

[1] Morton and Ruthven, the leading conspirators, informed Cecil in
a letter from Berwick, written on the 27th March, that the end proposed by them in the murder of Rizzio was to prevent the universal
subversion of religion within Scotland. Morton and Ruthven to Cecil,
27th March 1566. "R. O. Scot., Eliz.," xii., No. 41.

her, and she was thus kept in custody for three nights and two days. During that time the Earl of Moray and the other exiles, who had awaited in England the tidings of this deed of blood, hastened to Edinburgh and conferred with the King concerning their designs.

"They proposed that Mary should be put to death on the pretext of adultery, that all Catholics should be either slain or driven out of the kingdom, the sacrifice of the Mass and evangelical doctrine be prohibited, and Calvinism established and strengthened by every possible means. In fine, Darnley was to be crowned King, and the royal authority conferred upon him by universal consent. In order to induce the young man to believe that they really intended carrying this out, the crafty conspirators allowed certain proclamations to be issued in his name alone. Whether Darnley was shocked at the atrocity of the crime into which he had been led, not having expected so tragical an issue of his plot, or he now foresaw the Queen's removal would only lead to similar or still worse measures against himself, he argued that it would be sufficient, before deciding upon taking her life, to lay before her the compact they had made on the subject of religion, and if she refused to assent to it, they could then consider what step to take next. The conspirators accordingly commissioned him to extort the Queen's assent to the support of the Calvinist party, by entreaties or by threats and denunciations. He obtained admittance to the chamber where the weeping Queen was imprisoned, and thus addressed her: 'I could not bear to meet your sight, if I thought of the horrors of the deed in which I have had a share. But the imminent peril in which we both stand at this moment claims all our attention. I have gained admission to your presence by an artifice, and my object is not to excuse but to accuse myself. I acknowledge my fault without extenuating it, and entreat forgiveness, and, though my ingratitude does not deserve it, your own wonted clemency and kindness will easily grant it. By the hand I hold I entreat you to pity one whose crime has made him miserable, and recall him to your side. You will do so if you judge of what has passed, not in its terrible reality, or from my words, but according to your own readiness to forgive. This I hope you will do, and your tears and the marks of sorrow on your countenance, and the loss of the surroundings of your rank—all so many evidences of my guilt—prevent my saying more.' The Queen fell on his shoulder as he knelt and raised him from the ground, for he could scarcely stand, and, though herself greatly affected, said much to him, reminding him gently of the honours she had conferred upon him, and the ungrateful return he had made, yet speaking neither unkindly nor reproachfully, but rather endeavouring to restore his courage and hope; after which he related to her the whole course of the conspiracy and his own share in it. She then sent him back to the conspirators. He told them that the Queen would consent to all their proposals, and turning to Moray, remarked: 'There is one thing which seems to me of importance. The Queen promises to follow our advice, so that we can attain the end proposed without bloodshed or danger of popular tumult, which we have every reason to avoid if possible. I will convey the conditions of peace in writing to the Queen, and have no doubt she will subscribe them. But since they are likely to be of great interest and moment in future times, she ought not to sign them while in custody of a military force, or else it will always be said hereafter that her assent was wrested from her by violence. I will undertake to guard her for this night by means of my own servants, and place them at the doors as my own attendants, not as gaolers of the Queen.'

"This proposal led to much deliberation. Those who were most strongly prejudiced against the Queen thought they had better not lose so favourable an opportunity of accomplishing her death; but others apprehended that such a step would be the signal for a general insurrection and a civil war. The good fortune of the Queen did not desert her. All agreed to the King's proposal, and this the more readily, because Mary was commonly reported to have been thrown into such a state of dejection and consternation that she could scarcely be expected to live over the night, or the next one, at furthest. The guard placed by the rebels was therefore removed, and in the middle of the night the King and Queen mounting their horses, held in readiness for them at the gates according to her Majesty's orders given to Arthur Erskine, the master of the horse, rode first to Seton, the castle of the Lord Seton, and after resting there a little while, and obtaining fresh horses, reached in safety the strong fortress of Dumbarton before morning. The conspirators had recourse to different modes of escape. Some sued for pardon, others proposed to take up arms, while of the rest each took the line which seemed best to him, whatever it might be. The Earls of Glencairn, Argyll, and Rothes, Lord Boyd, and even the Earl of Moray himself, went off into Argyllshire, whence they sent messengers to demand pardon; and obtained it.[1] But Morton, Ruthven, Lindsay, and the

[1] " With incredible facility," writes Mr Hosack, " Mary not only pardoned Moray and his associates, but received her brother once more into her confidence. If it was amiable in the sister to forgive, it was unwise in the Queen to forget, his ingratitude and treachery. Mary was not aware that at the very time when he was disclaiming all connection with the murderers of Rizzio, he was using his utmost

others who had been guilty of the murder, finding themselves thus abandoned by their fellow accomplices, fled into England. The Earls of Huntly and Bothwell (who had escaped from the rebels through a window at the time when the Queen was made prisoner), having admitted the Earl of Athole, Hamilton, and certain others of the nobility into their counsels, collected a body of nine thousand armed men, and brought Mary back in safety to Edinburgh, where the persons involved in the late conspiracy met with but a very slight degree of severity. Morton, Ruthven, and Lindsay fled to the Queen of England, and begged her to stand mediator for them.

"The Queen now repaired to Edinburgh Castle to await the birth of her child. Frequent consultations were held how best to guard against possible surprise on the part of the exiled lords, and also against Moray, Glencairn, and Argyll, who, if more cautious than their associates, were not much more loyal. The three last named had been pardoned, and now frequented the Court. As the time for the birth of her child drew nigh, Mary, wishing to provide for every emergency, privately took into her confidence John Leslie, Bishop of Ross, Alexander Erskine, David Chalmers, and the Provost [of Edinburgh], who were Catholics. She drew up her will with her own hand, and nominated in it certain guardians for her son, in case she should die in giving him birth. She also left in writing a list of her jewels and other articles of value, and entrusted them all to the care of the Bishop of Ross. Further, she gave directions that during the time of her confinement, meetings to deliberate upon the

influence with his English friends, Bedford and Randolph, on their behalf." J. Hosack, "Mary Queen of Scots," vol. i. p. 144. Cf. Sir H. Ellis, "Letters on English History," ii. 220.

administration of the realm should be held within the city of Edinburgh, which were to be presided over by the Bishop of Ross and the Earls of Huntly and Bothwell.

"At length, on the 19th of June 1566, she was delivered of a boy, an extremely fine and beautiful child. The nobles were all admitted to see the heir to the throne; cannon were fired, and every testimony was given of general satisfaction and rejoicing. Envoys were at once despatched with the news to the King of France, the Queen of England, and the Duke of Savoy, both in order to announce the event and to request that these sovereigns should send ambassadors to represent them personally at the baptism. As soon as the Queen recovered her health, she resumed hunting and other favourite sports. While awaiting the arrival of the envoys, she examined the treasury accounts, and fixed the sums required to render due honour to the baptismal ceremony. She went on to Jedburgh, near the borders of Scotland and England, and captured a formidable band of robbers, of whom several were put to death. During the struggle the Earl of Bothwell was severely wounded by a robber of the name of John Loyd, and nearly died, but he managed to slay his assailant, and ultimately recovered, contrary to expectation. The Queen herself was suddenly taken ill at Jedburgh, and all supposed she was dying, but by God's favour her life was spared.

"About this time the most Reverend the Bishop of Mondovi was sent by Pope Pius the Fifth, as Legate *a Latere*, to console the Queen in Scotland, and bear her a present of 100,000 crowns of gold to supply the sinews of war against the heretics. This aid had been requested in her name by the Bishop of Dunblane and Master Stephen Woltar [Wilson]. The Pope further promised that he would never desert her, but would, on the contrary, render her yet more efficient assistance if it were needed.

"The Queen did her best, as well personally as through the Bishop of Ross and others, to induce the nobles to give free entrance into the kingdom to the papal legate. The Catholic nobility were most anxious for this. No argument, however, could move the sectarian nobles, and especially the Earl of Moray, to assent. It became necessary, therefore, for the Queen to send John Beaton into France to offer her excuses to the legate on this head. Beaton (who was a person of good family, an excellent catholic, and a man of high character in every respect) brought with him a portion of the money.[1]

[1] Cf. Labanoff, ii. 20; vii. 107.

Bishop Leslie's narrative receives an important confirmation from a letter written shortly afterwards by Father Edmund Hay, on his return from Scotland, whither he had been sent by the Nuncio. The letter is dated Paris, 6th November 1566. "The papal Nuncio," writes Father Hay, "is compelled to linger in France, for the Queen cannot decide any way of receiving him with the respect which is due to himself, to the papal see, and to her own dignity, without occasioning very great tumults. This is supposed to have been the cause which threw her into that state of mind which produced such a dangerous illness, which attacked her at Jedburgh about the 18th of October 1566. Thinking that her last hour had come, she summoned all the nobles together with M. du Croc, the French ambassador, and requested that they would come to her in her bed-chamber. When she saw that they were there present, she protested that it was her wish to die in the faith and religion in which she had been born and baptised. She assured them that she frankly admitted that she had been neglectful not only in the government of the realm, but also, and chiefly, in promoting the Catholic religion; and therefore she asked God that of His mercy He would pardon her offences in this respect, and would show her some way by which Catholic interests could be put into better order for future.

"Having said this, she turned her eyes upon the Earl of Moray, who happened to be present at the time along with the others, and spoke to him with a grave earnestness, chiding him because that he, driven

"In the month of December the prince was baptised by the Archbishop of St Andrews, with all the rites and ceremonies of the Catholic Church. The Count d'Eu[1] represented the King of the French, and the Countess of Argyll, took the place of the Earl of Bedford, the ambassador of the Queen of England, who, as a heretic, refused to be present at the rites of the Catholic Church. The Earl of Moray acted instead of the ambassador of the Duke of Savoy, who had been long waited for, and was still on the road. The baptismal font, sent by the Queen of England, was of pure gold. The child received the name of James. All the ambassadors were afterwards entertained at a banquet, with the principal men of the kingdom; they received valuable presents from the Queen before returning to their respective countries. Bedford, on leaving, carried with him favourable answers to two requests made by him in the name of the Queen of England. One was the pardon of the murderers of the secretary David; the other was the confirmation of the treaty made at Leith between the French, the Scots, and the English, containing especially the article which provided that the Queen of Scotland should never, under any pretext, interfere with the peaceful succession of Elizabeth and her heirs to the crown of England, provided she had legitimate issue. On the other hand, Mary named three ambassadors to the Queen of England, the

onwards by the blindness of error and the evil advice of some knaves, not only had invested superstition with the name of religion, but had gone beyond all the chiefs of that faction in cruelly persecuting the Catholic faith. He alone was almost the only cause why it could find scarce a resting place within the kingdom." (Archives, S. J.)

[1] According to the State Papers, it was the Comte de Brienne who represented Mary's royal brother-in-law, Charles IX. of France, as godfather. Cf. Teulet, "Papiers d'Etat," vol. ii. pp. 147, 151. Labanoff, vol. vii. pp. 107, 108.

Bishop of Ross, the Earl of Huntly, and the Lord Herries, charged to obtain a public proclamation from Elizabeth that, in case of her own death without issue, the English crown should descend to the Queen of Scotland as next heir. But just as they were preparing to set out, Morton, Ruthven, Lindsay, and the other rebels, who had taken refuge in England, having obtained their pardon, returned to Scotland, and at the intercession of Moray, by whom they were introduced to her presence, were restored to all their former influence with the Queen. They retained the strongest resentment against Darnley for having betrayed their plans to the Queen, and they anxiously sought an opportunity of vengeance. In a short time they disclosed their design to Bothwell, urging him to murder the King, and promising that if he consented they would persuade or compel the Queen to give her hand to him. Bothwell was a man of ambitious and haughty character, endowed with great bodily strength and masculine beauty, but vicious and dissolute in morals. He accepted the task assigned him, conferred with the different conspirators, obtained the adherence of each one, and having assured himself of their concurrence, proceeded to take measures to carry out his plan. Meanwhile Darnley had gone to Glasgow on a visit to his father, the Earl of Lennox, and was there attacked by an illness which confined him to his bed. The Queen went from Edinburgh to him; and, through her kind words and attendance, he so far rallied as to be able to return to the capital along with her, in obedience to the advice of the nobility and his physicians. He was taken to the house of the Provost of Saint Mary's in the Fields, and though it was a humble building, one perhaps scarcely adapted for the abode of royalty, yet it had been decorated with the royal furniture and hangings used by her Majesty, and was considered by the doctors the most healthy spot in the whole town. The Queen paid him daily visits, accompanied by many of her nobles, and the conversation sometimes lasted till midnight.

"The conspirators, of whom the leaders were Moray, Morton, Argyll, Bothwell, and the secretary Lethington, met privately, and after interchange of views they unanimously subscribed a written agreement to the effect that Darnley might lawfully be put to death, both because of the offence he had committed in rescuing the Queen from custody on the occasion of David's murder, and because he had endeavoured to make himself King against her wishes. They added, for the encouragement of Bothwell, that Mary could scarcely be much displeased at what they were about to do, since Darnley had not only frequently betrayed her interests, but had likewise inflicted many affronts and injuries upon her. On the 10th of March 1567 the Queen had been to see Darnley, and remained in conversation with him, amusing him with various games until a late hour of the night, when she took leave of him and returned to the palace of Holyrood. Darnley then retired to rest. Bothwell, who had previously prepared a mine under the house and filled it with gunpowder, came shortly after midnight along with some chosen partners in his crime, and fired a train connected with the powder beneath. The explosion which followed blew the whole house into the air, from its very foundations. And so tremendous was the report that it roused nearly the entire populace of the town, who all crowded to the spot, nobles and common people alike. The body of Darnley and that of one of his servants were found in the garden close by. Some thought they had been blown thither by the force of the explosion; but I am inclined

to think, with others, that they had been strangled by
Bothwell and his associates, and thrown into the garden,
before the mine was fired. As soon as the Queen heard
of this atrocious deed, she rose from her bed, summoned
the nobles who were in the palace, and expressing to
them all the grief and anguish she felt, demanded an
inquiry into the authors of the crime and their punishment with all possible severity. Then entering the
chamber which had been hastily prepared for her
mourning, she first of all returned thanks to God for
her preservation from so great a peril, for it looked as
though the contrivers of the plot had expected that she
would pass the night there with the King, and had thus
planned the destruction of them both. She remained in
that retreat many days, constantly asking if anything
had been done. On the day after the murder the council
sent a magistrate accompanied by several surgeons to
examine the bodies of Darnley and his servant, and try
to discover in what way they had been killed. Questions were put to the other servants who slept in adjoining buildings, and whose escape was matter of general
surprise; different witnesses were called, and nothing
was omitted that could lead to the discovery of the
authors of the crime. Bothwell himself showed greater
diligence in the enquiry than anyone else. At nightfall
the body of the dead prince was conveyed to the chapel
of Holyrood, attended by some gentlemen on horseback,
and was placed in the royal vault near the remains of
James V.; but no befitting funeral pomp would have
been permitted in Scotland at that time when so many of
the great lords were Calvinists. While the Queen still
mourned in complete retirement, the people began
to murmur and accuse Bothwell of the crime, and notices
to this effect were posted in the city during the night.

Bothwell was highly incensed, and complained to everyone that he was suspected of an outrage which he had never thought of. One person who charged him with it he challenged to mortal combat; and later on he petitioned the Queen to allow him to be put on trial, that he might prove his innocence. This was granted, and on the day appointed one Thomas Crawfurd, a relative of the baron of Kilburnie, came forward and in the name of the Earl of Lennox publicly charged Bothwell with the murder of the king. He denied the charge, and the case was then referred to the judges in the usual manner. Fifteen men of noble birth, earls and barons, were selected to try the cause, and having listened to the arguments of Bothwell's accuser, the Earl of Argyll, as president of the court, pronounced judgment in its name, declaring Bothwell to be entirely acquitted of the crime. This decision was entered on the public records and attested by the signature of all the members of the court.

"Meanwhile Elizabeth sent a spy, or rather traitor, as was usual with her, under the guise of an ambassador, whose mission was to offer condolences to the Queen. This man's name was Killigrew, and he began at once to concert measures with the disaffected nobles for the purpose of creating a revolution in Scotland and deposing the Queen. He made particular enquiries into the circumstances of the recent tragedy, and the light in which the populace regarded it, wishing principally to gain time in which to arrange his plot against the Queen's peace and honour.

"In the ensuing Parliament, which met as early as could be convened in April 1567, the Earls of Huntly and Sutherland were restored by general consent to their hereditary dignities and patrimony, which Moray had wrested from them with violence and fraud. The sentence of the court also acquitting Bothwell was confirmed by the three estates of the realm. Bothwell, thus formally declared innocent, began openly to treat with them about his proposed marriage to the Queen, and made every endeavour to win over their assent to it, tempting some with promises, and menacing others with the most atrocious threats. Finding his project universally received with suspicion and dislike, he resolved to take the matter into his own hands and carry out his design by force. With this end in view he induced the associates in his crime to put their names to a letter which he drew up himself, declaring that he was entirely free from any imputation of guilt, and that there was no one to whom the Queen could be more suitably married than himself. They signed the paper without difficulty, for their only hope of safety now lay in his accession to the supreme power, as they were well aware. Next he summoned the other nobles, who he knew detested him, to his own house, one by one, and with threats, and the menace of being seized by the Queen's guards whom he then commanded, compelled them to put their hands to the same document; which they did, having before them the plain alternative of subscription or else death. Bothwell's own wife, the sister of the Earl of Huntly, was still alive, and as it was necessary for him to obtain release from his marriage bond, he first endeavoured to prevail on her by flattery and entreaty to consent to a separation or divorce. He found, however, his prayers and persuasions of no effect, for his wife absolutely refused to take part in so iniquitous a proceeding, and he therefore determined to remove this weight from his neck by an act of violence. He carried Lady Bothwell to Crichton Castle, and when alone with her in her chamber presented to her a cup of poisoned wine, requiring that she should either drink it or sign her name to the paper approving the divorce. She agreed to have the notaries summoned, as a means of escaping the immediate danger to her life, but she would not sign until she had declared in their presence that she did this unwillingly and simply under compulsion. The only reason assigned by Bothwell for a divorce openly proclaimed his baseness and utter disregard of all decency, for it was the confession of his own adultery, committed with a woman of low rank, whom he produced in presence of the Calvinist ministers. He was in consequence proclaimed by them free from the bond of matrimony, and announcement was made from the pulpit, in particular by John Craig, a preacher of Edinburgh, that Bothwell was now at liberty to marry any woman he pleased. Moray, after long consultation with his friends as to what steps he should take, left France under some pretext or other, and passing through England began to raise money from his own resources and to assemble a body of troops.

"The Queen now went from Edinburgh to Stirling to see her son, who was carefully guarded in the palace there. As she was returning, Bothwell met her on the way, at the head of a very large force of nobility and armed men, and compelled her by fears and menaces to go with him, much against her will, to the neighbouring castle of Dunbar. There he extorted her consent to marry him, to place him in command of the castle of Edinburgh, after accompanying him thither, to pardon him for the violence he had used, and proceed at once to the celebration of their nuptials.

"At this marriage—which strictly, however, cannot be called a marriage at all, since it was celebrated contrary to the laws of the Church—only a few nobles were present. For all the ecclesiastics and the greater part of the secular nobility, who made open profession of Catholicism, publicly opposed such nuptials. Above all the Archbishop of St Andrews, the Bishops of Ross and Dunblane, the Earl of Montgomery, and the Lord Seton, all of whom had ever been foremost supporters of the Queen, used on this occasion their utmost efforts to oppose a proceeding which was illicit, and likely to bring great harm and shame upon her. It was on this account that they met with the undisguised enmity of Bothwell. On her return from that unlawful ceremony, the Queen, finding some of them in her apartment, could not help weeping. At once she sent for the Bishop of Ross, and with many tears unlocked the secret of her heart to him; she showed many signs of repentance, and promised that never again would she do anything opposed to the rites of the Catholic and Roman Church, or permit any such thing to be done in her presence, even if it should be at the peril of her life. On the Feast of Pentecost, which followed soon afterwards, she publicly received the Eucharist after sacramental confession, in order to repair by so excellent an example of piety the mischief caused by her fault. It must be added, as was indeed believed by most people at the time, with every appearance of probability, that Bothwell threw the Queen's mind into a confused state by means of magical arts, and so brought her to consent to this marriage. By what other means she can have been induced to take a step so improper and unsuitable, and so unlike the usual tenor of her life, I confess I cannot see.[1]

[1] Sir James Melville, who had been taken prisoner with her, records that such violence was at last used to her that she had no longer a choice. Bothwell, in his dying confession, said that he accomplished his purpose "by the use of sweet waters." Morton's roclamations charged him with using violence to the Queen, "*and*

"While these events were passing in Edinburgh, there met at Stirling the Earls of Argyll, Mar, and Morton, Lord Lindsay, the Barons of Tullibardine and Lethington, the Queen's secretary, who had recently left her service and abandoned her cause. These had lately attached to their party the Earls of Glencairn and Athole, together with Lord Huntly and a great many others. They united in opposition to the Queen, and proceeded to assemble an armed force, under the pretext that they desired to rescue her from Bothwell's tyranny, and bring him to justice for the murder of the king.

"A fortnight after the marriage, Bothwell persuaded the Queen to leave Edinburgh, partly to gain recreation and change for her, and partly to use her name and authority to turn Lady Bothwell out of Crichton Castle. They went to Borthwick, and had remained there two days, when in the middle of the night the Earl of Huntly surrounded the castle with five hundred horsemen at least. Morton arrived at dawn, with a large reinforcement, and Mar, Lindsay, and other nobles of the faction soon came up, with as many soldiers as they could collect, mounted and on foot. They were beginning a regular siege, when Bothwell managed to get the Queen away secretly to Dunbar, and the conspirators, baulked of their prey, returned to Edinburgh. The Most Reverend Bishop of Dunblane had gone to Paris, as the Queen's envoy, to explain to the most Christian King and to the Queen's uncles the circumstances attending her marriage, and to offer excuses for it, assuring them at the same time that it was her secret design to extricate herself from the labyrinth in which she was involved, as soon as she could find a chance of doing so. The tumults, above

other more unleisum means." It seems not unlikely therefore that he employed some sweetened potion.

described, prevented the bishop's return to Scotland, where his constancy in the profession of the Catholic faith was well known.

"Shortly afterwards the Queen, on leaving the castle of Dunbar, was met near Musselburgh by the conspirators with an armed force. Bothwell had only a few soldiers on his side, though these few were well prepared to fight. But before they engaged, Kirkcaldy of Grange asked for speech with the Queen, and assured her they had no intention of doing her any injury, but only sought to rescue her from the hands of Bothwell, provide for the safety of her son, and bring the Earl to justice for the murder of Darnley. They easily persuaded her to join their army, with only a few waiting-maids and attendants, as the best means of allaying the public excitement; and she recommended Bothwell, before she left him, to secure his own safety. He first went to Moray, thence he sailed to the Orkneys, and from that crossed over to Norway. Arrived there he proceeded by land to the King of Denmark, by whom he was honourably received in the beginning, but was afterwards consigned to a gloomy prison, where he ended his days. The Queen was at first kindly treated by the conspirators, as one whose term of power was drawing to its close. The next morning she was placed on horseback and conveyed to Loch Leven, and taken in a boat to the castle, where she was detained for a year in the closest confinement. The conspirators, having now attained their object, sent for Moray from France, and committed the government to his hands. They proclaimed the Queen's son, who was scarcely a year old, King of Scotland, appointed themselves his guardians, and proceeded to govern and misgovern everything at their pleasure. After a time the Lord Seton and John Beaton, formerly intimate friends of the Queen, and now old men, who had not ceased to devise plans for her liberation, succeeded in winning over George Douglas, who had charge of the gates of the castle, and by his means gained one of the servants. The latter, while his master was at supper, stole the keys of the apartment in which the Queen was confined, opened the door and took the keys to her. She left the castle by a postern gate, entered a boat, and was rowed across the lake by Douglas and his associate. These two on landing raised the concerted signal of her freedom, and a large body of horsemen who were waiting among the hills came forward to greet her, and received her with every mark of honour. Messengers were sent in all directions to announce the liberation of the Queen. The heartiest demonstrations of joy were visible throughout the kingdom; the nobles who remained faithful to Mary flew to arms and assembled their forces. Not to prolong the narrative of the almost endless calamities of this kingdom and of its unfortunate queen, we barely tell how, within a few days after she had been set free, she was defeated in battle by the conspirators at Langside, and hastened into England, to cast herself on the protection of her royal kinswoman. She was arrested by Elizabeth, and has now been kept a prisoner twelve years. Scotland during this time has been a scene of marvellous confusion. The Queen's most determined enemy and infamous betrayer, the Earl of Moray, was killed in sight of his own supporters by a noble of the house of Hamilton, and later a similar fate overtook the Earl of Lennox; while others who, on the Queen's forced retirement from Scotland, had attempted to seize her power and authority . . ."[1]

[1] This last sentence of Bishop Leslie's MS. is left incomplete. Latin MS. "Arch. Vat. Politicorum Var.," xvi. p. 297.

PART THE SECOND.

NARRATIVES AND LETTERS
ILLUSTRATING THE HISTORY OF SCOTCH CATHOLICS UNDER JAMES THE SIXTH.

I.

LETTERS AND MEMORIALS OF THE STATE AND PROGRESS OF EVENTS FROM 1570 TO 1603.

On learning the unexpected death of the Earl of Moray, Elizabeth was at first in considerable perplexity, as all her schemes now seemed baffled. But she was soon reassured by the intelligence that her minister, Cecil, and her other partisans had succeeded in raising the Earl of Lennox to the regency. Arriving suddenly from England with an English army, Lennox burnt the castles of a few of the Scottish nobility, wasted the Hamilton country, and put to a cruel death the Archbishop of St Andrews, Primate of Scotland. Already, in order to obtain power, Lennox had taken a share in the murder of Rizzio in 1566, though he knew that the attempt was directed not only against the unfortunate Italian, but also against the Queen, who was then far advanced in pregnancy. He who at that time had been capable of endangering the life of his own son's child, is not likely to have hesitated from any sensitive scruples to deliver up this valuable hostage to Elizabeth four years later; and it was upon this subject of negotiation that he began his correspondence with Elizabeth, who was now the arbitress of Scotland.

While such negotiations were in progress, Lennox, not content with the oppression he exercised towards all the friends of the captive Queen, was shameless enough to place among the attendants of the young Prince persons who taught him to apply to his mother terms that were "filthy and most dishonest."[1] Those who had gone so far in wickedness saw no other hope of safety for themselves than in building up an impassable barrier of prejudice between the son and his mother, and they appointed the godless Buchanan, whose hatred to Mary was well known, to be tutor to James VI. Lennox, however, speedily met with the punishment of his crimes; for, on the 3rd of September 1571, the Queen's party having surprised the Castle of Stirling, he was put to death, in revenge for the murder of the Archbishop of St Andrews. His place was taken by the Earl of Mar, who had the care of the young King of Scotland in Stirling Castle. James was then only six years old, and as he would not attain his majority till he was seventeen, the Earl looked forward to a prolonged tenure of office, if only the Queen was not allowed to escape from her prison and once more ascend the throne. Mar, the former tutor and guardian who had protected and instructed the young Queen, then a helpless child, in his priory at Inchmahome; who had resided for ten years at her Court in France; who had received from her so many marks of favour and friendship, did not scruple to piece together again the threads of the relations which Elizabeth had established, and which had twice been broken in her hands by the unexpected deaths of Moray and of Lennox. The proposal was that the imprisoned Queen should be given up, and put to death within four hours after she had crossed the Border.[2] Everything was

[1] Strickland, Letters of Mary Queen of Scots. London, 1848, vol. i. p. 233.

[2] Secret instructions for H. Killigrew, September 10, 1572; Murdin's "State Papers," p. 224, 225; Tytler's "Inquiry," vol. ii. p. 314; Letters from Killigrew to Burleigh and Leicester, Cotton. Lib. Calig., c. iii. f. 375, 19th September 1572.

agreed upon except the price which the Earl was to receive for the murder, since he would not assassinate his Sovereign for nothing. While only waiting for the reply from London to a last message on this subject, Mar went, perhaps imprudently, to dine at Dalkeith with his worthy friend the Earl of Morton, who was a secret aspirant to the regency. Next morning he was seized with an illness which would yield to no remedies, and expired as he was entering the castle at Stirling, October 28, 1572.

Morton succeeded to the inheritance. On the 24th of November he assumed the regency, which he owed to the patronage of Elizabeth,[1] who wrote to him a very flattering letter, and, without alluding to Mary's murder, offered to give him most effective support in money and troops.[2] On the 25th of April an English army appeared in the capital, and the battering train having at the same time arrived by sea, the siege of Edinburgh Castle commenced. Kirkaldy of Grange and Lethington, who had returned to their allegiance, looked with confidence to the arrival of assistance from France; but Verac, commissioned to bring them relief from the French King, was driven by a tempest into Scarborough, and detained in England. The last gleam of hope which their gallant defence had kindled in the desolate heart of Mary, was extinguished by the surrender of her last stronghold to the English forces under Sir William Drury, on the 29th of May 1573.

The Queen, now in prison in England, was more

---

[1] Great secrecy was to be used in the delivery of the money to Morton. The sum was £2500. Letter from Sir Valentine Brown to Lord Burghley, 26th December 1572, quoted by Tytler, vol. ix. p. 330.

[2] MS. Letter, B. M. Vespasian, F. vi. fol. 181 d.; Burghley to Walsingham, 3d November, 1572.

anxious than ever for the safety of her son, now that he was in the power of Morton.

"I am in great distress," she writes, "at not having any tidings of my son. Although the Earl of Shrewsbury, when I ask him, always says that he has not heard otherwise (thank God!) than that he is well; and this bearer, of whom I have made inquiry, has also assured me of the same, which, as neither you nor the Bishop of Ross have written anything to the contrary to me, consoles me; yet, as I cannot but feel apprehensive till I am thoroughly assured about it, I entreat you, Monsieur de la Mothe Fénélon, to obtain, if possible, of the Queen my good sister, permission to have tidings of him, from time to time, on which I can depend. He is all I have in the world, and the older I grow, the more foolish mother do I become, in which, however, I think I may be pardoned; and, being deprived of the sight of him, if, at least, I can be assured of his health, my ills would be half alleviated, and I could bear my afflictions more easily."[1]

Her principal and unceasing anxiety, as will easily be understood, was to withdraw her son, if possible, from the moral and religious influence of Morton, as well as from the grasping eagerness of Elizabeth, who kept returning to the subject in her correspondence with the Regent. It was in reference to this subject[2] that Mary renewed her former friendly relations with the Countess of Lennox. The countess had at last penetrated the terrible mystery of 1567. She could no longer doubt the innocence of her daughter-in-law, and the guilt of Morton towards her son.[3] The mother and the grand-

[1] "Labanoff," vol. iv. p. 100.

[2] We are not informed as to the exact date.

[3] Nothing can be more affectionate than the letter she wrote to Mary on the 6th of November 1575. ". . . I beseech your Majesty fear not, but trust in God, that all shall be well; the treachery of

mother devised plans for the safety of the child in whom the affections of both were centred—their "gentle and peerless jewel of Scotland." Believing his life to be in imminent danger while he was in the hands of his father's murderer, they proposed that he should be privily stolen out of Morton's hands, carried from Stirling to Dumbarton, and then embarked for Flanders, and consigned to the care of the King of Spain for his education. The arrest of the Countess of Lennox and her incarceration in the Tower of London put an end to the design of abducting the little king.

In February 1576 Mary enjoyed one comfort. Mr Hamilton, a faithful follower having returned from Scotland, brought the consoling intelligence which she communicates to La Mothe Fénélon in this brief but joyous sentence :—" My son loves me much !"[1] About the same time she received satisfactory news touching the arrival in England of a copy of Bothwell's confession, attested by the Danish bishop and nobles in whose presence it was uttered. Not the least interesting incident connected with the publication of Bothwell's confession, was the effect it produced on the mind of Mary's son. One day, while the young Prince was studying in his chamber at Stirling, his attention was caught by some words which the Laird of Tullibardine, the controller of the household, read aloud at that moment to another gentleman of rank. The young James rose, left his work, and coming suddenly upon them, demanded sight

your traitors is known better than before." She hopes that her grand-daughter, Arabella Stuart, Darnley's niece, "may one day serve Mary." She wishes Mary a "long and happy life," and subscribes herself "Your Majesty's most humble and loving mother and aunt. R. O." See the facsimile of the document, vol. v. "Lives of the Queens of Scotland and English Princesses," by Miss Strickland.

[1] "Labanoff," vol. iv. p. 265.

of the paper they were reading. Tullibardine would not at first allow him to see it, but James snatched it out of his hand, read it straight through, then gave it back and returned to his seat without another word. The rest of the day he was gayer than usual, conversed cheerfully with the gentlemen about him, and as he continued in the like animated mood from dinner to supper, all present were curious to learn the cause. After supper, Tullibardine commended him for his gracious deportment, and expressed pleasure at seeing him so cheerful. "Have I not reason, Tullibardine, to be so," replied the royal boy; "and to rejoice that very grievous accusations and calumnies having been all along impressed upon me against her Majesty the Queen, my mother, I have this day seen so manifest a testimony of her innocence?"[1]

Early in the spring of 1578, Mary exulted in the tidings of a bold stroke by which the Earls of Argyll and Athole had deposed Morton from the regency, and invested her son with the government of Scotland, though he had not fully completed his twelfth year. Athole's design in effecting this bloodless revolution is thus explained by one of his most intimate friends, the Bishop of Ross :—

John Leslie, Bishop of Ross, to Cardinal de Como.

"MOST ILLUSTRIOUS AND MOST REVEREND LORD,—I wrote not long ago to your illustrious Lordship, stating that we had no information of what was going on in Scotland, because the messengers whom we sent to that country were not permitted to return. Now, however,

---

[1] Keith's "Appendix," page 143. The Archbishop of Glasgow was informed of this by a gentleman to whom Tullibardine had repeated it.

two of them, sent into Scotland by us, came back here, by God's goodness on the 13th of May, namely, Captain Robert Stewart, a Scotchman of high birth, and another from whom I learnt, by letter and by word of mouth, what I am about to relate. In April last there was a meeting of the nobles held at Stirling, at which it was unanimously agreed that the King should be at liberty to leave Stirling Castle at his pleasure, and should traverse the kingdom and show himself to his subjects, in order that they might acknowledge and receive him as their sovereign. Further, the noblemen who were under bond for his safe custody were released from the obligation. They have now under discussion the constitution of his household, and the selection of a hundred men of noble birth, who are to be charged with his safety. On this account there are a great many on their way from France into Scotland, to be enrolled among the King's guards, and in the royal household. Fears are nevertheless entertained that, if the King should go anywhere with an insufficient military force to protect him, he may be carried into England at the instigation of Morton, who lately has held the administration in Scotland, and is said to have a private understanding with the Queen of England on this point. The alarm is all the better founded, because the illustrious Earl of Athole, who was one of the King's nearest kinsmen, and stood in the place of a parent to him, and who, out of Christian zeal for religion, had deposed Morton from the administration of the kingdom of Scotland, fell sick shortly after the convention of the nobles, and died, to the King's great regret and that of all ranks and orders in the kingdom. He died, as they affirm, not without suspicion of poison, administered to him at table, when Morton himself and several of his adherents were present with a large party. It is impossible to express how great a loss the Christian cause in the country has sustained by his death. He was a truly Catholic nobleman, and illustrious protector of the Catholic party. He had only one object, to which he directed all his efforts and all his influence—the restoration to the Scottish people of the Christian religion of their forefathers. He frequently wrote to me, declaring that he desired nothing more earnestly than that I should be permitted to return to Scotland, and that he could not rest nor enjoy any peace of mind until he had me at hand to assist the King and himself with my advice. There is, however, one very hopeful circumstance that the King has written to summon his cousin, the Lord d'Aubigny, from France, a man of sound judgment and marked prudence, and a constant upholder of the Catholic religion, and one whom the King is anxious to have at his side. There is every hope that in process of time he will be able to do much to settle the affairs of Scotland. The hand of the Lord is not shortened, as your illustrious lordship is well aware. We have lost the Earl of Athole, but God is able, in the words of Holy Scripture, to raise us up another saviour. There are many left who have not bent their knees before Baal. The Earl's death has occasioned me no little grief, since he was one of my most intimate friends; yet I shall not cease to promote the cause of religion and good government in my native country, to the utmost of my power. Yesterday I saw the most Christian King of France, and the illustrious Duke of Guise, and gave them all the information I could. They promised every assistance in their power, and engaged to arrange everything, with the utmost dispatch possible, for the expedition of Lord d'Aubigny. There are, moreover, many earls and other nobles, of good principles, besides men of inferior rank, who will have no difficulty in repressing the efforts of these wicked men, if they can only receive assistance from some Christian Prince. I have no doubt your most illustrious Lordship will inform the Holy Father of all these circumstances. I continually pray Almighty God for the safety of his Holiness, and that he will preserve your Lordship long in this life.

"Your illustrious Lordship's
"Devoted Servant,
JOHN, BISHOP OF ROSS."

PARIS, *May* 15, 1579.[1]

The Same to the Same.

"MOST ILLUSTRIOUS AND MOST REVEREND LORD,—I have received a letter from your most illustrious Lordship, in which you ask for information relative to the Parliament held in Scotland in April, from which you had conceived great hopes of the restoration of religion in that country. All good men looked forward confidently to this assembly of the nobles, because the illustrious Earl of Athole had raised a standard round which the well-wishers of the State were eager to rally. His influence with the young Prince was almost like that of a father, and he had brought not only the King himself, and most of the principal men of the Kingdom, but some of the Calvinist ministers as well, to agree to my returning to my country with safety, on condition that I would abstain from raising any subject of controversy, and join with the others in consultation as to the mode of carrying on the administration. This was indeed the matter of most pressing necessity, and I could have introduced

[1] Endorsed. Illmo et R^{mo} D^{no} D. Card^{li} Comensi Dno Meo Observandissimo. Romæ. Forwarded by Dandini, 17th of May. Original. (Secret Archives of the Vatican Nunciatura Franciæ, vol. xiv. fol. 230).

the subject of religion gradually as time went on, and the progress of business brought it under notice. It was another step in my favour that he induced the King to approve and endorse all my proceedings in Germany on behalf of the Scottish nation, a verbal account of which has been rendered to his Majesty, who desired to have the written documents submitted to him. I am about to send them through the hands of the Lord d'Aubigny, a French nobleman of the royal house of Scotland, one devoted to the Catholic religion, who is proceeding to Scotland with great authority, being specially summoned by letters from the young King, his kinsman. I have learnt these particulars partly from the letters of the Countess of Athole, and partly from other sources. Unhappily our hopes of success have been in great degree overthrown by the perfidy of Morton. He has poisoned the Earl of Athole, as every one believes—a grievous loss to our cause. Previously to his death the Earl received the Sacraments of the Church with every indication of piety, deliberately made his will and arranged his affairs, and wrote a private letter to the young King, pointing out how he could best avoid the treachery of his enemies, and what counsellors he ought to call to his assistance. Since his death matters in Scotland have continued to get worse and worse. Morton exercises an intolerable tyranny. He has proscribed the ancient house of Hamilton who are the next heirs to the crown after Mary Queen of Scots, and the young King, her son. He holds all their castles, and has put to death many members of their family, and keeps others in prison. Among these last is the Earl of Arran, who is the head of the family, though unfortunately out of his mind. Others he has interdicted from fire and water, especially two of the Earl of Arran's brothers,

John the Commendator of Arbroath, who was at Rome in the time of the late Pope Pius IV., and Claud, Commendator of Paisley, both favourers of the Catholic Cause, as well as many others who have succeeded in making their escape. These he has accused of parricide, declaring them, by a cruel edict issued in the King's name, to be murderers of the Regent of Scotland, and pronouncing them guilty of high treason. The relatives of the Earl of Athole are reduced to silence, and prevented from complaining of his death or bringing the authors of it to justice. The atrocious nature of these injuries is deeply felt by noble and generous minds, and may not improbably bring about a reaction. The relatives of Hamilton and of Athole are not likely to submit to such treatment, but will defend their rights by force of arms, if it cannot be done in any other way. Having crushed the Hamiltons, Morton proceeded to exercise the same severity against the Gordons, who are of their kin; besides being allied to them by marriage. The chief of the Gordons is the Earl of Huntly, a young man eighteen years of age, of excellent disposition, and well brought up in the Christian Faith; but he has escaped to Paris, having obtained leave through the Earl of Athole before that nobleman's death. We shall keep him for better times, like another Joas rescued from the cruelty of Athaliah, in hopes that he may restore the worship of God in Scotland, one of these days. The men who took part in the civil wars sometime back are apprehensive, not without reason, of an interruption of the peace which they had concluded with Morton. In order to prevent any from seeking safety in flight, Morton has published a letter written in the name of the young King, filled with falsehood and misrepresentation, and sufficiently indicating the cruelty of his mind and his detestation of the Hamiltons. I shall use every exertion in my power to discover, if possible, some means of defeating this man's machinations, and securing the safety of our young Prince, who is in imminent danger of being either given up to the English or put to death by the treachery of Morton. Our hopes are certainly lessened but not overthrown. Many good men remain, who in conjunction with the Hamiltons, the Atholes, and the Gordons, may prove strong enough to overthrow Morton's tyranny. The young Earl of Athole, the worthy son of an excellent father, a young man of eighteen years of age, and who inherits his father's piety and virtues as well as his possessions, is complaining loudly among all orders and degrees in Scotland, of the iniquitous murder of his parent, and is entreating the assistance of the great men of the Kingdom, the nobles, and everyone else. He is thus coming forward as a leader of opposition to Morton, and unless the latter can obtain aid from abroad, which he usually does, his usurpation may still be easily overthrown. . . ."

"Your illustrious Lordship's
"Devoted Servant,
"JOHN, BISHOP OF ROSS."
PARIS, *June* 20, 1579.[1]

Shortly after Athole's death, the General Assembly met at Edinburgh, and having chosen Mr Thomas Smeton for their moderator, appointed a council of the brethren to wait upon the King, with some requests to which they besought his attention. These were that he should interdict all parents, under heavy penalties, from sending their children to be educated at the University of Paris,

[1] Endorsed:—Illmo et R^{mo} D$^{no.}$ . . . Card. Comens. Domino meo observantissimo (Secret Archives of the Vatican).

or other foreign colleges professing the Catholic religion; that he should cause the University of St Andrews, some of whose professors had recently left the Protestant Communion, to be reformed in all its colleges and foundations; and should take Order for the banishment of the Jesuits, whom the Assembly denominated "the pestilent dregs of a most detestable idolatry."

Father John Hay, of the Society of Jesus, had just succeeded in penetrating into Scotland, where his presence caused no little excitement, as will appear from the following letter:—

Fr. John Hay to Edward Mercurian, General of the Society of Jesus.

"RIGHT REVEREND FATHER IN CHRIST—PAX CHRISTI, —I cannot say how much I was delighted with your Paternity's letter, in which you reply at length to one addressed by me to you from Bordeaux, just as I was setting out for Scotland.

"Your epistle reached me at the moment when the Calvinist ministers, who, alas! have ruled with an iron rod for many years past in Scotland, had decided to summon me by royal letters before the Council. It seemed like an interposition of Divine providence that at the very moment I was undergoing persecution a letter from your Paternity, so full of energy and wisdom, should have come to strengthen me in my resolution of adhering to our faith and rule, so that I more easily repulsed the attacks made against me. It would only fatigue your Paternity if I were to recount all my adventures in my long and toilsome expedition. I there-

[1] John Hay, of the family of Hay of Dalgaty, born in 1546, entered the Society on the 25th January 1566. He died at Pont-à-Mousson on the 21st of May 1607.

fore merely note down what will convey information as to the state of the Kingdom of Scotland, in the hope that this realm may be the sooner cleansed from the filth of heresy which has so long defiled it.

"I embarked at Bordeaux on the 23d of December, on board a Scottish vessel with a crew composed evidently of Calvinists (except two who were Catholics secretly), and I was often obliged to discuss with them the mysteries of our religion. When they were unable to answer my arguments they said their ministers would help them. I protested that I was not only waiting but desirous to meet their ministers in controversy, if the King commanded me to do so. The voyage, which was a very tedious one at that time of the year, occupied a month, and on the 20th of January we reached in safety the harbour of Dundee, having by God's mercy escaped from imminent peril of our lives. There was no little commotion in the town at the news of my arrival; for the people who had originally adopted the Lutheran heresy from the Germans, and then abandoned it for that of Calvin, now defended these latter errors with greater pugnacity than in any other part of Scotland. The majority, however, were well inclined, had they been let alone, towards the Catholic faith; and the magistrates, fully aware of this circumstance, were dreadfully afraid lest my expostulations might bring the people to reject the impieties of Calvinism, and yet did not know how to provide against the danger. If they were to incite the citizens to lay violent hands upon me, they foresaw that they would expose themselves to great risk from the vengeance of my kinsmen and clansmen; but it was no less evident that they would incur the hostility of their ministers if they allowed me to remain in the town unharmed. It was eight o'clock in the morning when our vessel cast anchor, so that the citizens received the first intimation of our approach from the report of the discharge of our cannon. I meant to have gone that night to a farm three miles off, belonging to my brother; but the master of the inn where I put up dissuaded me from doing so, assuring me that I was in no sort of danger, if only I kept my counsel about matters of controversy, and he declared he could send me safely on to the North of Scotland. I thought I could not well reject this man's advice, as my brother was under some obligations to him, though I saw very plainly what was about to happen.

"On the following day, the minister was so frightened at my arrival in the town that he stopped short in his sermon, and left it unfinished, as many of his hearers noticed; he determined at once to take measures for preventing my coming being ever repeated. He therefore proposed to the magistrate that I should be detained at the inn, until the Royal Council had received information of my arrival in Scotland. At the same time he felt that this alone would be little use, as the people were certain to assemble in large numbers to hear me, which, indeed, they had already expressed their intention of doing. He therefore secretly sent one of his boon companions to inform my host that the magistrates meant to detain me in custody. My host having communicated this piece of news to me, I exchanged my cloak for a coarse woollen plaid, such as the peasantry in Scotland commonly wear, and left the town instantly, with a boy for my guide. I sent the lad back again to bring me a horse, for though the journey was not long, yet having been out of health, I found I was not strong enough to make it on foot. I had scarcely left the city when I encountered a number of persons of rank, and was questioned with much curiosity as to who I was, and where I came from. I would not reply till I had ascertained that I had got beyond the boundary of the jurisdiction of Dundee; and when they learnt that I was a man of education, that I was withdrawing from the control of the magistrate, and that the latter had threatened to detain me in custody at the suggestion of his minister, one of them asked whether I was a Jesuit. When I answered frankly that I was one of those whom they called Jesuits, he told me not to be under any uneasiness, and that the minister had better look out for himself, since my kinsmen lived close by, and would be sure to pay him out very handsomely for any wrong done to me. He inveighed sharply against the minister, and invited me to rest at his house. But as I was anxious to push on to the north, I resolved to decline any invitation, however generous. On the evening of that day four municipal officers of the town came to look for me at the inn, and on hearing I had gone off, instead of taking this at all ill, they commended the conduct of my landlord highly. They quite understood they had gone as far as they durst without offending any of my clansmen; though, in order to avoid incurring suspicion from the chief ministers for neglect of their duty, they summoned into court the master of the vessel which had brought me to Scotland. He answered with great spirit that he had done nothing in opposition to the laws of the country, and had only brought to his native land a Scotchman who was almost worn out with sickness, was under no accusation of treason, and had no design of disturbing the tranquillity of that part of the country by simply coming to see his friends, with the hope of recovering his health. He said, 'If you want to bring him to trial you had better obtain an order from the

King, and I will answer for his appearance if he is summoned before the Council.' Most of the sailors who had come with me from Bordeaux, took up my defence with warmth when they heard that their minister threatened proceedings against me; and they roundly asserted that the members of our Society were far beyond the ministers in holiness of life, and if the question were to be decided by force of arms, many more would stand up for the Jesuits than for the ministers.

"The minister of Dundee began to assail the holiness of our institute with great acrimony in his sermons, the result of which was that the people took to making enquiries for themselves, with respect to our mode of life, manners and discipline, from such persons as had lived in France. Several of them commended our rule, and drew this argument in our favour from the name Jesuit. 'Since they imitate Jesus Christ, those who so cruelly oppose them must be under a great mistake, and in profound ignorance of what the Christian religion is.' The word Jesuit was in everybody's mouth, and nothing else was heard at table, among the higher classes, in taverns, in the market, or in sermons delivered in the church. It was reported all over the kingdom that twelve members of the Society, men of the most eminent piety and learning, had landed at the port of Dundee, and had begun to prove that all the ministers were ignorant deceivers. This rumour caused so much dismay among the ministers that they almost despaired of maintaining their influence in Scotland, and set about exhorting their hearers to constancy and perseverance in the cause, since they could not conceal that their Church was threatened with a grave and pressing peril. The Jesuits (they said) were a new race of persons, far worse than the Papists (as they call the Catholics), and so skilful in the use of

K

controversial weapons, that wherever they go they easily lead the minds of men astray.

"I was obliged to stay three days at my brother's farm, having left my books and papers in the ship, but through the care of two of the sailors, and of my landlord, I did not lose a single leaf. Some Hebrew books fell into the minister's hands, who immediately returned them to me as soon as he knew I was going into the north. I received a message from my brother Master Edmund Hay,[1] a man of eminence and a Catholic, held in great repute among the people of our country for wisdom; who most kindly entreated me, if I retained any human regard and benevolence towards those attached to me by the ties of consanguinity, not to go to my brother in the north until I had paid him a visit at his house. Accordingly he kept me with him twelve days, my brother having thrown out some hopes of coming into that part of Scotland himself. The latter had heard nothing all this time of my arrival in the country, except by report; and although everyone affirmed I had reached Scotland, he refused to believe it, because the people on his land at Dundee had neglected to inform him of it. I found that the family who were to receive and entertain me on my progress northward were Catholics, ladies advanced in years, and so steadfast in their faith that no threats of the ministers could deter them from the open profession of it.

"My brother feared my arrival might seriously involve

[1] Mr Edmund Hay, advocate, was one of the counsel for the Earl of Bothwell, on his trial for the murder of Darnley, and in the process of his divorce. (Buchanan's "Detection," and Goodall's "Examination," i. 368). He signs a contract as a procurator, Jan. 2, 1572. ("Register Book of Contracts of the Commissariat of St Andrew's.") Crawfurd seems to have confounded the Advocate with Father Edmund Hay, S.J. (M'Crie's Life of Andrew Melville.)

the family of the Hays; for at this period, the influence of the ministers was so great that they were able to place the government of the country in the hands of any persons they liked, or to remove them at pleasure. Since that time (thank God) the numerous instances of dishonesty in which they have been detected, have taken effect, and they are now regarded with utter and universal contempt. The Earl of Errol, Constable of the Kingdom, and head of the family of the Hays, came to see me at my brother's house, his own residence being only five miles distant, and he earnestly entreated my brother to allow me to spend some time with him, offering to conduct me to the King, and confidently promising that I should sustain no injury at the hands of the ministers. My brother, however, would not part with me, hoping that by this means he would be able to soften the hatred of the ministers against me. As soon as my arrival in the north was known, the people showed extraordinary anxiety to hear me preach, and not unfrequently there were larger numbers assembled in the churches of the neighbourhood than had been known within the memory of anyone living; many persons coming two days' journey on purpose. The most marvellous and incredible reports were circulated regarding me. I had seen and copied the dogmas of the Christian faith written with the finger of God upon the tables of stone given to Moses; others said, I had been carried down into hell; others, that I was clothed only in sackcloth, and gifted with such a wonderful and miraculous power of healing that there was no sickness or disease, how severe and dangerous soever, which I could not remove with perfect ease. Multitudes of people afflicted with hopeless ailments came in crowds to my brother's house to be cured, and I could scarcely get them to believe me when I assured them I had no skill in medicine, and had never studied it, but had in fact come to Scotland myself for the recovery of my own health.

"All this greatly tended to increase the dislike of the ministers for me, bitter as it had been before. The first thing they did was to obtain an order from the King, that no one in future should enter the kingdom without reporting his arrival to the Council, and appearing in person before them; and next, they procured letters summoning me to present myself before the Council on the 24th of March. They were in good hopes I should be alarmed, and quit the country before that date, until the event convinced them of their mistake. One of great note amongst them, and in high repute for learning, who had disputed with me on the subject of the invocation of the saints, while I was at the house of my brother, Master Edmund Hay, advised his brethren not to challenge me to controversy, if they wished to preserve the high opinion which the people had hitherto formed of them. In the month of July the ministers held an assembly at Edinburgh, and resolved, among other things, that I should be compelled to quit the country. As soon as I heard that the ministers had once more obtained royal letters to this effect (what had become of the former ones I know not), I wrote to the Constable of the kingdom, from my sister's house, requesting him to meet me at Stirling, where the King then resided, on the 10th of August; because it devolved upon him (the King being too young) to defend me from so great an outrage. He happened to be at my brother's house when my letter was delivered to him, and on reading it replied immediately that my demand was perfectly just, and that he would not fail me on the day appointed. This answer to me he showed to my mother and to my brother, and desired the latter to acquaint him as soon as the royal letters were published. Others of my kindred, and some of the Protestants, declared that they would also accompany me. After waiting several days for the letters from the Court, and concluding as time went by that they could not have been issued, they unexpectedly arrived by the hands of an official messenger after sunset on August 6th. This was a great annoyance to my brother, partly because the time allowed did not admit of notice being given to the Constable and to my other kinsmen, and also because it was a thing unheard of in Scottish history for even a thief to be summoned from our part of the country to appear before the Royal Council, without at least six days' interval for the journey, this being the shortest space permitted by the law. He thought, however, that it was better to submit, and I asked him to let me go without any other companion than one attendant, for he was engaged in building his castle, and his servants were so much occupied in the work that I saw he could not leave home just then without serious inconvenience. For his part he wanted me to remain at home, lest in my weak state of health I should be quite knocked up by the fatigue of the journey. But when he perceived me bent upon going, he arranged his home affairs as well as he could in the emergency, and we set out together at mid-day on the 7th of August, with a retinue of attendants, and were not out of boot and saddle till we arrived at Perth, eighty miles from my brother's residence. We encountered heavy rain, followed by intense cold, and my brother, who had not left his home for two years before, was seized with a severe attack of fever; some of his followers were also laid up with various maladies, and one of them died in consequence after our return to the North. On August the 9th we reached Stirling, the ministers not expecting our arrival. They had intended to proclaim me a rebel, in case of my not coming at the time appointed, and were in fear that if I had been allowed the six days' notice required by law to perform the journey, the constable and other of my kindred who would likely have accompanied me in considerable numbers, might support my cause by force of arms, and place the Calvinist's tenure of power in jeopardy. I met, the same evening, a superintendent and chief leader amongst the ministers, who followed his salutation with the information that he had many weapons ready for the attack upon me. The next day, August 10th, as soon as I had entered the castle, where the King resided, I was addressed by another minister with whom I had formerly been on terms of much intimacy, when he was a Catholic. This was the man who had advised the others to have me summoned before the Council, though when I charged him with it he denied the fact. When I asked him why he had urged on his colleagues to this unjust persecution of me, he replied that my name had been quoted in the remotest corners of the kingdom, and that various injurious sentiments uttered by me against his Church, were everywhere in the mouths of the common people. 'You must judge,' I said in answer, 'whether it is a right proceeding for men of your standing and character to drag me from the further end of Scotland to the bar of the Council on the plea of these vague popular rumours. I am sure of this, that no King of the Scots is ever recorded to have issued an order so unmerciful as that which I have received at the suggestion of the ministers.' Not being able to think of any plausible excuse, he threw the blame on the negligence of the officers. We were joined by the superintendent, who had told me of the darts which he had prepared against me, and they both requested me to undertake a private discussion on religion with some of the ministers of their Church. I said I would not attempt anything of the kind, without the order of the King. Upon the entrance of his Majesty into the hall, where the principal ministers of State were already assembled, the superintendent whispered something into his ear which I did not catch; though afterwards I found I had rightly conjectured the nature of the communication, which was, as he himself told me, a request that the King would allow my cause to be heard that day. I was waiting anxiously at the door of the Council chamber, expecting to be summoned by the King to plead my cause, when a royal messenger came up, and calling out my name with a loud voice, proceeded to read to me a letter signed by the King and two of the principal councillors of State, commanding me to remain in my lodgings until I had given a reply to certain questions which would be put to me in examination. I then perceived, for the first time, the object of this new contrivance; the heretics were afraid lest, if I came into the presence of the King and the Council, they might be compelled to dispute with me concerning the mysteries of religion in public. My brother related the whole history to some of the statesmen, who told him in reply that the ministers were liars, and that not only any one professing the Christian faith, but even a Turk or a Jew, was at liberty to travel all over the country, if he liked. The attention of the Council that day was occupied with the election of a Chancellor of the Kingdom, and with a question respecting the capital punishment, by hanging, of two men who had published libels reflecting on the character of certain persons of rank. August 13th, some members of the Council were appointed to consult with the ministers as to what was to be done with me; and they decided that three ministers should ascertain from my own mouth my sentiments on the mysteries of religion. The same day, accordingly, these three came to my lodging, accompanied by several other ministers, among whom were the two superintendents. We sat in the garden, and the minister, whom I have named above as having been intimately acquainted with me in former times, produced a book containing heads of religious belief extracted from the writings of Calvin, and approved by a decree of Parliament, at the time of the rise of the heresy in Scotland. He began by saying, 'We can determine at once whether you hold the same sentiments with the Scottish people on religious matters, if you assent to these articles of religious doctrine which the states of Scotland have promulgated as true, and have ratified by an Act of Parliament.' I told him he was giving himself a great deal of unnecessary trouble, since he was already perfectly well acquainted with my sentiments on religious matters; and that it was not for me to pass judgment upon the decrees of the Parliament of Scotland. On hearing this he put away the book. I acknowledged I was a Catholic, and held the same opinions as my forefathers regarding the dogmas of religion. On which he impudently declared that the members of his sect were Catholics as well, and retained the religious sentiment of their forefathers. A dispute followed which was only brought to a definite issue by my asserting that I approved the decrees of the ecumenical Council of Trent. 'So do we,' he said. To this I replied, I assent to all the definitions of the Council. 'We,' he owned, 'cannot approve them all.' Finding that the man spoke

so unreasonably, and was not contented to receive my
open profession of my faith, I bade him report to the
King and the Council what I had said, adding that I had
acted in the straightforward manner which became a
Christian and a Catholic. Upon this, and on the suggestion of the superintendent, he proceeded to interrogate
me in detail on certain articles of religion, to all which I
replied according to the sense of the Catholic Church.
Then he asked whether I was willing to discuss the subject with them. I said I had come to Scotland with a
view to the restoration of my health, and my medical
advisers had strictly forbidden me to expose myself to
any violent action or agitation either of body or mind;
but if they felt so very strong a desire for disputation,
they had only to obtain a safe conduct from the King,
and they would attract to Scotland not Scotchmen only,
but men highly gifted with sound learning and every
virtue, from many other nations as well, who, I would
undertake, could give them full satisfaction in this
respect, and something over. The King's chaplain, one
of the three sent to confer with me, observed that a good
general does not recall the enemy whom he has once
expelled from the citadel; his duty, on the contrary,
still obliges him to repel the attacks of the invader.
This speech was interrupted by the others with hisses
and marks of disapproval, so that they evidently did not
much relish it; and the minister who occupied the place
of honour, asked me again whether I would consent to
hold a disputation. I said that if the King commanded
me, I would willingly do so, even at the risk of my
health, provided the discussion was carried on in the
presence of the King and his ministers. They said they
preferred a private discussion, because in a conversation
of that sort the reasons and arguments advanced on both

sides could be more conveniently fought out in detail, point by point. Then I gave for answer :—'If you go back to the farthest antiquity, you will find very little or rather no advantage gained by disputing with heretics. Should you really wish to know the arguments by which Catholics defend their religion, you had better study their books. I am pretty certain you have confidence in yourselves and your cause, and do not want to learn anything of me; and I in turn consider that I know quite enough about, not the Catholic religion only, but that of the Calvinists as well, to make me independent of any instruction from you. If, however, you wish to engage in controversy with me, obtain an order from the King, and you shall find me, God willing, ready and prepared.' They then asked me if I would go to the College of Glasgow. I said, I had no objection if the King ordered it, but it must be understood that I would not consent to be present at any of their sermons. They asked why, and I answered, because if I was seen at a sermon people might take great scandal, for it would be reported and generally believed that I had abandoned the Catholic faith.

"The ministers returned to the Council, and announced my constancy and my resolute adherence to the Catholic religion. The officers of State urgently pressed for an order from the King requiring me to quit the kingdom within ten days; but this was opposed by three of the principal nobles—the Earl of Morton, who had formerly been Regent of the kingdom; the Earl of Argyll, Chancellor; and the Earl of Buchan. These thought it would be sufficient if my brother gave security that I would leave Scotland by the first of October. Meeting the ministers next day I told them I should be sorry to have to return to France, especially as I had derived great comfort from my visit to Scotland. Political life was a succession of changes. Their dominion, I hoped, would be very soon overthrown, and the ruler whom their influence now consigned to a life of poverty and exile, would then return and oust them from their places. The others having gone back to the castle, there remained with me a young man who, I thought, was not a minister but a student, for he was scarcely twenty years old, and yet he began to inveigh at great length against the Supreme Pontiff. I considered the best way of stopping his mouth was to remind him of the character of Beza, the god of their idolatry. Do not, I said, continue to talk against the life and manners of the Pope, a subject of which you are entirely ignorant; but read the verses which Beza wrote about himself, and you will, I assure you, find him a profligate person, since he proclaims himself under the dominion of vices which ought not to be named in the hearing of a Christian man. He reported to the other ministers what I had said about Beza, and this so exceedingly enraged them that they would have laid a complaint against me before the Council, had not the superintendent, their chief man, interposed his authority, and forbidden it. The superintendent invited me to supper the same evening, but as it was Friday, and the Vigil of the Assumption of the Most Blessed Virgin, though I sat with them at table, I would not take supper; observing this, they sent for some raisins for me. The ministers feasted sumptuously, and freely ate of flesh meat, though they pride themselves on their obedience to the laws, whereas a royal decree is still in force which forbids any one to eat flesh either on Friday or Saturday. After supper they all conducted me to my brother's lodging. The next day, two, who hold the principal authority among them, dined with us. We discussed many subjects at dinner, but said nothing about religion. I asked them to give me their true opinion on the religious question, and asserted, in my brother's hearing, that I would willingly quit my native land for the sake of my religion, and was ready even to shed my blood for it. I acknowledged, however, I was very rejoiced and glad that the King had not adjudged me to be a rebel, for loyalty had always been the characteristic of the Hays, and none of them had ever been charged with any treason.

"While all this was passing at Stirling, my relatives, and especially the Constable of the Kingdom, felt the greatest anxiety about me, as he would have been unable to render me any assistance, in case my life had been exposed to danger, owing to the distance, and the unjust use of the royal authority made by the ministers in my regard. It happened, however, that one of their body from Aberdeen was returning northward about this time, and the Constable, being a citizen of that town, sent to him, and enquired as to the progress of my affairs, and heard with great joy that my life was in no peril. I soon left Stirling and repaired to the North, to visit my mother, brothers, and other kindred. I heard the ministers severely blamed wherever I went, for declining my challenge to a public dispute, and for compelling me to leave my own country. Most of those who agreed with the ministers in doctrine had formerly been under the belief that out of the whole number of Catholics there was not a single one who would venture to engage with them in controversy; but now, having learnt that these ministers had positively refused to enter the arena of public disputation in the presence of the King and of those of noblest rank in the kingdom, the high estimation they had formed of the learning of their teachers was marvellously lessened. By way of assigning some plausible excuse for this refusal of a public discussion, they said the King was only a boy, and were dreadfully afraid that the arguments of the Catholics, if he were permitted to hear them, might shake his confidence in the religion in which he had been educated from his infancy. But, say what they would, their refusal left upon them an indelible and disgraceful mark of ignorance in those matters with which their profession required them to be familiar; and by all circles of society, at table and elsewhere, it is admitted that their system has sustained a great diminution of strength and stability.

"A few days after my departure from the King's castle I went back to Dundee; because as his Majesty had allowed me a fixed time for remaining in Scotland, I decided to take the earliest opportunity of returning to France. I had scarcely entered the town when my arrival became known to all. On going down to the harbour with my host, I perceived that the captain hesitated, and for some reason was unwilling to perform his engagement. My host desired him to state plainly any difficulties he might feel. He said, 'You know quite well how ready and glad I should be to assist you and your friend, only I am afraid of incurring the enmity of the town councillor.' One of these councillors encountered my host on his way home, and blamed him for receiving me into his house. My host answered that there was no law forbidding it, but he was summoned next day to a meeting of the council, and reminded that the master of the ship which had brought me to Scotland had been so powerfully influenced by my exhortations in favour of the Catholic religion, that he openly expressed his abhorrence and contempt for the form of religion which had been approved by the Estates of Scotland. The opinion of the councillors was supported by the minister present; and he adduced by way of illustration the sad example of certain persons who, having rashly exposed themselves to the danger of catching a contagious disease, had fallen victims to their temerity. They enquired what could have induced my host to receive me under his roof, since my presence was fatal, not indeed to the bodies of men, but to their souls. My host spoke out boldly and to the purpose in my behalf, rebuking the minister's insolence with wonderful force and energy, and informing him that the members of his order at Stirling had invited me to supper with them. My host bitterly lamented, in conversation with me, the miseries into which Scotland had fallen, of which he truly declared these ministers were the cause. As long as they teach, said he, that all our works are grievous wickedness, can they wonder if we become wicked in earnest? It is all the same whether you practise piety and holiness, or take a man's life away, if there be no difference of reward for good and for evil. Just then some messengers, whom I had sent the day before to my brother's seat in the neighbourhood, for the purpose of bringing me some fresh horses, returned with them, and I set out at once for the harbour, taking my way through the principal streets of the town, lest I should appear to be in any degree influenced by the threats and intimidation employed; and having dined at the house of my brother, Master Edmund Hay, I wrote thence to the palace, and through the influence of my relatives, obtained a letter from the King, strictly prohibiting all seamen in any part of the kingdom to place any obstacle or difficulty in the way of my crossing over to whatever foreign land I wished to reach.

"It was in my power to embark at Dundee, with or

without the consent of the councillors of that town, but I did not wish to bring my host into any trouble or difficulty on my account, and decided to make for the famous port of Leith, at which, the wind being unfavourable, I did not arrive till the twelfth day. I dined almost daily in Edinburgh, the capital, and there not one ever gave me any sort of offence, even by a word, though nearly all knew perfectly well who I was. Not only this, but the minister of Leith very kindly asked me to his house, where we entered on a discussion about the difficulties in Scripture. He thought these perfectly simple and easy, and that there was no obscurity at all; I maintained, on the contrary, that they were often hard to explain, and in order not to seem to have advanced such an opinion without ground, I cited the well known words of St Peter on the subject, and further asked him to explain the apparent discrepancy between the statement of St Stephen in Acts vii. as to the number of the sons of Jacob who went down into Egypt, with that of Moses in Gen. xlvi. He first turned to Luther's commentary on the book of Genesis, but finding that this book had not been finished, he went to Lyranus, and having read there many discordant opinions of a number of learned men, he acknowledged himself unable to solve a question of so much difficulty. I advised him to study the old ecclesiastical writers, from whom the modern German authors derived their commentaries.

"I met and saluted the officer in command of the royal garrison, a General of distinction and a Catholic, as he was returning from the sermon. He asked me if I would come and listen to a sermon, but I said I never attended the preaching of the ministers, lest the people should suspect me of favouring their doctrine. He took me to the Castle, and assured me with many speeches that if at any time his influence or authority could be of use he would willingly serve me. I also held a conversation with the first counsellor of M. d'Aubigny, an able man and a Catholic, and found him greatly in hopes that through his mother's care and exertions the King may one day reject the infidelity of the heretics, and return to the Catholic religion of his forefathers. I had intended to call upon M. d'Aubigny himself, but as he had scarcely returned yet from his attendance on the King, and the day fixed for the limit of my residence in Scotland had gone by, I left to my great regret, without seeing him. I do not doubt that, were a few men of influence to set themselves resolutely to the task of raising and reanimating the prostrate cause of the Catholic religion in Scotland, it might shortly be restored to its former condition. No one would believe the detestation which the common people feel for the Calvinist ministers. As long as the Catholic religion flourished among the Scottish people, all the necessaries of life and the materials of food and clothing, were plentiful and cheap; but, since heresy came in, the land has been left uncultivated, while dearness and scarcity of provision of all kinds prevail everywhere. The people acknowledge this, and lament it, confessing that the misery which they suffer is a just punishment for their crimes. They have, moreover, discovered to their cost, though too late, that their ministers are acting in direct violation of the promises and professions made by them when they first obtained admittance to the country. At that time the ministers inveighed insolently and vehemently against the riches and luxury of the Ecclesiastical order, and promised to the people the abolition of tithes, but their subsequent conduct has proved how little generosity and sincerity were contained in these professions. For the first three years they did not exact tithes, but the people were afterwards compelled to pay up the arrears of these three years all in one sum, to their extreme inconvenience.

"It would be no injustice to call such ministers disciples of Epicurus, and not of Christ. Some have married the wives of other men while their husbands were yet alive, and, by their countenance and example have encouraged others to do the same. Their tables are furnished splendidly and luxuriously, they are unrelenting in the exaction of usury; and in a word there is scarcely any wickedness which they do not daily practise. They are ambitious beyond all bounds in grasping at honours and preferment. For a long time they claimed the right to occupy the seats which the Bishops had formerly held in Parliament; and, when this was refused them, they began to cry out loudly that all ministers of the Church are of equal authority and dignity. There is consequently a violent controversy raging on this point between the ministers and those who style themselves bishops, abbots, or priors; indeed the ministers themselves, while their number is daily falling off, do not exhibit much concord or agreement among themselves. As the apostate monks gradually grow old or die, more and more difficulty is experienced in finding men to supply their places, and one preacher has not unfrequently to be put in charge of three or four parishes at once. Under these circumstances, the people in the north of Scotland began this summer to pay their devotions at a distance from home on certain Sabbath days, in pursuance of an old and pious custom of their forefathers; and three hundred of them or more were frequently seen in the church at Turriff, clothed only in linen garments, and imploring the aid of God and the Saints, and especially of the

Blessed Virgin. Not a few went on pilgrimage to the church of our Lady of Grace, situated on the river Spey, and of all these expeditions common report pronounced me the leader, though in fact I was a long way off at the time. Rosaries were also offered for sale in the market at the fair of Turriff. It is not difficult to conjecture the real feelings of the people on religious matters, from such indications as these. Tracts and public addresses were also published in considerable numbers, in which the profligate conduct of the ministers was very roughly handled. The ministers are so odious to the nobility that they would be only too glad to shake off their yoke, for it was in consequence of the political confusion which they introduced that the principal nobles of the kingdom were divided into two camps, and involved in civil war with one another, and have never been able to agree together as they did before. Were they to do so, the ministers would all be expelled. Those who first seized upon the revenues of the Church have since been reduced to such extreme poverty that their indigence and degradation have passed into a proverb, and are the subject of common and daily reproach.

"I cannot recall without the greatest pain, complaints which I heard expressed by the poor people against their ministers, accustomed as they had been to the most generous treatment from the churchmen of old times. Now the revenues of a single monastery which formerly supported two hundred people in honesty and comfort, are scarcely sufficient to maintain the profligacy and extravagance of even one spoiler. In a word, the people would not be heretics if it were not for their ministers, and the tyranny of a certain number of men of abandoned life, who have either taken possession of the revenues of the Church by force, or daily outrage public feeling by licentiousness and vice; so that, as St Augustine wrote, quoting the language of St Cyprian, heretics are always men who would be lost even if they were in the Church.

"I should never get to the end of my letter if I were to put down everything that has come to my knowledge. I will, therefore, before finishing, very briefly declare the reasons which have brought men of sense, and those well acquainted with the state of Scotland, to the conclusion that the restoration of the Catholic religion in this country is not impossible. If the King could be rescued from the hands of the heretics, he might very easily be persuaded to cross over into France, for he is reported to be very anxious to do so. As the illustrious Lord d'Aubigny, his kinsman, is now very high in his favour, and the King is now no longer shut up in a fortress, there is every reason to hope that an arrangement so advantageous to Christendom may easily be carried out, especially if the Holy Father would desire his Nuncio at the Court of the most Christian King to give encouragement to M. d'Aubigny, by his advice, and, if necessary, by pecuniary assistance as well.

"In the next place, supposing this measure does not produce the improvement we expect, owing to the miserable condition of the country, then the Holy Father might send a legate into Scotland to demand the concession of freedom of faith and worship to all the Scottish people. It would, however, be important that the legate should be accompanied by some men of piety and learning, as well as of public celebrity and fame, who could withstand the controversial attacks of the ministers.

"Lastly, if the most Christian King cannot be induced to give his consent to such a scheme, advantage should be taken of the first movement of civil war in Scotland, to send members of our Society into the northern districts of the country to secure the expulsion of ministers from their benefices, which could easily be effected by transferring the revenues of all benefices held by heretics to the Catholic nobles, on condition of the restoration of the ancient worship.

"The illustrious Lord Adam Gordon, brother to Father James Gordon, entreated me to pass the winter in Scotland, because he was in expectation of civil war breaking out at an early date, promising at great length to protect me from any violence in case the public peace was disturbed. This I would have done had not my brother given his word to the King that I would leave the country.[1] Besides which it would be necessary to have some books written in the Scottish language, both for moral instruction and for discussing the controverted points of religion. I send my letter to the Supreme Pontiff open, that your Paternity may read it, and judge whether it be best to send it on. I do not doubt your Paternity will shortly send me into Scotland to cultivate that neglected vineyard of our Lord, and I am certain every Scottish member of our Society, if he had the permission of your Paternity, would gladly expose his life to hazard, in the hope of being of use to his afflicted country. For myself, God forbid that I should allow the noisy threats of the ministers to deter me from ardently desiring to be sent to Scotland again. My brother's promise only extended to my leaving the

---

[1] Caution by William Hay of Delgatie, in £1000, that Mr Johnne Hay, Jesuit, his brother, shall go abroad, "wind and wedder servand," before the 1st October next, and that he will do nothing meanwhile " offensive to the trew and Christiane religioun established."—" Register of the Privy Council," vol. iii. p. 204.

country, and my return would not therefore expose him to any risk at the hands of the ministers. I have determined, however, in all things to obey the directions of your Paternity, and I earnestly entreat not only that I may be encouraged by your holy sacrifices and prayers, but that you will ask and obtain for me the strength requisite to fulfil the obligations of our institute. May Almighty God long preserve your Paternity to us.

"Your Paternity's unworthy son and servant
in Christ,
JOHN HAY."
"PARIS, *Nov.* 9, 1579."[1]

As the year 1579 passed away, it became apparent to all who regarded the state of the country with attention, that it could not long remain without some sudden change or convulsion. Morton's great wealth, his energy, courage, and experience, made him still a powerful enemy, and it was rumoured that he had plotted to seize the King and carry him to Dalkeith. The emancipation of the royal youth was effected suddenly, and by his own act, or more truly by that of his kinsman, Esme Stuart, Count d'Aubigny. This young man, who was a nephew of the Earl of Lennox, had come over from France with the express object of destroying Morton. He succeeded in winning the friendship and confidence of James VI., and was able to cheer and encourage his flagging hopes. Together they prepared the plan for their common deliverance with boldness and energy. When all had been arranged, Morton was arrested at the Council table on the 31st of December 1580, as an accomplice in the murder of Darnley. In spite of the prayers of Elizabeth, of her menaces,[2] and even of her armaments, the King,

[1] Archives of the Society of Jesus.
[2] Walsingham wrote to Randolph, "that if a hair of Morton's head

who was now in his fifteenth year, and was supported by all his people, refused to relax his hold on his prey. Morton expiated his crimes on the scaffold at Edinburgh, the 2d of June 1581.

Delivered from this formidable adversary, the friends of Mary Stuart in Scotland rallied joyfully round James VI. A golden opportunity presented itself for the return to Scotland of the Scottish priests who were then abroad. "Their number in Paris," says Father Tyrie, "was considerable. They were men of high character and admirable learning; and they would most gladly have undertaken the mission. But some influential persons, who measured everything by the dictates of human prudence, fearing that the King might possibly incur danger hereby, decided that the attempt should be postponed until some other opportunity offered." Father Persons, however, who saw clearly the bearing which the religious condition of Scotland must have on England, sent thither a secular priest named William Watts, and shortly afterwards a Jesuit, Father William Holt, that both these might inform him of the state of the country. In a letter to the General of the Society of Jesus, Father Persons thus exposed his plans:

Fr. Robert Persons to Fr. Aquaviva, General of the Society of Jesus.

"26th *September* 1581.

"Our chief hope is in Scotland, on which depends the conversion not of England only, but of all the north of Europe; for the right of succession to the English crown, were touched, it should cost the Scottish Queen her life." Feb. 9, 1580-81.—"R. O. Scot. Eliz.," vol. xxix. No. 32.

on the death of the present occupant, passes to the Queen of Scotland and her son. Of this son some hopes have begun to be formed, especially since the execution of the Earl of Morton, and it is very desirable to take him in hand while he still professes obedience to his mother, to whom he is just now very much devoted; and the heretic party have recently given him great offence. We thought the opportunity should not be neglected, and regretted that it had not been more warmly taken up by those who are most especially interested in it, that is, by the Scots themselves; though indeed it concerns us, on many accounts, as much as it does them. We accordingly collected contributions from our Catholic friends, sufficient to purchase all the requirements for a priest in the discharge of his office, and sent him to Scotland, accompanied by a servant, with directions as to the subjects he was to introduce in conversation with the King, if he obtained admittance to his presence; and if not, with the Scottish nobles. First, he was to request him to take the persecuted Catholics under his protection, particularly such as escaped into Scotland, on the ground that the Catholics were the only party who favoured his succession to the crown of England. Then he was to dwell upon many grave reasons which ought to incline the King to view the Catholics and their religion, with favour, and hold the heretics in abhorrence. These were, the security of the King's own crown; the prospect of the English succession, which he could secure only by their help; the friendship of the neighbouring Catholic princes; regard for his mother, so unjustly deposed and imprisoned; the murder of his father by heretic hands; the numerous plots which these people had laid against his life, and which the aid of Catholics had, by God's goodness, enabled him to discover and escape. The priest was then to offer the King the assistance of the Catholics of both countries, and that of us priests especially, in recovering Scotland for the Catholic Church, a work we were ready to undertake, though it cost us our lives. He set out with these instructions, entered Scotland, and by the grace of God accomplished his mission with great success, as will appear from his letter which follows. The most important and principal part of what was said to him, was of a confidential character; and he would not write it down, but repeated it by word of mouth to his servant, with directions to tell it to me and to no one else. The servant, not finding me in London, did not venture to reveal to those who were left in my place what his master had told him. He gave them, however, his master's letter, which was forwarded to me at once; and, he further added, what indeed appears from the letter itself, that they had met with an excellent reception in Scotland, and that the Scots pledged themselves to give every assistance to me, and to those whom I should send. This man also said that a day was fixed for me to meet a large number of the Scottish nobility, namely, the 26th of September in this present year (1581), an engagement which unfortunately I cannot keep, because it is the very day on which I am now writing. The following is a copy of the letter in question:

"'As soon as I arrived in Scotland I was obliged, if I would avoid running still greater risk, to repair to the residence of the Warden of Scotland,[1] a Calvinist, who resides at a place called Cesfurd. He enquired

---

[1] John Lord Maxwell was appointed Warden of the West March on the 29th of April 1581. William Ker of Cesfurd was Warden of the Middle March.

the cause of my arrival, on which I said that I was a refugee for conscience' sake, that protection was not refused even to criminals in distress, and ought still more readily to be conceded to exiles for religion. "But," replied the Warden, "there is no greater criminal than the professor of a false religion, and enemy of the Church of Christ." This, I replied, was very true, but the question was, who are the enemies of the Church? He said there was no doubt whatever that they are the Papists. I smiled at this, and proposed that we should adjourn the controversy until after supper. Accordingly when we had supped, they held what they call a chapter. One of the ministers, for there were three present, read a Psalm, and then delivered a short address, during which the Warden with his wife, and many gentlemen of noble birth and high position, who were also present, listened reverently with heads uncovered. I sat with my hat on, which occasioned surprise to many of them, and when the address was finished, with every mark of respect to the men of rank who were present, I explained why I had refused to uncover my head during the minister's speech. "At any rate," replied the Warden, "you should have shown respect to the word of God." I said, "the Scripture wrongly expounded is not the word of God, because it contains what is false, which God's word cannot." On this response, he invited the minister to defend his cause. The minister, who had heard our conversation, at first declined to take any further part in the controversy; but being urged by the Warden, we entered on a discussion as to whether it belonged to the Church alone to pronounce judgment on the sense of the Scriptures. This dispute detained us a considerable time, and the Warden was so displeased with the opinions

advanced by the ministers, and with their mode
of argument, that he said he should not be so
ready to condemn Papists in future. . . . After this
he promised, before them all, to give me a safe conduct
to every part of Scotland, and ordered it to be immediately written out and given me, as well as another for
my servant. He added that he should like to talk more
with me on these subjects, or with anyone I should send,
to whom he promised every kind treatment and security.
I then left him and went to the Baron of Grencknols,
who is disposed to favour the Catholic cause, in the
frigid manner which is customary here. I opened my
mind freely to him, and told him of the desire which
existed on the part of the English priests to incur any
danger, and to lay down their lives for the salvation of
Scotland; adding that some of them had now determined
to give all the assistance in their power to the Scottish
priests, in order to effect this end, and try what could be
done by God's help. He rejoiced and gave thanks to
God for inspiring this holy resolution, and when I
suggested that he should take care of his own soul and
return to the communion of the church, he complied with
the request more readily than even I had made it.
Previously, however, I omitted to say that he had
earnestly desired me to give him some recommendation
to the Queen of Scotland, by means of which Mr Redman
(Father Persons) will be able to conjecture what he requires, if he comes into this country. Thence I proceeded to the house of another nobleman, a member of
the Seton family, and a violent heretic. At his table I
heard an endless series of the most horrible blasphemies,
but said nothing until supper was ended, when I talked
with him for an hour and a half, I think, in protest
against this blasphemous violence; many arguments being

brought forward on both sides. In the end he thanked me very kindly, promising to be less vehement in his attacks upon Catholics in future; and he assured me that he should always be happy to receive me or any other English Catholic under his roof. At last I reached Edinburgh, where the King was then staying. I conversed with many of the nobles, and among them Lord Seton, the father of my late host, and the Prior his son, and others, explaining the cause of my coming, and our eager desire for their salvation. They treated me with kindness, and introduced me to the King, but my conversation with the latter must not be committed to these sheets. From the court I retired to the country seat of the Baron Seton, where I found a number of Scottish nobles assembled. They all joined in assuring me, and desiring me to repeat to Fr. Persons,[1] that whenever he came (and they advised him to do this soon), they would ensure him protection, as we were English subjects and not amenable to their laws. They made further promises relating to the King, which I omit here, and extended their assurance of protection not to ourselves only, but to any others we might send, giving a secret token which I will explain in another letter. I here supply the names of several noblemen who favour the Catholic cause, and who could easily be persuaded, by God's help, to become Catholics, if proper pains were taken, although at present they are far from a state of grace. These are the Duke d'Aubigny,[2] the Earl of Huntly, the Earl of Eglinton, the Earl of Caithness, Baron Seton, Baron Ogilvy, Baron Gray, Baron Fernihurst, and some others, to whom our labours would neither be unacceptable nor

[1] In the Latin original, "Mr Redman."
[2] "On Monday the 8th of August (1581), D'Aubigny was proclaimed solemnly Duke of Lennox" (Calderwood, iii. 567).

profitless, on condition only that we do not put them to any expense. This is an important point, and Fr. Persons would do well to take every care to provide for the expenses of the men he sends hither, at any rate for some time; otherwise he will find it very difficult to effect anything, or rather I should say he will do no good whatever. They must also be carefully selected, and eminent both for virtue and learning, indeed if he has none such ready to send, he should wait till he has. It would be better that no one came at all, than any who are unfit, and who would do a great deal of harm, in a country where the work has to be begun from the beginning, and at a time when the authority and reputation of the Catholic Church depend entirely upon the learning of her defenders. Fr. Persons should have many prayers said for this undertaking, which is one of great importance, and deeply affecting the welfare of all Europe, as you will have perceived. If ever labour and prayer were needed, it is now.—Farewell.'

"I received the above letter on the 15th of September, and as the shortness of the time and the great number of my engagements made it impossible for me to keep the appointment and be in Scotland on the day named, I did what I could; that is to say, I wrote to Lord Seton, explaining the cause of my delay, and encouraging him, by all the considerations I could think of, to persevere in the desire he felt for his own salvation and the salvation of others, adding that I would, in a short time, write to him again and enter fully into the whole question. I also wrote to England begging that a correspondence should be opened by any means that were possible with the Queen of Scotland, on the points above mentioned, and promising to come myself very shortly to arrange other matters, since I understood that my presence was much desired. I also wrote to the priest whom I had despatched to Scotland, directing him to remain near the borders of that country sometime longer, until he heard from me again, and I sent him as much as I could afford for his maintenance. I now, therefore, as regards this matter, rely entirely upon the answer you send me; first, as to whether I am to proceed in it or not? All the English Catholics most earnestly and anxiously advise me to do so, because upon the conversion of Scotland every human hope of that of England absolutely depends. If this King is once for all confirmed in heresy, with which there is no doubt he is very dangerously infected, there will be no help or refuge for the unhappy English Catholics; whereas, at present it is an immense consolation to them to have Scotland open to them as an asylum. It is at present easy to obtain access to the King, and he is not at all unimpressionable, but this may not continue always. It may also suit us to spend some time in Scotland in order to avoid a particularly cruel storm of persecution, and though the Scots themselves are not without men excellently fitted for the work, they are very few, and not nearly sufficient for so extended a vineyard, especially just now when they are most required. Scotland is to be won, if at all, within the next two years; while in many parts of the country, power lies in the hands of men not greatly opposed to us, especially to those of us who are foreigners. There are no laws affecting us, and our language is common both to us and the Scots. I have arranged to get Catholic printed books sent to Scotland in future, just as to England; I refer to books in the vernacular, to controversial and devotional works such as have hitherto never, or very rarely, been seen in Scotland, for there is no printing press in the country, and the heretics get all their books printed in England. It is owing to this want of books that Scotland is much more under the influence of heresy than England."[1]

Watts returned to London in January 1582, and having addressed to Dr Allen at Reims a report upon the condition of Scotland, and the dispositions of the King and the gentry towards the Catholic faith, he went back to Edinburgh to continue the work assigned him. Allen forwarded to the Cardinal of Como, the Pope's Secretary of State, that part of the letter which regarded the general affairs of Scotland.

Cardinal Allen to the Cardinal of Como.

"REIMS, 18*th February* 1582.

"MOST ILLUSTRIOUS AND REVEREND LORD,—We have had this winter, in Edinburgh, the capital of Scotland, two priests engaged in the task of ascertaining the sentiments of the Prince and the nobles on the question of religion. One is a member of the Society of Jesus,[2] the other a scholar from our college.[3] Their letters had already filled me with hopes, as I stated before, and at the beginning of the present month of February, one of them came into England, to London, in order to be able to write to me more fully about increasing the numbers of the mission, and about the state of public affairs and of religion. I will arrange all these matters with the

---

[1] H. More, S.J., Historia Missionis Anglicanæ. Folio. St Omer, 1660, p. 116.

[2] F. William Holt, who arrived in England with F. Gaspar Heywood, soon after F. Campion's apprehension, July 17, 1581, and had been despatched by Father Persons to Scotland.

[3] William Watts.

Rev. Father General of the Society, but I think the contents of the accompanying enclosure ought to be communicated to our most Holy Father by your Highness. They are of great moment, and should be kept profoundly secret. It is of much importance to all the Christian world, that the Prince who is one day, by God's grace, to rule over the whole of our island of Britain, should become a son of the Church."[1]

From London, Feb. 8, 1582.

The following is a statement of the present condition of the kingdom of Scotland:—" The King has so far been badly taught by the heretical ministers, and knows hardly anything about the Catholic faith; yet he is not so obstinately confirmed in heresy but that we are in hopes he will readily listen to the arguments of Catholics. He has indeed promised the Queen, his mother, to do so, in reply to her requests to that effect conveyed in her letters; for he is much attached to his mother, though he never sees her.

"Many of the nobility are inclined towards the Catholic cause, and are anxious for the restoration of our religion in their country; but they do not think they are strong enough to effect this without assistance, because, while they are afraid of interference from England, they see no prospect of any aid from abroad. They propose nevertheless to employ such means as are in their power, suggesting that some learned men should talk to the King, and that public disputations on religion between Catholic priests and heretical ministers should be held; in furtherance of which they are prepared to obtain the authority of the Queen. If this is

[1] Printed in Theiner, Annal. Eccles., tom. iii. p. 370.

found to be impossible, they would then get her Majesty's license and permission to convey the King, her son, if necessary, to some Catholic country, where he could be better instructed in the true faith, and trained to the duties of sovereignty, and obtain the friendship of more powerful princes, without at the same time sacrificing his own dignity or rights. At present, they are of opinion that, owing to the peculiar situation of England and Scotland, foreign alliances would be rather a source of danger, unless supported by armed forces from abroad; while from the King of France, they have no expectation that they would obtain any assistance. They would seek this willingly from the Supreme Pontiff, or from the King of Spain, were there any chance of its being accorded. A small foreign force might be sufficient, and Italian troops would be the best that could be employed.

"The nobles of highest rank, as well as many other persons, gladly receive our English priests, nominally as fugitives from England for some offence against the laws, which in truth most of them are, but in reality from a desire to be present at Mass and hear their sermons, as the difference between the two languages is very slight. Many of the nobility do not conceal their determination of quitting their own country and providing for the salvation of their souls in foreign lands, if freedom of conscience is not speedily allowed them. An additional motive for this course is the risk to which both they and their young King are perpetually exposed at the hands of the heretics of Scotland and of England, as well as the conviction that the King has no chance of obtaining the succession to the English crown (to which he will become entitled as heir to his mother on the Queen's death), otherwise than by means of the

Catholics and the profession of the Catholic faith. Ambitious views in this direction have very considerable influence both ways.

"The principal supporters and agents of the King of Spain are the Duke of Lennox, the Earl of Huntly, the Earl of Eglinton, the Earl of Argyll, the Earl of Caithness, Lord Hume, and Lord Seton, with some other men of high position. Lord Seton, who is the father of the Lord Alexander Seton, educated some years back at the German College, in the Roman Seminary, offers to procure the signatures of these and some other noblemen to a bond or engagement, and to give his eldest son as a hostage for its fulfilment, if by that means the aid of a foreign force can be obtained from any prince.

"The opponents of the cause are, first, the ungrateful Lord Arran, who has lately been made an earl by the King's desire, together with a certain number of ministers. Most of the inhabitants of the towns are heretics; yet in Edinburgh there are a good many Catholics scattered up and down, and one of us gave communion to a hundred last Christmas.

"Scotchmen are generally agreed that Scottish priests cannot at present reside in the country, either so safely or with so much advantage as English priests, who, according to what I have just said, are received everywhere in the character of exiles.

"The Queen of Scots has always been afraid that, because of ancient animosity between the two nations, English priests could not labour with advantage in Scotland. But we have not found this to be the case, and the nobles are of opinion that few Scottish priests should be sent at first, and a rather larger number of English, but not too many. The English priests require nothing but altar vestments and travelling expenses, yet cannot do anything without this assistance; at the same time, they are so full of hope, and ardent love of their mission, that they are perfectly willing to risk their lives if there be any prospect of accomplishing their end.

"In the opinion of the Scots themselves, the most convenient course to take would be that the King of Spain should send an envoy to the King of Scotland on some other pretext, but accompanied by men of learning and zeal for the faith. These persons would thus be able to reside near the Court, and would have an opportunity of suggesting arguments to the King and to the inmates of the palace in favour of the Catholic faith, as well as the steps to be taken for its promotion. They might even propose a marriage between the King and the daughter of the King of Spain, if his Catholic Majesty approved this project; but of this the Scots entertain very little hope, on account of the poverty of their own sovereign.

"We celebrated daily and preached during the Christmas season in the house of Lord Seton, the greater part of his household, which is very numerous, being present.

"Priests coming from France can land in any part of Scotland they prefer; but the most convenient port is Leith, as it is only six miles from the residence of Lord Seton. One of them should land and apprise Lord Seton of their arrival. Men of learning and controversial powers are urgently wanted, and especially in addition to those whom it is hoped Fr. Robert[1] will bring from the Society, they want Father William Reinold, of your college, and Richard Barrett, of the Roman College, if you can do without them.

"With the consent of the Catholic nobles, and the

[1] Father Robert Persons.

advice of my colleague and fellow-priest, I have crossed the frontier of the two kingdoms, and come to London, without incurring any particular risk, that I may communicate with you more rapidly, and you may form an opinion as to what ought to be done with regard to the supply of priests and other matters. My colleague remains at Lord Seton's, to watch the Catholic cause, until I return. My intention originally was not to have left London before receiving a reply from you, or from Father Robert; but upon consideration, they now think it best for me to return at once, through fear the roads, or the passage of the Scottish border, should be closed by some insurrectionary movement which, it is said, Arran and the ministers are setting on foot against the King and the Duke of Lennox, in opposition to the expected change of policy. A messenger arrived here from Scotland yesterday, with the information that the Estates are to be once more assembled by the King's authority, in order to rescind the decrees passed against the Catholics in Scotland, and are summoned to meet in the Duke's palace, a place where Arran and the false ministers have never ventured to appear. The heretics are consequently taking up arms, with the object of excluding the Duke of Lennox, who is a foreigner, from any share in the government.

"The above is the position of affairs in Scotland down to last January. Your Reverence can write in cipher on any subject, either to London or to Edinburgh, in Scotland.

"The custom of fasting has been entirely abandoned in Scotland, owing to the fact that our priests are sometimes detected too soon by refusing to eat, thus putting a hindrance in the way of their usefulness. Your Lordship would do well to enquire whether his Holiness would grant them a dispensation to eat flesh, in case of urgent necessity. We require one priest who can speak French well, for the Duke [of Lennox] does not know any other language, and business has very often to be transacted with him. Send your own men as early as possible; we will prepare the way for them, and avert the dangers to which they would otherwise be exposed from the jealousy of the heretics. I need not add my entreaties that you will use every effort in this cause of Christ, which you have taken up; and that you will have prayers offered for us. Farewell, my most revered Lord. The illustrious Lord, in whose cipher I write, aids and consoles us in every way, and makes us the amplest promises in the name of his master. He is writing fully to-day on these matters to yourself, as well as to some of the sovereigns."[1]

A wide door was apparently opened. Queen Mary herself earnestly desired that some one should be sent to promote the cause of religion with d'Aubigny and her other friends; and she believed that her son, now a youth of fifteen years of age, might easily be brought to better sentiments. Though trained up a Protestant, he was docile in disposition, and seemed to have a great regard for his mother, while the administration was now almost entirely in the hands of Catholics. Mary, therefore, wrote to the Duke of Guise, requesting him to arrange with the Apostolic Nuncio[2] at Paris, and with the Provincial of the Jesuits, to have some of the Fathers sent to Scotland. She entreated Persons himself, in a

---

[1] Endorsed: Illmo et Rev^{mo} in Christo patri ac domino, domino Cardinali Comensi, domino suo benignissimo.—Archives of the Vatican. " Nunziatura d'Inghilterra," vol. i. p. 216.

[2] Julius Cæsar Castelli, Bishop of Rimini.

message sent by letter to Bernardine Mendoza, to undertake the direction of the province, and not waste his time writing books, when the salvation of a kingdom was at stake. Many petitions were presented to him on the subject, and indeed there was nothing Persons himself desired so much; nevertheless he thought it prudent to send into Scotland Fr. William Crichton, who might discover exactly how things stood and what measures it was in the power of the Society to take for the relief of that kingdom.

Crichton went to Scotland in the beginning of Lent 1582. "At the time of his arrival only one of the members of the Royal Council, Lord Seton, remained constant to his religion. This nobleman willingly received Fr. Crichton into his house, and treated him with kindness and respect. All the others had subscribed to the heretical confession of faith, through fear of the tyranny of those who had seized upon the government, and especially of the heretical preachers. The guardian of the young King, then still a minor, was his cousin, the Duke of Lennox. Fr. Crichton considered it best to enter into correspondence with this nobleman, whom he knew to be a Catholic at heart, although externally complying in every respect with the requirements of the ministers; and it was not without great difficulty that he obtained an interview with Lennox, for he had to be introduced into the King's palace at night, and hidden during three days in a secret chamber. The Duke promised that he would have the King instructed in the Catholic religion, or else conveyed abroad, in order to be able to embrace it with more freedom. To secure this concession, he made some on his side, chiefly of a pecuniary nature; and such as seemed very insignificant when compared with the object in view. The articles of this agreement were drawn up by Fr. Crichton, and signed by the Duke's hand in evidence of his assent to it, so that the Pope, then Gregory XIII., might possess in the Duke's handwriting a proof of the accuracy of Fr. Crichton's verbal statement. Armed with this document, Father Crichton at once crossed over to France, and arrived in Paris, where the Duke of Guise—the King's relative, the Archbishop of Glasgow, Father Tyrie, and the other Scotchmen, all considered the Catholic cause as good as gained."[1] They therefore despatched Crichton to Rome, and Persons into Spain. The object of their mission was that they might secure the safety of the young King, and of the Duke d'Aubigny, by assembling a strong military force to guard them, and might at the same time provide a Catholic bride for the Prince, in the hope of making his conversion more probable. The Catholic King had two daughters old enough to be married, and the object was to obtain one or the other of them for James. The Pope felt the calamities of Scotland deeply, and was roused to exertion by the dawn of hopes so bright. He not only approved the plan and took it up eagerly himself, but wrote to urge it on King Philip as a matter greatly interesting all Christian people, and one which the King ought zealously to forward. No time was to be lost in assembling the armed force required for the guard. The Pope subscribed 4000 gold crowns, the King 12,000, promising the same amount every year, and an increase if necessary; the sum just named being sent at once.[2] "But," says Fr. Crichton, "the plan, which might have been easily

---

[1] Manuscript account by Fr. William Crichton. Archives of the Society of Jesus.

[2] Fr. Persons in his Autobiographical Notes, summing up the results of his first visit to Spain in 1582, writes thus: "At this my being

carried out in two months, was spread over two years; and so came to the notice of the English Court." Elizabeth took the alarm, as did the Scotch Presbyterian ministers. The rumour spread that *Popery*, as well as *Prelacy*, was about to be re-introduced, and d'Aubigny's professed conversion to Protestantism was regarded as a sham. It was at this crisis that, on August 23, the Earl of Gowrie and the Confederate Lords seized the person of the young King, who, suspecting nothing, was then on a visit to Gowrie, at his Castle of Ruthven; though surrounded with all the outward tokens of respect, he was soon made to feel himself really a prisoner in their hands. The Duke of Lennox escaped to Dumbarton Castle; but James, if we can trust the account given by Bowes, "having been sharply threatened by the Lords, that if he did not cause the Duke to depart, he should not be the longest liver of them all,"[1] ordered Lennox to leave Scotland.[2]

Persons was still at the Court of Spain, when this revolution was announced to him. Philip expressed much grief at the young King of Scots' misfortunes, and the dangers which beset both his soul and his life; but he acknowledged that he saw no remedy, and all that could be done was to watch the further course of events.

In spite of so great a blow, and the premature death of his friend, who had taken refuge in France, the Scot-

with the King of Spaine I obtained 24,000 crowns to be sent to the King of Scots, which were paid by John Taxis in Paris." Stonyhurst Archives, Grene's MSS., p. 230.

[1] "R. O. Scot. Eliz.," vol. xxxi. No. 8, Jan. 5, 1582-3.

[2] The Duke of Lennox, "passing through London, on his way to take refuge in France, was poisoned, as is supposed, and died a few days after his arrival in Paris." Fr. Wm. Crichton's MS., Archives of the Society.

tish King did not entirely lose courage. He wrote to his mother that, in the midst of all the troubles he suffered for love of her, he had never failed in the duty and affection he bore her, and that he only loved her the more in proportion as his trials grew heavier.[1] Shortly after, the cheering tidings reached Mary in her prison that her son had regained his liberty and his power, on the 7th July 1583, by an act of vigour and determination. Elizabeth made an ineffectual attempt to recover her former influence in Scotland, by inciting the Lords of the English faction—Gowrie, Angus, Lennox, and Mar—to undertake yet another aggressive attack upon the young King. Their consent only led to failure, and this enabled James to bring the vengeance of the law to bear upon Ruthven, Earl of Gowrie, whose long catalogue of crimes extended as far back as the murder of Rizzio. In a letter to his royal mother, the King expressed his determination of punishing all who had been guilty of treason against her, without allowing a single one to escape, whom it was in his power to secure. "As regards your deliverance," he added, "in pursuance of the intention which I have long entertained, your Majesty may be assured I shall, in a short time, send one of my servants to receive your blessing, and inform you of my plans; and also to demand from the Queen of England your liberation, which I wish above all other happiness in this world. Most especially I promise your Majesty, you shall receive from me every satisfaction that a good mother can hope for from a humble and obedient son; for this I shall be to you all my life. With such determination, and having humbly kissed your hand, I pray God the Creator, madame, that He

[1] Cf. Letter of James quoted by Miss Strickland, "History of Mary Queen of Scots," vol. vii. p. 322.

will grant to your Majesty a long and happy life in perfect health."[1]

James was, no doubt, perfectly sincere in what he wrote. He loved and respected his mother; he detested the criminal perpetrators of so many murders and so many calumnies; and yet, the hour drew near, in which, driven to act, he was to fail at the critical moment and disappoint the promise of his earlier life.

The overthrow of the Ruthven usurpation had enabled the young King to establish his authority on a firmer basis than before, by surrounding himself with his mother's faithful friends. He became every day more inclined to the Catholic cause; and, on the invitation of some Catholics of rank, was induced to enter into a secret correspondence with them, and not only to approve their plan for releasing his mother from her severe and perilous captivity, but to give them all the assistance in his power. He had become very weary of the subjection in which Elizabeth held him, surrounded as he was with spies who reported to her everything he did, and the persons with whom he conferred. He therefore urged upon the Duke of Guise the immediate execution of his design, and went so far as to seem very much inclined to adopt his mother's proposal that he should marry the Duke of Guise's daughter. Early in January he sent the laird of Fintry and the Master of Gray, whom he had selected as being most devoted to his mother and himself, with a letter to the Duke, and instructions to arrange everything with him. They were charged to urge the Duke to undertake the expedition, and were to do all they could to induce the Kings of France and Spain, as well as the Supreme Pontiff, to encourage it by their authority

[1] 23rd July 1584, W. Murdin, "State Papers," London, 1759, fol., p. 434.

and by a supply of money. Fintry and Gray, to all appearance, eagerly undertook the commission. Lord Seton, who had been sent as ambassador from the King of Scotland to Paris, for the purpose of negotiating the course of action with the French King and the Duke of Guise, informed the Pope that there was every reason to believe, from what he had heard, that the King of Scots was seriously disposed in favour of the Catholic cause.[1]

Lord Seton to Pope Gregory XIII.

"To our most holy Lord,—I need not explain to your Holiness the part which I have taken in defending the Catholic religion, and the authority of the Supreme Pontiff, for I would rather leave this to others. Having been sent hither by my most serene master, the King of Scots, to implore the aid of the most Christian King, in our dreadful emergencies, I could not do otherwise than write to your Holiness some account of the state of our affairs. Briefly, after the ministers had succeeded in sending the Duke of Lennox away from Scotland, the King was so offended that he would hold no communication with them, though previously he had always acted in accordance with their advice. They took offence in turn, and set on foot a violent insurrectionary movement against his authority, partly by means of the agents of the Queen of England, and partly through their own rebel leaders. Being reduced to extremity, he has implored the aid of the most Christian King, and more

---

[1] Letters of James VI. to the Duke of Guise, 22d January and 19th February 1584; letter to the Pope, 19th February 1584, published by Theiner, "Annales Ecclesiastici," vol. iii. pp. 801, 802, 806, ("Archivio Vaticano, Anglia," vol. ii. fol. 274); cf. "R. O.," Wade to Walsingham, May 5, 1581, from Paris.

particularly that of his relative the Duke of Guise; a proceeding which has raised the hopes of Catholics to the highest point. So favourable an opportunity never occurred before, and could not have been expected or looked for; and it is doubly important that it should not be lost. The King has so high an opinion of the Duke of Guise, that we are in hopes he will be guided in everything by his advice; indeed he has not only written as much to the Duke, but has charged me with a message to the same effect. Our hope is that your Holiness will both animate and encourage the Duke to make some effort in the cause of religion, and also give him substantial assistance. God Himself, beyond all our hopes, seems to have provided your Holiness with this opportunity of extending religion and of obtaining never ending glory. The King's age, his perilous and critical position, the unbridled insolence of the ministers, are all circumstances in our favour. But it is of the utmost importance to lose no time, or the chance will pass away. The Queen of England is straining every nerve to crush the King of Scots by a rebellion in his own country, and if successful, she will suppress the Catholic religion altogether. The Duke of Guise, to whom I have transmitted the King of Scotland's letter for your Holiness, will doubtless explain matters in detail. But I would implore your Holiness not to let the existence of these communications be known to anyone, for this would, at the present juncture, place the King in the most extreme difficulty. At a later period we hope, by the aid of your Holiness, that he will be free to declare himself openly a son of your Beatitude. At present he is so situated and so completely in the power of his enemies, that he is scarcely at liberty to do anything whatever; from this condition it is for your Beatitude to rescue him. God preserve you long to his Church.—Your Holiness's most humble servant, SETON."

"PARIS, *March* 14, 1584." [1]

Father Holt, who had recently experienced much kindness from the Scottish King,[2] was equally sanguine, and wrote hopefully of the King's conversion, as will appear from several letters addressed to the Scots in Paris.

Father William Holt's letter from Edinburgh.

"*March* 20, 1584.

"I wrote a few days back touching events in this country, but Gray's arrival in town has put me in possession of further particulars, which I now send to be communicated to the Duke of Guise, as his occupations do not allow him to write.

"The King of Scotland has the best disposition towards us, and remains firm in these sentiments, but complains of your delay in sending to him. He says he has

---

[1] Theiner, "Annales Ecclesiastici," vol. iii. p. 598.

[2] Fr. Holt had worked with no little success, as long as the Catholics remained in power. But after the raid of Ruthven, the machinations of the stricter Calvinists frustrated all his endeavours, and in March 1583, he was apprehended near Edinburgh by order of the heretical counsellors of State, in whose power the King then was. From several letters between Walsingham and Elizabeth's agents in Scotland we learn the efforts made by Elizabeth to obtain possession of the prisoner's person, which would have inevitably resulted in his torture and death; had not the young King, supported by the French Ambassador, refused to deliver him up, and put off his importunate enemies with fair promises. On one occasion Bowes tells Walsingham that the French Ambassador, in his late interview with the King, had laboured earnestly that Holt might be speedily examined and handed over to him to take to France. He has also been advised of an in-

involved himself in much difficulty on our account, and has never received any reply to his letters. As regards the affairs of state—the King's most faithful counsellors are the Earls of Huntly, Crawford, Montrose, and Morton, and Lords Herries, Home,[1] Gray, Colonel Stewart, commanding the guard, and some others. Angus is under arrest,[2] but goes about free. On our side are Mar, Glammis, Boyd, and many besides. Gowrie will shortly be banished from Scotland, unless he exerts himself to prevent it. Argyll, Glencairn, Arran, Marishal[3] are at Court, and take a moderate line, but they must be considered as our opponents.

"These last have lately been endeavouring to persuade the King of Scotland to choose a wife from the royal family of Sweden. This is done at the instigation of the Queen of England, whose agent here, Andrew Keith, acts through Arran. Their object is to detach the King from the friendship of the Catholic Princes. Our friends have done all in their power to prevent it, and Gray, in particular, has worked for this end with great industry, and to good effect. Colonel Stuart, as I said just now, is entirely on our side, and is very anxious to be commended to the Duke of Guise. It would be of

tention of withdrawing Holt, and a report was bruited through Edinburgh that the prisoner and his keeper (Lord Seton, who secretly entertained F. Holt) had actually fled. So he (Bowes) obtained from the King a promise for Holt's detention, and to have him sharply examined within four days, and after his examination to be delivered to the writer for further examination on behalf of her Majesty. ("R. O. Scot. Eliz.," vol. xxxi., and Cott. MSS., "Caligula," c. vii. 67.) An account of the examination will be found in the Tanner MS., vol. 79 folio 187.

[1] They were members of the Privy Council.

[2] Angus, prosecuted as a Ruthven raider, made his escape to England towards the end of April (1584).

[3] Members of the Privy Council.

great advantage for the Duke to recognise him, by letter or otherwise; for the Colonel has the King's full confidence, and devotes himself day and night to provide for his master's safety. He has contracted an intimate friendship with Gray, and is much guided by his advice, so that the latter can easily influence the Colonel in any direction the Duke of Guise may point out. God knows how long the opportunity is likely to last.

"The English troops are said to be near the frontier, ready to act in conjunction with the King's enemies, and he is likely to be overwhelmed by this combination, unless some effectual move is made to counteract it.

"The King's leaning towards the Catholic religion may be gathered from several indications. He has sent one of the ministers away from Edinburgh, and another out of Scotland;[1] is on bad terms with them all, and, when anything is referred to him, he puts difficulties in their way rather than removes them. On the other hand, he regards all the Catholics most favourably, and enjoins Gray and Fintry to use no concealment in their efforts on behalf of the Catholic cause, through fear or friendship for anyone, promising them his protection if they should be molested by the ministers. He shows me greater marks of favour every day, and has not only permitted, but even approved of my remaining in the kingdom. He condescends to make use of my assistance in some important affairs, but this he wishes to remain a profound secret, for the present, in order to prevent any risk to himself from the outcries of the ministers, until

---

[1] On the 17th of February (1584) Andrew Melville was ordered to enter himself a prisoner in Blackness Castle, but he fled to Berwick. Melville was followed in his flight by several of his brethren, who had reason to dread the displeasure of the King. ("Register of the Privy Council of Scotland," vol. iii. p. 631, and *seq.*)

circumstances shall allow of his declaring himself more openly. He has evidently made up his mind to grant full liberty of worship to all the inhabitants of the kingdom, provided he can do so consistently with his own personal safety, and the peace of the country. I do not say this only on conjecture, but from information received through one of his most intimate friends, who, though himself a Protestant, assures me that the King entertains this intention.[1] I will write more fully on the subject another time. The great hindrance is the King's want of money, which is such that he can scarcely manage to pay his own guards. The noblemen around him have spent all they possessed on the measures necessary to insure his security, and unless a supply be obtained very shortly, the downfall of all our hopes is imminent. The King will be exposed to the utmost risk, and compelled to change his policy, just at the moment when he has resolved to follow the guidance of the Catholic Princes, and attach himself to their views, for the rest of his life.

"He is reported to have said that the Catholics were far more faithful to him than the Protestants; an additional reason for transmitting without delay the subsidy promised through M. de Meyneville.

"Two English Catholic noblemen,[2] who have lately taken refuge here, are in high favour with the King, as well as a third, who has been with me all along; and he has resolved to avail himself of their help in some

---

[1] *Cf.* Correspondence between Davidson and Walsingham. "R. O. Scotl. Eliz.," vol. xxxiv. n. 58, 59.

[2] "One of them," says Bowes, "is thought to be Sir Robert Gerard." They were entertained at Seaton. Robert Bowes to Sir Francis Walsyngham, March 4, 1584. ("R. O. Scotland Eliz.," vol. xxxiv. 23.)

important matters. It is desirable that his disposition towards the English Catholics should be made known, as they will thus be encouraged to forward his views. The kindness he shows to a few of them is in fact open to all, and each one would be sure of the same liberal treatment were he in want of it. The King perfectly well understands, and we daily impress it on him, that he will never obtain the crown of England but by the aid of the Catholics, and that he cannot safely trust his mother's enemies in Scotland. I did not hear his Majesty say this himself, but I had it from men of undoubted veracity, whom I have lately spoken with. They told me more, which I judge prudent not to write at present. This much is certain—the King cannot declare himself more openly without extreme peril, unless he receives assistance first. That this may be done as soon as possible, we most urgently entreat, and he himself as earnestly desires. Gray is desired by the King to request that the six thousand gold pieces, which the King asked for in his last letter, may be sent to him; and that further sums be got ready at Paris, so that, if his affairs succeed, he may be able to assemble an army and invade England. I write in Mr Gray's[1] house at Edinburgh, where I have been concealed for some days.

WILLIAM HOLT."

" *March* 20 [1584.]"[2]

[1] The Master of Gray, under an exterior which was remarkably graceful, carried a heart as black and treacherous as any in this profligate age. He pretended to be a Catholic, and had always professed the deepest attachment to Mary Stuart, who trusted him with much of her secret correspondence. Gray not only betrayed her cause, but recommended the assassination of the unhappy Queen.—(Courcelles to Henry III., 31st December; Egerton, 97. "Calderwood," iv. p. 613).

[2] Archives of the Society of Jesus, Latin MS.

Letter from Fr. Wm. Holt at Edinburgh.

"The King is excellently disposed and resolute in our interests. He has communicated his purpose to Colonel Stuart, having first obtained from him an oath of fidelity and secrecy. The Colonel is ready for anything, and the Duke of Guise should at once write, to thank and encourage him. Gray, by the King's order, has treated with Huntly, Crawford, and John Maitland, who are all engaged on his side, but know nothing of the plan; Gray only having spoken in general terms. They have promised to assist him to the utmost, so that as soon as the design is made public, we may depend upon their aid. The King is quite resolved to send some one to you with fuller powers than heretofore, and gets more eager every day, intending to take the field in person. We hear every day of fresh plots against his life, contrived by enemies both at home and abroad; and these he cannot long withstand except by your aid. So make haste. He has heard of some danger threatening him from his rebellions subjects, and from the Queen of England; and is consequently assembling an armed force, though he has no money with which to pay it. The Colonel is entirely with us, and very active. The ministers are in open opposition to the King, and in defiance of his authority hold nightly assemblies within their place of worship. They have been treated with very little consideration of late, and probably keep their vigils with greater zeal on that account. Huntly is full of courage, Arran detested by every one. I have much to do, and, thank God, am safe and free, through the King's bounty and kindness. I have better hopes of him than ever, for he does not refuse to converse about religion. John Seton is said to have landed.

"The King has lately written to the Queen, his mother, in very consoling terms, promising all that could be expected at the present juncture."

"*From* EDINBURGH, *April* 1, 1584."

Another from the Same, April 8.

"The King loves secrecy, observing it himself, and expecting others to do the same. Be expeditious in his affairs. All is being done here with zeal and fidelity, and procrastination on your side will be ruinous. The favours bestowed on Catholics by the King have roused the suspicions of many Protestants. We are only waiting for measures in support of his authority, and for replies to our letters. I think he will shortly send me on a commission to you. God be with you."

"EDINBURGH, *April* 8, 1584."

Another from the Same.

"*April* 7.

"The ship being still in the harbour, it occurs to me to add a few words about the excommunication. I have no doubt you have done all that is necessary, but it must be drawn up in such terms as to compel the Catholics to take up arms against the excommunicated princess under penalty, or else it is very likely they will not be ready. Fintry's letter will tell you how great the harvest is here, and how few the labourers. During the last few months, since the King quarrelled with the Ministers, a great part of the country has abandoned them, and begun to ask for Catholic preachers. Tell me when you write, whether the matter you are engaged in is likely to succeed, and what I am to do here."

"EDINBURGH, *April* 7."[1]

[1] Archives of the Society of Jesus, vol. Scotia, Latin MS.

From all accounts, such a favourable opportunity for prosecuting the enterprise had not occurred before; but there was no time to be lost. "If it be not carried out this year," said Allen, "I give up all hope in man; and the rest of my life will be bitter to me." The Archbishop of Glasgow, writing to the Cardinal of Como, expressed the same anxiety.

The Archbishop of Glasgow to the Cardinal of Como.

"The state of Scotland was never more hopeful, as appears from their choosing for ambassador to France a Catholic, one who has shown himself most resolute of all during this crisis. He has been ordered to settle nothing with the French King without previous consultation with me; I hardly know why. It seems to me most important not to delay, for as things now stand the King's crown and life are in most critical danger; and it is evident that we must look very shortly either for success, or for his death, and the utter ruin of everything. Our hopes depend in a very great degree upon his Holiness; if he comes to our aid in time, all may be well. As regards the others, I fear their help will be given too late, unless they can be induced to act more promptly than is their wont."[1]

The only thing lacking was the final decision of the King of Spain, without whose fleet, troops, and money, nothing could be effected. But, whether it arose from his habitual procrastination, or from want of money, Philip II. let the propitious moment pass by unemployed, until events happened in France and elsewhere which turned the Duke of Guise's thoughts into another channel,

[1] Theiner, "Annales," vol. iii. p. 598.

and, without extinguishing, cooled the ardour of his zeal for the enterprise which he had hitherto so warmly advocated.

Beaton, however, would not wait till the plans of politicians had become a failure, and as it was obvious that the daily loss of souls in Scotland was great, he encouraged the exiled priests[1] to return without delay, and entreated the Pope to send some priests of the Society of Jesus who were of Scottish birth.

The Archbishop of Glasgow to Pope Gregory XIII.

"Paris, 25*th June* 1584.

"Most Holy Father,—They write from Scotland that the harvest is great, the labourers few, and that it is desirable to send some to them for the purpose of keeping the Catholics firm, and assisting those who are

---

[1] There is in the secret archives of the Vatican a paper entitled: "The humble petition to his Holiness of Priests of the Kingdom of Scotland now in exile and desirous to return to their country even at the risk of their lives." The Petition contains the "names of those who are prepared to return at once, but cannot move from where they are for want of means. They nearly all live in Paris or the neighbourhood. Signed by—

"Fathers Hunter, Doctor of Theology; Gray, Public Professor of Theology; Chalmer, Preacher, Theologian; John Hay, Doctor of Theology; James Lang, Doctor of Sorbonne; Andrew Gallway, Licentiate in Theology; James Schin, Doctor in both Laws; James Mertin, Theologian; William Meldrum; Patrick Dunglas, Candidate of Theology; James Finlason, Candidate of Theology; William Viddirpon (*sic*); James Friserel, Theologian. Three Priests from the Semminary at Pont-à-Mousson. Fathers Archibald Hamilton, Candidate of Theology; Alexander Hamilton, Canon of St Quentin; John Hamilton, Professor of Philosophy at Paris; Robert Balfour, Philosopher."

On the back, *Scotland*. Copy in an Italian hand of the end of the XVIth century. Archiv. Vaticano. Nuntiatura Angliæ, vol. ii. 4 pp.

ready to return, and might be easily reclaimed. On this account, we request your Holiness to desire the Rev. Superior of the Society of Jesus to send some priests belonging to that order and of Scottish birth; and especially Father Edmund Hay, James Gordon, James Tyrie, William Crichton, and others whom he considers fit persons. We, on our part, have sent Dr James Cheyne, to whom your Holiness has granted an ordinary pension, which he finds sufficient. But there are no benefices to support the Fathers in Scotland, and neither their own relatives nor the Catholics in general, are always willing to supply the need, for Catholics have chaplains of their own to say Mass in their houses, and the relatives of our Fathers are often heretics. Under these circumstances, it will be desirable for your Holiness to send the same instructions to your present Nuncio, which were given to the most Reverend Bishop of Ariminum, his predecessor; namely, that he should assign an annual and sufficient pension to such priests as we shall deem suitable for this mission. Your Holiness will, in this way, act for the best interests of those kingdoms, and there is hope that a harvest will quickly follow, by the grace of God, to His glory and the consolation of your Holiness; a result for which we have laboured with tears and prayers during many years."[1]

In compliance with the Pope's desire, and at the earnest request of the Catholic nobility, in 1584 Father Crichton was sent to Scotland again, and with him Father James Gordon; but their vessel was seized on the high seas by the heretics of Holland, who were in rebellion against their own sovereign. The vessel was set free, there being no war at that time between the

[1] Theiner "Annales," ii. p. 602.

Scots and the Dutch; but a merchant who had hired her for the voyage, and had discovered the character of Father Gordon and Father Crichton, accused them of being enemies of his party in Scotland, and the Dutch detained them on this account. The merchant then became apprehensive that the Earl of Huntly, who was Father Gordon's nephew, might kill him in revenge for the betrayal and denunciation of his uncle to the Dutch; and he accordingly succeeded in procuring Father Gordon's liberation, and the substitution in his place of Mr Ady, a secular priest, then proceeding to Ostend. Here Father Crichton was recognised as a Jesuit, he and his companion were condemned to die for the murder of the Prince of Orange. Obviously no one else but the Jesuits could have done the deed; they therefore, the rebels resolved, must all be hanged. A gallows was erected for the execution of Father Crichton; but just at this juncture a treaty was concluded in England between the Dutch and the Queen of England. Elizabeth, on learning that Father Crichton was a prisoner at Ostend, requested the negotiators of the treaty to have him given up to her, and sent a ship across to Ostend for the special purpose of conveying him to England.[1]

Father Gordon's arrival and missionary labours in Scotland form the subject of the following letters.

Fr. Edmund Hay to Fr. Claud Aquaviva, General of the Society of Jesus.

"VERY REVEREND FATHER,—I learn by a letter from the Laird of Fintry, the nephew of the Archbishop of Glasgow, dated from Scotland in the middle of Sep-

---

[1] Father Crichton's MS. account. Archives of the Society of Jesus. Latin MS.

tember, that Fr. Gordon has arrived in that country, and gone to the house of the Earl, his nephew. Also Fr. Crichton, together with the chaplain of the Bishop of Ross, has been taken prisoner by the English on their way from Flanders, or rather, as we had heard before, from Flushing, and is now a prisoner in London. We are ignorant how it happened that Fr. Crichton was the only one taken, for Fintry does not mention this in his letter, and Fr. Gordon has not yet written. As there is no doubt he is really in prison, we have taken the only step in our power. The Archbishop of Glasgow has written to Mauvisière, the resident envoy of the King of France in London, entreating him in the most urgent terms to go and see the Father, if this be possible, and learn all about him from his own lips. If this be impossible, he is to make every inquiry and write directly and say what steps we can take with the view of effecting his liberation; providing meanwhile for his wants, as far as can be. We have ourselves taken precautions for this end, through the very kind assistance of Mr Matthew Zampini, a person favourably known to Father Claudius.[1] He has an Italian friend in London, who, for some years past, has rendered valuable assistance to Catholics imprisoned for their faith. He has now written to this friend, begging that he will not allow the Father to want anything, and will ascertain how he is, either from himself or through others. Fr. Gordon had scarcely reached Scotland when he was betrayed by the sailors and other companions of his voyage, the same in all probability who betrayed Crichton, and he was denounced to some of the few ministers left. This was done with the addition of a statement of a most astonishing character, and artfully adapted to drive the ministers wild.

[1] Father Claude Mathieu, Superior of the Jesuits in France.

They declared that there were thirteen Fathers of our Society on board the vessel, and that they were all given up to the English, with a great number of chalices and other sacerdotal ornaments. This so enraged the ministers, who quite believed it, that they did all they could in their sermons to induce the people to credit the story, adding that the King had been already subverted by our Fathers, and heard the Mass every day. This is very crafty as well as malicious, for their object is to bring James into detestation with the nobles and the heretical populace, and once more turn all the united violence of the sect against the throne. The unfortunate prince was obliged to meet this trick with another, and published a proclamation forbidding any Jesuit to enter the kingdom in future, requiring also Fr. Gordon to quit Scotland within a month, and meanwhile not to come within ten miles of the court. If the ministers complain hereafter that this proclamation was a *ruse*, it will probably be answered, or at any rate might be said with truth, that the story which occasioned it was equally false. Fintry writes that Fr. Gordon has nothing to fear, and will soon be set at liberty by the Earl's influence. The King has restored the Bishop of Dunkeld, and, I think, the Archbishop of Glasgow, but this good prelate does not want his Holiness, or those at Rome, to be made aware of it until he hears from his nephew that the matter is settled, which he hopes he will soon. I trust that all who have decided to help this prince will do so without delay, that he may no longer be afraid to enquire freely about religion, or say what he thinks on the subject, and may act towards the ministers as he thinks right, and they deserve. Father Robert feared for his life, and is gone to Rouen, or else to Flanders, leaving in my hands the case of the Scottish mission entrusted to him by your Paternity. The Archbishop of Glasgow thinks I ought to be one of the first to sail, perhaps with Fr. Tyrie. To prevent Fr. Gordon being alone, and to help him if he has not been very successful, your Paternity should consider in our Lord to whom you will entrust this charge. But I will write again on this subject, with God's help. I commend myself to the Holy Sacrifices and prayers of your Paternity and all at Rome.

"Your Paternity's unworthy son in Christ,
"EDMUND HAY."
"PARIS, *October* 29, 1584."[1]

The Archbishop of Glasgow to Father Claud Aquaviva.

"15*th Feb.* 1585.

"VERY REVEREND FATHER,—I must first express my great gratitude to your Paternity for having acceded to my wishes by permitting the Father Provincial to send Fathers Hay and Tyrie, whenever I shall consider the opportunity favourable. I faithfully promise to make use of this advantage as may seem best for God's glory, and the salvation of souls. Fr. Gordon has written again. I cannot, however, as yet read his letter for want of the counter-cypher, but I hope to receive this soon from Fr. Claudius,[2] who I hear has arrived at Pont-à-Mousson. Meanwhile I hear from my nephew, in whose house both Fr. Gordon and Fr. Holt are entertained, that the Fathers do not advise any Scottish priest, especially a man of much note, being sent to that country, as they are afraid that the King may be compelled, for the pro-

[1] Archives of the Society of Jesus, vol. Scotia (I.), Latin MS.
[2] F. Claude Mathieu, Superior of the Jesuits in France.

tection of his own life from the attempts of the heretics, to take some severe measures, against the Fathers themselves, and the Catholics in general; and thus our difficulties for the future would be increased. As the harvest, with God's help, seems likely to be great, they recommend that two English priests should be sent without delay, and should land at Aberdeen. I am thus able to conjecture pretty well what Father Gordon's letter contains, though as yet we cannot read it. But since my nephew adds that he will send a messenger at the beginning of March, to give full information, we have decided to do nothing until that time, when we hope the information brought by him will enable us to write fully, not only to your Paternity, but to our Most Holy Lord Gregory XIII. as well. I implore your Paternity meanwhile to have our King earnestly recommended to God. The English Council is straining every nerve to procure his destruction by treachery if they cannot by open violence. We trust that, with the aid of your prayers, God may be good to him, so that he may not be entrapped. Christ Jesus keep your Paternity ever safe and mindful of Him.—Yours most affectionately in Christ.

"JAMES, ARCHBISHOP OF GLASGOW."

"PARIS, *Feb.* 15, 1585." [1]

"Among the other causes which contributed in no small degree to the growth of the Catholic religion in Scotland, was the personal influence of Father Gordon. He was a kinsman to the King, and not only touched the hearts of many persons by his holiness of life, but, further, being a man of great learning, he openly defeated the ministers of the heretics in the public discussions which were held.

[1] Archives of the Society of Jesus, vol. Francia, 1540-1604. Latin MSS.

It happened also, most opportunely, that while the King was expostulating with the young Earl of Huntly for not embracing Calvinism, Huntly replied that there was an uncle of his own in Scotland, to whom he would much more willingly entrust the salvation of his soul than to any of that heretical ministry. 'Let him come,' said the King, 'we are not afraid of him.' Father Gordon put on the habit of the Society, and made his appearance before James and eight ministers. They asked him first, for a definition of justification; and, in reply, the Father gave them the definition laid down by the Council of Trent. They said, 'if that is your opinion of justification, the Pope of Rome will have you burnt, for the Papists ascribe it to good works.' Father Gordon held to his ground, and they then proceeded to argue against the Mass. The Father proved the truth of the Mass by the most cogent arguments, when the King, perceiving that the ministers said nothing to the purpose, himself took up the argument against him. The debate ended in noisy clamours and strong language, and was adjourned till the next day. But the King, having observed that Father Gordon was skilled in controversy, and that the ministers were sure to be vanquished, prohibited any discussion being held except in his own presence; and in future, whenever the ministers assembled for this purpose, he invariably went out hunting. Father Gordon followed his Sovereign to the chase, and everywhere else, for two whole months, always seeking an opportunity to make some effort for his conversion. Finding his endeavours fruitless, he proceeded to the north of Scotland. Here, at the request of a number of noblemen, a day was appointed for him to hold a public discussion on matters of faith with Mr George Hay, the most learned of the ministers, a man of good birth, fairly versed in Greek and Latin literature, and occupying the first place among their preachers. He admitted that the doctors of the Church during the first five centuries held what was true, but when he proceeded to defend the opinions of his sect by garbled quotations contained in the writings of their doctors, Father Gordon protested that the ancient writers did not maintain such sentiments. Then the minister, sending to his own house, which was at some leagues distance, procured a whole horseload of books, and among them the writings of the ancient doctors. By means of these, in the presence of a great concourse of nobles and ladies, Father Gordon vanquished the minister by bringing forward complete sentences and not isolated phrases, from the ancient writers to whom the minister had appealed. This occurrence made a great noise, and produced much effect, for a large number of persons returned in consequence to the religion of their fathers, and others were encouraged to persevere therein. Among the former was Francis, Earl of Errol, Master of the horse."[1]

In 1585, Father Gordon was reinforced by Fathers Edmund Hay and John Dury, both coming for the sake of concealment, as domestic servants of one Robert Bruce, a Scottish priest. The King knew all about it, but said nothing. "John Dury, by his learning, his indefatigable labours, and the sermons whereby he seemed able to turn the minds of men in any direction he wished, converted to the Catholic faith almost all the inhabitants of Dumfries, together with Lord Maxwell, the governor of the town and district."[2] "In spite of the persecution

[1] Fr. Crichton's MSS., Archives of the Society. Cf., "History of the Society," by Fr. Jouvency, S.J.

[2] This nobleman, however, afterwards returned to his errors, or pretended to do so, and was killed in battle, and his hand was cut off. He used to pray that it might be, if it ever subscribed to heresy.

against the Catholics, at that time sufficiently violent, Father Dury determined to sing the whole of the office of the festival of the Nativity of our Lord, together with the three Masses, solemnly, in a monastery situated outside the town, and on the other side of the river, guards being posted on the bridge, to prevent anyone crossing without a written order. But the people were so eager to hear him preach, and to witness the solemn office, that those not allowed to cross the bridge forded the stream, though the water was up to their waist; and thus, wet through, they passed the night of the vigil of the Nativity, hearing the office in the Church. Not one of them sustained any harm, a fact attributed to the miraculous power of God, and the merits of the Father. Great numbers of people visited him for confession and advice regarding religion, many of whom came at night, not venturing to appear by day through dread of persecution and the watchfulness of the spies.

"The Father was at length so worn out that his recovery from fatigue was despaired of. On this account Fr. Edmund Hay, Superior of the mission, sent for him, but he died on the road, in the house of the illustrious Lady of B——, on the 20th of October, 1588. He requested permission of the Lady to speak a few words to the family before he died, as she had many sons and a numerous household, all in some sort heretics. He spoke on the certainty of the Catholic Religion, and the vanity of any hope of salvation outside it, with so much force and efficacy as to draw tears from all, and obtain the conversion of many of them, among these being several sons of the lady of the house. Soon after this he rendered up his soul to God."[1]

[1] Father Crichton's MS., Archives, S. J.

Father James Tyrie to Fr. Claud Aquaviva.

"VERY REVEREND FATHER,—We have had a visit from an Irish Bishop who has been sometime in Scotland with Fathers Hay and Gordon, and was entrusted by them with letters for your Paternity and the Fathers here; but being in peril, and fearing these letters might fall into the hands of enemies, he threw them into the sea, an act which has occasioned us no little distress. From letters written by Robert Bruce, and others which have reached me, I extract some particulars which I think worth sending to your Paternity. Fathers Hay and Gordon are in the North of Scotland, with the Earl of Huntly; Fathers Holt and Dury, in the West with the Earl of Morton. The number of Catholics increases rapidly every day, and the Irish Bishop assures me that during the short time he remained in Scotland he administered the sacrament of Confirmation to at least ten thousand persons; from which circumstance the correctness of his statement may be conjectured. The Queen of England has written to James, strongly urging him to take some measures against the Fathers of our Society, and the King, whose Ministers of State are all in favour of Elizabeth, has published a proclamation requiring us all to leave the kingdom within one month, and forbidding any one, on pain of death, to receive us into their houses. But the best informed persons do not regard this as a real peril, and not one, whose doors were open to us before, has closed them now. The King is in greater danger than he ever was before. Your Paternity will learn everything fully from Chisholm's letter, for if I were to detail all particulars of the condition of the country, I fear I should trespass too long on your patience. I will not detain you from more important occupations. God keep your Paternity long in safety to us and all His Church.

"Your Paternity's unworthy servant,
"JAMES TYRIE."

"PARIS, *Sept.* 31, 1585."[1]

The return, even of a small number of Catholic priests to Scotland, says Fr. Tyrie, was followed with remarkable success. From that time the face of the country was entirely changed, and so manifest did the great increase of the Catholic body become, that it could easily have shaken off the yoke of the heretics, and the Catholics in England might have neutralised the power of their enemies in that realm.[2] But the hopes of the Catholic party were soon to be blighted by a fresh outbreak of the tempest.

Father James Tyrie to Father Aquaviva.

"VERY REVEREND FATHER IN CHRIST,—PAX CHRISTI. —I have lately heard from Fathers Hay and Gordon, who desire me to salute your Paternity in their name, and to say that the present troubled condition of Scotland, together with the uncertainty of all future prospects there, prevents their having any clear intelligence to send. Father Holt went to visit the Catholics in the

---

[1] Archives of the Society of Jesus, vol. Francia, Latin MS.

[2] Fr. Tyrie's statement receives an important confirmation from a letter of Thomas Rogers to Walsingham. "The Jesuits," he says, " have certified lately that they proceed according to their wishes in Scotland, and have reconciled 10,000 of late, and daily expect numbers, and also to gain the King, which is the mark they shoot at.' (R. O. Domestic Eliz., vol. xxxix., No. 47, October 18th, 1585.) D. Bernardino de Mendoca in a letter to Philip II., dated November 28th, 1586, states that "the Jesuits have converted three of the

north, and I hear he has now returned westward to
Father Dury. All four are well, and full of resolution,
determined on no account to quit a country where they
are reaping so fine a harvest, whatever turn matters may
take. Before the storm burst, our Catholic friends had
obtained a royal letter granting us perfect freedom of
action and license to remain in the kingdom; and
another forbidding any one to molest us. Before, however, these letters could be published, there was a complete
revolution in the Government.[1] The King is still in the
hands of his enemies, and exposed to extreme peril,
because, of course, were he to escape, they are likely to
pay severely for their violence towards him. But we
have great hopes of assistance from the Lord Claud
Hamilton, who has been for some months in France, and
by God's help has been brought to the Catholic faith.
He was always devoted to the King, and long ago
warned him of this conspiracy, but the King was too
confident in his own powers, and neglected to take proper precautions. His Majesty has written to him with
his own hand, urging him to come to Scotland for reasons
which he will learn on arrival. This indicates that the
King is planning the recovery of his freedom, and hopes
to effect it by the aid of the first man in the kingdom, if
only he were present. God turn all to good! Fathers
Hay and Gordon write that they have expended all the

principal noblemen and a great many gentlemen of note, and have reconciled over 20,000 persons." (Teulet, Papiers d'Etat., vol. iii., ed. in 4°, p. 503).

"El Padre Etmon [Edmund Hay] Escoces, de la Compañia de Jhesus, que fue en Escocia con otro compañero, afirma por sus cartas haver reconciliado à la Yglessia Catholica romana, en seis messes, pas- sadas de diez mill almas." (Teulet, vol. iii. pp. 408, 409).

[1] The Ruthven Lords had returned to Scotland. (See Tytler, vol. viii., p. 242, et. seq.)

money they received from us at setting out. They likewise say that it is necessary to send plenty of books in the Scottish idiom, especially the New Testament, which was translated into that language some years ago, and illustrated with comments from the writings of the old Fathers, and with meditations also in Scotch. They think this will contribute more than anything else to the conversion of the country; but the books are rather expensive, and there is not money enough to purchase the number of copies required. I have mentioned the subject to the Archbishop of Glasgow, who is anxious to do all he can, but has not the means to carry out his wishes. It is impossible to send letters to the Queen of Scotland otherwise than open, since she has changed her prison; and if they contain anything about religion they are not permitted to reach her hands. I must therefore beg your Paternity to advise me what to say, for I turn to you as to an anchor of refuge. I believe the Apostolic Nuncio is going to write to his Holiness on the matter. . . .[1]

"Your Paternity's son and servant,
"JAMES TYRIE."

"PARIS, *Jan.* 18, 1586."[2]

The storm alluded to by Father Tyrie was the sudden return of the banished Lords to power. As early as September 1584, Elizabeth had been informed of the design of the Scottish and English Catholics to rescue Mary Stuart from her hands. The Master of Gray, James' ambassador, had revealed to her the arrangement between Mary and her son, by which she was to resign the Kingdom into his hands. The exile or the imprison-

---

[1] The rest of the letter treats of French matters.

[2] Endorsed: To the Very Rev. Father in Christ, Father Claud Aquaviva, Superior General of the Society of Jesus at Rome. (Archives of the Society, Latin MS.)

ment of her friends; the reception of English and Scotch Jesuits into Scotland; the negotiations of the Scottish nobles now in power, with the bishops of Glasgow and Ross, Mary's ambassadors at the courts of France and Spain; all were so many facts, which clearly demonstrated that Mary guided both King and nobles as she pleased. This appeared an alarming state of things to Elizabeth, and Gray artfully offered to overwhelm all the secret plots of the Catholics. Angus, Mar, and the other banished Lords, who were then in London, received Elizabeth's permission to set out for Scotland. On the 31st of October, 1585, they concentrated their troops at Falkirk, and from this marched to Stirling at the head of eight thousand men. James, then engaged in pursuing the sylvan sports which had lately become not only the amusement, but the business of his life, was surprised and taken. Arran, his Prime Minister, secretly fled. The young prince was forced to submit, and the exiled Lords now ruled everything at their pleasure.

The situation in which James found himself was terrible. He was surrounded by implacable enemies, always plotting for his overthrow, and as fiercely embittered against the son as they had been against the mother and the father. In London, the same opponents who had persecuted his mother kept the rebels against his authority in pay; and English territory was always ready to receive them when they required a refuge, in which they could speedily gather fresh resources. If ever the isolated and helpless prince obtained the services of a loyal and capable minister, dark threats and darker bribes, and inducements to treachery, came to corrupt the latter's wavering fidelity. Thus it was that the son of Mary Stuart, incessantly exposed to the most formidable engines of attack which, one after another, the genius of Elizabeth could devise, and to the treacherous suggestions of favourite ministers, who were secretly in the pay of his enemy, led astray also by his own ambition and self-love, and so poor that he had scarcely anything of royalty left him but the name, at length clung to this title with such obstinate pertinacity that he was bent on wearing it by himself alone, refusing to share it with another. Accordingly he rejected, after having in principle accepted, the association in the royal authority which Mary had offered him. Guided by his greed of the English Crown, and lured by a secret promise of the succession, James abandoned his mother, became the sworn pensioner of her enemy, and in July 1586 formed an alliance, defensive and offensive, with Elizabeth, pledging himself to maintain the religion now professed in both countries against all adversaries, notwithstanding any former engagements to the contrary.

While James consented to become the avowed persecutor of that religion which his mother believed to be the truth, Walsingham, who had boasted that the death of Morton would cost the Queen of Scots her head, succeeded in entangling a number of young Catholic gentlemen in a scheme which included the dethronement of Elizabeth. It was known as Babington's plot,[1] and one of its principal

[1] It seems pretty clear that they were induced to engage in it through the artifices of Walsingham or his agents. Blackwood states (Jebb, De vita et rebus gestis Mariæ, 1725, vol. ii., p. 281) that two years earlier Gifford was acting as Walsingham's spy at Rheims, and had come twice to London to incite Savage to regicide (cf. Howell's "State Trials," vol. i., p. 1120). And both Morgan's correspondence and Châteauneuf's "Memoir" (Labanoff, vol vi., p. 279) mark out Gifford as the prime mover in the plot. When Gifford returned to England, in December 1585, he went straight to Philipps's house, where he lived during the month of January, "practising secretly among the Catholics"—that is, insinuating himself into the confidence of Babington and his friends, and opening Walsingham's route of communication with Chartley.

associates was an agent of the Minister, who, by dint of unheard of craft and treachery, succeeded in engaging Mary and her secretaries to correspond with the conspirators.[1] This was all that was wanted to effect her destruction, for her death had long been resolved upon.[2] Elizabeth shrank from incurring the infamy of bringing her royal cousin to a public trial and execution. "Surely," said she to Davison, "Paulet and Drury" (the latter had been lately appointed additional keeper of Mary) "might ease me of this burden. Do you and Walsingham sound their dispositions."

A letter was accordingly forwarded to Sir Amias Paulet on the same day, in the name of both secretaries. It informed the two keepers that her Majesty charged them with "lack of care and zeal for her service," otherwise they would long ago have "found out some way to shorten the life of that Queen."[3]

"God forbid," replied Paulet, "that I should make so

[1] Mary denied the authenticity of the letters produced against her. Mr Hosack proves that in her alleged answer to Babington's letter there are distinct traces of the forger's hand ("Mary Queen of Scots and her Accusers," vol. ii., p. 364).

[2] On the 10th of September, 1572, Killigrew received instructions to press the Scottish Regent and Morton to relieve the English Queen of her unwelcome guest. On the 9th of October, Killigrew was able to write to Burghley that Mar and Morton were "willing to do the thing he most desired." Certain noblemen, to be named by the Regent, were to repair to England as hostages, and pledge their lives that Mar and Morton should kill their Queen. (Killigrew's letters, quoted by Mr Hosack, "Mary Queen of Scots," vol. ii., p. 508 et seq.) Before any agreement was concluded the sudden death of the Regent Mar put an end to the negotiations, but two years after the atrocious scheme was revived, and Killigrew was once more sent to Scotland to ascertain the terms upon which Morton would murder the Queen of Scots. (Letter of Killigrew to Walsingham, 12th July 1574, quoted by Mr Hosack, "Mary Queen of Scots," vol. ii., p. 184.)

[3] "The Letter-Books of Sir Amias Poulet," edited by John Morris, S.J., 8vo, 1874, p. 359.

foul a shipwreck of my conscience, or leave so great a blot to my poor posterity, as to shed blood without law or warrant."[1] Mary's two gaolers having refused to dip their hands in her blood, nothing remained but a public execution. The form of a trial was therefore gone through; a commission of Peers sat as her judges at Fotheringay Castle. With one exception they found Mary guilty. Her life now lay at the mercy of Elizabeth. Much pressure was brought upon the Queen to induce her to consent to Mary's death. She at length listened to the representations of her ministers, signed the warrant, and bade Davison get it sealed at once, that she might hear no more of it. On the 19th of November, 1586, Lord Buckhurst, by order of Elizabeth, proceeded to Fotheringay to read the sentence of death. He bade Mary "look for no mercy, seeing that as long as she lived the received religion in England could not subsist."[2] Whereupon Mary "seemed with a certain unwonted alacrity to triumph, giving God thanks, and rejoicing in her heart that she was held to be an instrument for the re-establishing of religion in this island."[3] Again, upon the eve of her execution (8th February 1587), the Earl of Kent declared to her: "Your life would be the death of our religion, and your death will be its preservation"; to which she replied: "Ah! I did not flatter myself with the thought that I was worthy of such a death, and I humbly receive it as an earnest of my acceptance into the number of God's chosen servants."[4] The same day

---

[1] "The Letter-Books of Sir Amias Poulet," edited by John Morris, S.J., 8vo, 1874, p. 361, 362.

[2] Instructions to Lord Buckhurst and Beale, in Labanoff, vol. vii.

[3] Buckhurst's Report, "State Trials," i., 1201.

[4] "Mort de la Royne d'Escosse," Jebb, vol ii., p. 612. Cf. Tytler, "Hist. Scot.," vol. viii., p. 393-470.

Pope Benedict XIV. thus expresses his conviction that the religion

at supper, addressing Burgoigne, who waited on her:
"Did you not mark the power of truth," said she,
"during the discourse I had with the Earl of Kent, who
was sent hither, I suppose, to convert me? They told
me I was to die for attempting the life of the Queen of
England, of which you know I am innocent; but now
this Earl lets out the fact that it is on account of my
religion. Oh, glorious thought! that I should be chosen
to die for such a cause."[1] As she made herself ready for
the block, tenderly reproving her maids, she exclaimed:
"Do not weep; I am very happy to leave this world.
You ought to rejoice to see me die in so good a cause."[2]

Mary had declared upon oath that she had never been
party to any design against the life of Elizabeth, and the
same affirmation she repeated in the course of her prayer
on the scaffold. Kneeling at the block, she said several
times aloud, "Into Thy hands, O Lord, I commend my

which Mary professed was the real cause of her death:—" Si vera mortis causa examinetur, cum illa constituenda sit in odio catholicæ religionis, quæ, ipsa superstite, in Anglia perstitisset, si invicta perpendatur constantia, qua oblatam repulit deserendæ catholicæ religionis conditionem; si admirabile animadvertatur robur, quo mortem sustinuit; si attendantur, prout attendi debent, protestationes ante obitum et in obitu emissæ, se semper catholicam vixisse et propter Fidem Catholicam libentissime mori; si non omittantur, prout omitti non debent, evidentissimæ rationes quibus ostenditur nedum falsitas criminum Mariæ Reginæ oppositorum, sed etiam *iniquam mortis sententiam, specie tenus calumniis innixam, vere processisse ex odio catholicæ religionis*, et ut hæretica dogmata *in Angliæ regno immota persisterent*, nihil fortasse deerit ex iis quæ pro *vero martyrio* sunt necessaria."—De Canonis. SS. L. III. cap. XIII, n. 10, Roman edition of 1748. Opera omnia. Prati, 1840, vol. iii. p. 119.

This passage is quoted by Pius VI., Bull. Rom. Contin., t. ix., p. 613. Romæ, 1845.

[1] Jebb, Ibid.

[2] MS. Narrative of Mary's Life and Death, quoted by Miss Strickland.

spirit," and with admirable resignation received the fatal stroke of the axe (8th February 1587).

The intelligence of Mary's death was received in Scotland with a burst of national indignation. So deep was this feeling, that the nobles, in a transport of pity and enthusiasm, threw themselves upon their knees before the King, and, amid the clang of their weapons and their loud imprecations against Elizabeth, besought the King to avenge the deed.[1] But James had no intention of risking his chance of the English succession by any act of indiscreet hostility,[2] so he was content to accept Elizabeth's apologies, and with her apologies to accept the bribe of a fresh pension and an English dukedom.[3]

The Catholic party, however, commanding nearly all the northern counties, and having with them the sympathies of the people, who were enraged at the execution of the Queen, attained in a short time a strength on which James had not calculated. They knew that Philip II. of Spain had made stupendous preparations for the invasion of England, to avenge the damages done to Spanish commerce by the English government, and the assistance given to his rebellious subjects in Flanders; while it was also intended to hurl Queen Elizabeth from her throne and restore the Catholic religion in England. Might not this be an opportunity of punishing Elizabeth for her recent insult to Scottish

---

[1] Carlyle to Walsingham, 3d August 1587. (Tytler, ix., p. 14.)

[2] Cf. Letter of Walsingham to Sir Richard Maitland, printed by Spottiswood, pp. 359-62.

[3] R. O. Scotland Eliz., vol. xlii, no. 108. William Asheby to Lord Burghley, 6th August. On the 14th of December, 1588, the Master of Gray, writing to Archibald Douglas, complains that the King " has received only a fiddler's wages.' Vol. xlii., no. 116. Cf. vol. xxxix., no. 85. The Master of Gray to Sir Fr. Walsingham, 17th May 1586.

national pride and the royal blood of the Stuarts? Might there not be a Scottish invasion of England, or might not Scotland be utilised in some other way for the purposes of Philip in his enterprise? It was not only among the remnants of the Catholic party in Scotland that these speculations were entertained. While such well known Roman Catholic nobles as the Earls of Huntly, Crawford, and Errol, and Lords Maxwell and Herries (with other Lords, lairds and ladies, scattered freely about through Scottish society), were actually welcoming the prospect of a Spanish invasion, as being likely to restore Scotland to the old faith, or at least to ensure its restoration in the future, there were important Protestant magnates, such as the Hamiltons and Bothwell, who were not indisposed towards a temporary Spanish alliance against England as a means of retaliation for Queen Mary's death.[1] Either through policy or necessity, James was soon utterly estranged from England, and, with his connivance, messengers were sent to Spain, who held out hopes to Philip of Scottish assistance in his great enterprise against England.[2] Elizabeth began to be in serious alarm, and instructed Lord Hunsdon to open a communication with the Scottish King. The promise of a yearly pension of five thousand pounds, the fear of cutting himself out of the succession, again made him a friend to England. In proof of his sincerity against the Catholics, he summoned his forces and started for the West March, to put down the rebellion which Lord Maxwell, recently

---

[1] The Register of the Privy Council of Scotland, edited by D. Masson, LL.D., vol. iv., p. xxxiv.

[2] Teulet, Papiers d'Etat iii., pp. 472, 516. Cf. Tytler, "History of Scotland," ed. 1853, vol. ix., p. 14. Cf. R. O. Domestic Eliz., vol. xxix., No. 39. Thomas Rogers to Walsingham, Aug. 11, 1585.

returned without leave from Spain, had managed to raise in those parts, and which was intended to open a door for the Spaniards, should they seek a landing in Scotland. A proclamation was issued against all the Catholic clergy who could be found in Scotland, and against every one who should harbour them. No Scottish auxiliaries were permitted to pass over to the service of Spain, and soon the news flew from place to place, that the invincible fleet had been smitten by the skill of the English admirals, and afterwards scattered by a succession of violent storms.[1]

Delivered from her fears of a Spanish invasion, Elizabeth urged James to assail the Catholics, and assisted him with money to proceed against them.[2] The principal nobility found themselves excluded from court, and loaded with accusations as though they were rebels, while their followers were harassed and annoyed. Informed that their enemies were flocking in great numbers and inciting the King to attack them, the Earls of Huntly, Errol, and Crawford took up arms; and, lest any one should suspect them of rebelling against lawful authority, they sent a deputation to his Majesty, with the request that he would grant to his faithful Catholic

---

[1] In England the crisis had roused the loyalty of the nation. Catholics and Protestants, noble and merchant, all alike came forward; some fitted out vessels at their own expense, and there was not a man in all England who did not show himself ready to die in her defence. On receiving a false report that the Armada had been dispersed by a tempest, Elizabeth, with characteristic parsimony, gave orders that four of her largest ships should be dismantled. But Howard of Effingham, the brave old Catholic admiral, retained the vessels, and offered himself to defray the charges.

[2] Letter of W. Asheby to Lord Burghley, 6th Aug. 1588. R. O. Scotland, Eliz., vol. xlii., no. 116.

subjects the right of professing the old Catholic faith.[1] They well knew that it was not of his own accord, but in consequence of wicked counsel, that the King had published severe edicts against Catholics. Now was the time for his Majesty to extricate himself and his faithful nobles from a situation involving continual danger. Let him only say the word, and they would be answerable for its execution. Unwilling to decline, yet reluctant to accept their offers, James exhorted the Earls to disband their troops; it was easier, said he, to approve than to carry out their schemes. Huntly and his followers having ascertained that the King could not be rescued from the hands of the Presbyterians without great risk, disbanded their forces and relinquished their design.[2]

James was now bent upon matrimony. Frederick the Second, King of Denmark, had lately offered to pay up the money for which the Orkney and Shetland Isles had been given in pledge, and as Scotland had no wish to give them back, it was thought that the difficulty might be got over by choosing one of his daughters, who would most likely bring the islands as her dowry. This proposal was agreed to by Frederick. His daughter Anne was betrothed to James, and Keith, the Earl Marshal, was sent to Copenhagen to act as proxy for the King in the marriage ceremony and to bring home the bride; but contrary winds prevented her setting sail, and James, at last losing all patience, gallantly proceeded in quest of her. He joined her at Upsal, but as nothing could make him brave the long sea voyage again, before the winter was over, they returned together

---

[1] R. O. Robert Bowes to Lord Burghley. Scotland, Eliz., xlix., no. 45. 11th Nov. 1592.

[2] Con. De Duplici statu, p. 147.

to Copenhagen, and did not come to Scotland till the next spring, May 1, 1590.

Hope seemed to dawn with her arrival, for though the Princess had been brought up in the Lutheran religion, she regarded Catholics with favour. The serious struggle between the principles of the Reformation and the ancient faith seemed to be lulled. Had the Kirk contented itself with this triumph, and rested satisfied with the King's present dispositions, which appeared wholly on its side, everything might have remained quiet: seeing that the Catholics were ready to abstain from all practices inimical to the Protestant religion, on the single condition that they should not be persecuted for their adherence to the ancient faith.[1] "But," says Tytler, "the Kirk was not disposed to take this peaceful course. The permission even of an individual case of Catholic worship, however secret; the attendance of a solitary person at even one Mass, in the remotest corner of the land, at the dead hour of night, in the most secluded chamber, and where none could enter but such as knelt before the altar for conscience sake, and in all sincerity of soul; such worship, and its toleration for an hour, was considered an open encouragement of antichrist and idolatry. To extinguish the Mass for ever, to compel its supporters to embrace what the Kirk considered to be the purity of Presbyterian truth, and this under the penalty of life and limb, or in its mildest form of treason, banishment and forfeiture, was considered not merely praiseworthy, but a point of high religious duty; and the whole apparatus of the Kirk, the whole inquisitorial machinery of detection and persecution, was brought to bear upon the accomplishment of these great ends. Are we to

[1] Tytler, "History of Scotland," vol. ix., p. 65.

wonder that, under such a state of things, the intrigues of the Catholics for the overthrow of a government which sanctioned such a system were continued; that, when they knew, or suspected the King himself to be averse to persecution, they were encouraged to renew their intercourse with Spain, and to hope that a fresh outbreak, if properly directed, might lead either to the destruction of a rival faith, or the establishment of liberty of conscience." [1]

A discovery, which occurred at this time, corroborates these remarks. In the month of December, 1592, the Catholic nobles sent a messenger to the King of Spain, bearing their promise that they would give him all the help in their power if he made an attempt of some kind or other upon the Queen of England. Were he to decline this, they undertook to make war upon her themselves with their own forces, provided he sent them some little assistance. It happened, however, that Lord George Ker, the bearer of these letters, was seized; and although most important facts had been intrusted to his fidelity, yet, under fear of torture, he made very compromising revelations, and so placed many of the leading nobles of the realm in a position of utmost danger. The Earl of Angus and the Laird of Fintry were immediately apprehended, and sentence of capital punishment was pronounced upon both of them. The Earl of Angus escaped from Edinburgh Castle by bribing his guards, but the Laird of Fintry was executed. He was held in the highest esteem in Scotland on account of the purity of his life and his wonderful prudence and learning. He might have saved his head if he had accepted the proposal made to him, of embracing the Protestant religion. But he answered very

[1] Tytler, vol. ix., pp. 65, 66.

resolutely that it would be a bad bargain for him, if he were to prefer earth to heaven.[1] The Earls of Huntly and Errol, with many others, who also had been discovered, incurred the same danger, and were summoned to compear before the Privy Council on the 5th of February. On the day fixed for the trial they did not appear, but confined themselves to their strongholds in the north; upon which the King made instant preparations to march against them.

James advanced without opposition to Aberdeen, the Catholic nobles having fled before him into the wilds of Caithness; and their immense possessions were then declared forfeit to the crown, though the sentence was not enforced. The King's clemency was strongly blamed by the General Assembly, but had James granted what the Assembly asked, an ecclesiastical court need only declare a man to be a Papist, and he would become at once an outlaw. A Catholic had but to let a priest come under his roof, and he was liable to the confiscation of his goods.[2] James was unwilling to put such laws against Catholics into execution. Thirteen of his nobles and a considerable part of the population of the kingdom, especially in the north, were still attached to the Catholic religion. The ministers, however, would have no mercy upon them; they sought to confiscate the estates of the Catholics and drive them into exile. With this view they held secret meetings, organised plans of insurrection, and aimed at getting the whole power of parliament into their hands. The excitement culminated in a riot in Edinburgh, by which James thought his royal life was endangered. He came to the conclusion that

---

[1] Fr. Tyrie's Report. Cf. "Record Office, Scotland, Eliz." vol. 1., No. 4.
[2] "Book of the Universal Kirk," pp. 381, 382. Calderwood's "History," vol. v., p. 248.

the Presbytery could not be bridled, and that it must be destroyed; under these circumstances he determined to raise the Catholics once more to power.

With the advice of his councillors of state James sent Father Gordon and Father Crichton secretly to Rome, for the purpose of laying the whole matter before the Pope, and arranging with him the means of restoring the Catholic religion in Scotland. Gordon accomplished this mission according to his instructions, and returned to Scotland in company of Father William Crichton and the Pope's legate, George Sampiretti. The last named was the bearer of a large sum of money which he was to give to the King of Scotland, promising him a monthly allowance of ten thousand ducats, on condition of his protecting the Catholics and allowing them to remain unmolested in the exercise of their faith.[1] On the 16th of July, 1594,[2] the party landed at Aberdeen. Father Gordon, being well known to the officials and to the provost, was easily recognised; and the news of his arrival produced a very unfavourable impression on the ministers, who suspected that his coming was connected

---

[1] "For then," says Fr. Crichton, "our king had so great fear of the number of Catholics, the puissance of the Pope and Spain, that he offered liberty of conscience and sent me to Rome, to deal for the Pope's favour, and making of a Scottish Cardinal; as I did show the king's letters to Fr. Persons, and prayed him to concur, at least to give some satisfaction to our king." MS. Letter of Father Crichton to Father Parsons, June 4, 1605, Stonyhurst archives, vol. Anglia A. iii. 55. Cf. Archives, S.J., De Missione Scotica puncta quædam notanda historiæ societatis servienda. MS. by Father William Crichton, S.J., Latin MS. Cf. Lord Walter Lindsay of Balgaries' "Account of the present state of the Catholic religion in the realm of Scotland in the year of our Lord, one thousand five hundred and ninety-four." A very rare Spanish pamphlet in Blairs College Library.

[2] R. O. Scotland Elizab. liii., No. 81. Colville's letters, pp. 108, 111.

with some new scheme. They were afraid to seize him through fear of his nephew, the Earl of Huntly, of whom they stood in great awe, but they seized the Pope's legate, along with the money and letters in his possession. When the Earls of Errol and Angus heard that the legate had been imprisoned, they immediately took measures to get him liberated; and being joined, within three days, by the Earl of Huntly at the head of seven hundred horsemen, they threatened to set fire to the town unless the prisoner was at once released. Alarmed by this threat, the provost yielded up the captives to their rescuers.[1]

Meanwhile the popular agitation had increased instead of abating, and probably under the pressure of this, James once more changed his mind and resolved that the laws against Catholics should be enforced. Accordingly on the 12th of November 1593, a fresh decree condemned many thousand Catholics to the sad alternative of renouncing either their religion or their country. The Earls of Angus, Huntly, and Errol, Sir Patrick Gordon, and Sir James Chisholm were to be "free and unaccusable, in time coming," of the crimes laid to their charge in regard to the Spanish blanks, provided that they refrained from any such trafficking in future, banished all Catholics from their presence, and received a Presbyterian minister into their houses, whose duty was to resolve their doubts and prepare them for subscribing the Confession of Faith.[2]

On the 30th of May the Parliament met. Huntly and his followers had not complied with the decree, and now

---

[1] Archives, S.J. Father Crichton's MS. Cf. Lord Walter Lindsay's account, and extracts from the Council Register of the burgh of Aberdeen, 1570-1625, 16 July, 1594; Rymer's fœdera, July 19, 1594.

[2] Calderwood's "History," vol. v. p. 284. Spottiswood, *lib.* vi.

rigorous measures were resolved upon. Their estates were declared forfeited, and commission was given by James to the Earl of Argyll, to pursue them with fire and sword.[1]

Argyll was Huntly's ancient enemy, and accepted the commission with alacrity. Two ministers were despatched to urge him to undertake the work, " as a thing acceptable to God."[2] Argyll resolved to take instant action, and in the beginning of October set out on his expedition, at the head of a force of six thousand men. " Huntly and Errol thought it would be more for their honour, in so just a cause, to die sword in hand, than to be murdered in their own houses. They quickly collected fifteen hundred horsemen from among their friends and retainers, with a few foot-soldiers, and invoked the Divine assistance by confession and communion. Father Gordon, with two or three other Jesuit Fathers, heard the confessions of the whole army, and gave them communion. They asked to have their weapons sprinkled with holy water, and marked a white cross upon their arms and coats, to let the enemy see that they were fighting in defence of the cross of Christ. Gordon of Auchindoun, Father Gordon's brother, being desired to fasten the cross upon his armour, answered that he would show how truly he held it in his heart, but was so occupied in arranging his troops that he had not a moment to spare. On their engaging in battle at Glenlivet Auchindoun was killed, but the victory remained with the Catholics. The heretics were routed with great loss, of the Catholics a few were slain and many wounded, but it was observed that none of those who bore the cross lost their lives. The Earl of Errol received two wounds; and his

[1] " Book of the Universal Kirk," pp. 404-8.
[2] " Histoire of King James the Sext," p. 338.

horse, no less than eight. They attributed their victory to the prayers of the Fathers of the Society, who continued on their knees all the time of the engagement."[1]

At the news of this reverse, James, in spite of the severity of the season, advanced with his army to Aberdeen, taking with him Andrew Melvil and a body of the ministers of the Kirk, to be witness of his behaviour towards the Catholic rebels. No resistance was made, and he dealt as he thought fit with the strongholds of the Catholic Lords. But the extreme measure of transferring their forfeited estates to those who would hold them with a sure grip was still delayed. He persuaded Huntly and Errol to withdraw from the country for six months, on condition that their property should be safe, and that no injury should be done to their followers and clansmen. The two Earls might easily have held their ground in Scotland by armed resistance, but they were willing to satisfy the King, of whose good will towards them they felt persuaded; and accordingly, accepting the terms offered, they left Scotland in April 1595, and went to Germany.

From this time the ministers ceaselessly urged upon James to send Father Gordon at least into exile as being the author, they declared, of this rebellion. The King consented, and though he paid many compliments to the pacific temper and patriotic loyalty of the Father, he not the less insisted on his going. Fr. Gordon most earnestly entreated that, before he went, he might have the opportunity of engaging in public disputation with the heretical doctors, in the presence of the King and the council. He offered to surrender his very life were he defeated in controversy, provided that if he prevailed, liberty of conscience should be granted to Catholics.

[1] Fr. Crichton's MS.

Nothing would induce the ministers to accept conditions so obviously just. Gordon quitted the country with the full prestige of victory. Crichton was also compelled to leave Scotland; he passed across to Flanders, and devoted all his energy to the foundation of the Scottish Seminary at Douay.

The place of these Fathers was secretly filled by William Murdoch, sent over from Pont-à-Mousson, and by John Morton, a Scotchman. The latter was immediately recognised and apprehended, but shortly after was set free by the King's order, and made to return into Belgium. Murdoch and Abercromby (for William Ogilvie seems to have died about this time), remained in hiding, to gather up the fragments of the wreck of the Catholic cause. Their life is thus described by Father Abercromby.

Fr. Robert Abercromby to Fr. Claud Aquaviva, General of the Society of Jesus.

". . . We live in caves, in secret and unfrequented places, perpetually moving from place to place, like the gipsies, and we never lodge two nights in the same locality, for fear of falling into the hands of the enemy. Spies and officers are posted at all the inns, and in every parish, to discover our whereabouts, and give us up to the authorities. On my first arrival I was taken prisoner, together with my companions, by Bothwell, the Admiral of the kingdom. After being robbed of all I possessed, I was committed to a guard of soldiers, whom I had to keep at my own expense, and who were charged to hold me in safe custody. We were released after fourteen days' detention; and the greater part of our goods was restored to us. For three years the persecution was not severe, as we were allowed to go where we liked, and say Mass in private houses. But in course of time matters grew worse, and the violence of the ministers increased. They procured from the government royal edicts, or, as they are called, "Acts of Parliament," declaring all Jesuits and Seminarists to be traitors and rebels, subject to the penalties of high treason, whom any person whatever was empowered to capture, and put to death if they resisted. All who received them into their houses, had dealings with them, or showed them any kindness, were pronounced rebels and traitors to their country. The Parliament decreed also that it was treason to say or even hear Mass, and they published many other Statutes or 'Acts,' directed against Catholics, whom they call Papists. This name is more odious and abominable than that of Turk, Saracen, or Jew. It is worse than calling a man a heathen, or a member of the vilest sect on earth. We are consequently obliged to travel by night; or, if we do so in the day time, we have to abandon the high roads and ordinary routes, and proceed across rough and pathless ground, or over the hills, where we are sure not to meet any one. We dare not enter an inn except after dark, nor leave it again until the next night comes on. This is rather hard upon me, since I completed my sixtieth year on the feast of our Lady in the past Lent. A hot meal would be a luxury to me, even though I am uncertain of my life every mile I go.

"Among our enemies who abound plentifully, the most inveterate are the preachers of the Word, as they are called. One especially named Bovis [Bowes],[1]

[1] In March 1591 we find Robert Bowis (*sic*), Esquire, resident ambassador for the Queen of England, in her name requesting King James to order the "apprehension of an Irishman, lately fled out of Ireland, being a Papist and adversary to the true religion professed in both the realms."—"Register of the Privy Council," vol. iv. p. 597.

Elizabeth's envoy in this part of the country, is a deadly enemy of the Catholic religion, and more particularly of our Society. This man, some four years ago, when there were only four of us in Scotland,—Gordon, Ogilvie, MacQuhirrie, and myself,—went to the King and said, 'Most gracious Prince, in addition to other evils, your Majesty has four terrible plagues in your kingdom.' He then named us, and proceeded, 'Gordon is a learned man, but without knowledge of political affairs; Ogilvie has such ill health, that he can do but little in opposition to our religion; MacQuhirrie is young and inexperienced; but the fourth is an old and tried hand, who leaves not a corner of the country unvisited, and this one must absolutely be taken out of the way.' Bovis has since continued to denounce me in the most violent language to the King; but seeing that the latter paid little attention to him, he next offered 10,000 pounds Scots to four different noblemen if they would apprehend me, as they themselves related to their friends. I have hitherto escaped, for it would be very unfair that I should be sold for more than my dearest Lord was. Now our enemies are become more violent, for they declare that the victory would be as good as won, if three men were cut off—meaning the Earl of Angus, the Laird of Boniton, and myself. They have had a portrait of me painted, that I may be more easily apprehended. So far I have escaped their hands, in the name of the Lord. The ship is about to sail, and I must conclude, but let me first say a word as to the fervour of some of our Catholics. I sometimes go to an inn, and indeed more than one, where the master of the house is a Catholic, but his wife and the rest of the family are heretics. I am lodged in an inner room, where the Catholic friends of my host cannot come to see me by the door-way, for fear of being observed; so they put up long ladders at the back of the house, and come in and leave by the window. Persons over sixty years of age will sometimes visit us in this way during the night, but the inmates of the house cannot imagine who they are, since no one is seen entering the house. I have an infinite number of things to say, but there is no time. I commend your Reverence to our Lord, and myself to your sacrifices and prayers. I send greetings to every one, especially to those whom I know, and I beg the prayers of all.

"Your Reverence's brother and servant in Christ,

"ROBERT ABERCROMBY, S.J.

"Scotus."

"*From* SCOTLAND, *9th June* 1596."[1]

In a meeting of the Estates, held at Falkland upon the 12th of August, a petition was presented from the Earls of Huntly and Errol, praying to be allowed to return to Scotland. Alexander Seton, the President of the Court of Session, supported it, arguing in his speech that, if they were driven to despair, the Earls might, like Coriolanus the Roman, or Themistocles the Athenian, join the enemies of the State, and endanger its well-being.[2] It was arranged that they should be allowed to return, and remain in the country till May of the following year, with the hope that by that time they would be reconciled to the Church.[3]

The Kirk, however, apprehensive that the State was negligent of its duty, placed the Catholic Lords under the supervision of a police of its own. Certain clerical detectives were appointed by the General Assembly to attend upon the Marquis of Huntly, the Earls of Angus

[1] Archives of the Society of Jesus, vol. "Scotia," Latin MS.
[2] Calderwood, vol. v. p. 438.
[3] Melville's "Diary," p. 249. Calderwood, vol. v.

and Errol, and the Lords Hume, Herries, and Maxwell. The most important of the instructions given to these detectives are : " First, Ye shall address yourselves with all convenient diligence and necessary furniture to enter in their company and families, there to remain still with them for the space of three months continual ; during the whilk time your principal care shall be, by public doctrine, by reading and interpretation of the Scriptures ordinarily at their tables, and by conference at all mete occasions, to instruct themselves in the haill grounds of true religion and godliness, specially on the heads controverted, and confirm them therein," &c.[1]

As Mr Hill Burton truly observes : "There are tortures attributed to the Inquisition which some men would rather endure than this scheme, dooming them and their families to be ever haunted by a pragmatical priest of a hostile Church armed with powers of exhortation, inquisition, and rebuke. Though their authority only lasted for three months, one of their duties was to procure successors for life, with this small difference, that while they themselves were merely to receive temporary hospitality, the permanent tormentors were to be put on a permanent establishment at the expense of their victims."[2] Some time before this domiciliary intrusion was adopted, the General Assembly had set it forth that one of the national sins for which the wrath of God was let loose on the land was " the not planting sufficient pastors " in the houses of the Popish Lords.[3]

The proceedings against the Catholic Earls had given so much ascendancy to the zealots of the opposite side, that no power in the State seemed sufficiently strong to

---

[1] " Book of the Universal Kirk," 985.
[2] Hill Burton, " History of Scotland," vol. vi. p. 75.
[3] Calderwood, vi. 114.

restrain them; and they soon became dangerous to the safety of the King himself.[1] They declared that the Catholic Lords were encouraged by the King, and that no good had ever come to the country through the Guisian blood.[2] The dread of Popery had engendered a stern spirit, which knew no compromise. Huntly and Errol must die the death. James was so completely brow-beaten by the violence of his assailants, that he promised he would require the Catholic Lords to conform to the Church established, before he would consent to the withdrawal of the forfeitures. He therefore wrote a peremptory letter to Huntly, informing him that the time had come when he must either embrace the Protestant faith, remain in Scotland, and be restored to his honours and his estates; or leave the country for ever, and never look to be a Scotsman again! The letter concluded with these words:

"Deceive not yourself, to think that by lingering of time, your wife and your allies shall get you better conditions. I must love myself and my own estate better than all the world, and think not that I will suffer any, professing a contrary religion, to dwell in this land."[3]

In an evil hour Huntly, Errol, and Angus, that they might save their properties for themselves and families, agreed to submit exteriorly at least and for a time; and

---

[1] Elizabeth had already written to James, in 1590, a warning which must have added to his fears. "Let me warne you that ther is risen, bothe in your realme and myne, a secte of perilous consequence, such as wold have no kings but a presbitrye, and take our place while they injoy our privilege. . . . Yea, looke we wel unto them."—"Letters of Elizabeth and James VI.," edited by J. Bruce, Camden Society, 1849, 4to, p. 63.

[2] James had received a severe warning from Elizabeth. (Camden Soc., 1849, p. 63.)

[3] Letter quoted by Tytler, vol. ix. p. 232; by Spottiswood, p. 438.

on the 29th of June 1597 they subscribed the Confession of Faith. Father Gordon, who at this moment arrived in Scotland, states, in the following letter, that he had foreseen this sad misfortune.

Fr. James Gordon to Fr. Claud Aquaviva, General of the Society of Jesus.

"VERY REVEREND FATHER IN CHRIST,—PAX CHRISTI, —I will proceed to give an account of our adventures during the past three months. We waited some time at Calais for a favourable wind, and at length set sail early on the morning of the 4th of June. Upon the third day we reached the coast of Scotland, close to the English frontier, and four days later arrived at our destination.

"It is situated in the North of Scotland, near a castle where the Earl of Huntly was then residing. We had a servant of the Earl's with us, whom he had left in Belgium when he went away. I sent this man on to the Earl before we ourselves disembarked, to let him know of our arrival, and explain the cautious manner in which we were coming on shore. I did this on the supposition that the Earl was still what he had been before. But I found, on the contrary, that a great change had taken place in him during my long delay in Flanders. This was what I had feared; and it is a great misfortune for the Catholic cause. Huntly listened to the blandishments of the King and of his heretical friends; was persuaded to confer with the ministers; then went to their temples to hear their sermons, and ended by openly, at least in words, if not sincerely, renouncing the Catholic religion, for which he had so gloriously combated. This miserable example has been followed, with fatal facility, by two other Catholic nobles, the Earls of Angus and Errol.

"These three were the only men of high rank who had hitherto remained sincere Catholics and defenders of the Catholic cause. The Catholic barons and nobles of inferior rank were thrown into great perturbation by this desertion of their leaders. Almost all have wavered, and most of them have trod in the footsteps of the two earls, and have either renounced their religion, or at least consented to attend heretical worship. Catholics everywhere yielded to grief and terror; every day we heard of some deserting their faith either by interior defection, or at any rate in outward profession. The ministers triumphed openly. Such was the state of things in Scotland when we arrived, and it is very little, if at all, improved now. The few of our Fathers who were left (three in all) had to fly for their lives, and conceal themselves wherever they could. Up to this time they had found themselves secure in the north of Scotland, under the protection of the Earls of Huntly and Errol, but henceforth they were obliged to go elsewhere.

"The heretics had taken precautions that the Earls should not receive any Jesuit, myself especially, nor admit any person suspected of being a Catholic into their households, nor have any intercourse with such persons, nor yet receive letters or messages from them. Should any Jesuit arrive in the north, the Earl of Huntly, who exercised the royal authority there, was to apprehend and give him up to the ministers, as well as those who received and encouraged him.

"This Huntly had bound himself to do under a penalty of 20,000 pounds Scots, a sum equal to the same number of Belgian florins. My arrival, under these circumstances, gave him very great uneasiness. He had written to me a few months before entreating me not to return to Scotland, conscious, no doubt, of his meditated apostacy. This letter never reached me, but I received one of an earlier date advising me to come. I wish I had gone at once; but God disposes all things, and I arrived too late. The Earl's confusion was very great, for he could not but feel the disgrace which his abandonment of his faith and treacherous desertion of religion had brought upon him in the eyes of the Catholics. His long-standing friendship with me, and our kinship in blood, made it impossible for him to take me prisoner or give me up to the ministers. On the other hand, he foresaw and feared the anger of the King, the rage of the ministers, the fine in money, and the risk, as he averred, of the total loss of his rank and fortunes to which he had been only very recently restored. He replied to me, therefore, by the servant whom I sent to him from the ship that he was unable to receive me on his domains, or speak to me without the knowledge of the King, but that he should write to the King without delay to apprise him of my arrival, and await his Majesty's answer. He was resolved to follow the royal commands whatever they might be, for fear of the loss of his property and position. I therefore, with my companion, went on to another part of the country, in the vessel which had brought us, and reached next day the safest harbour in Scotland, one which on that account is called the Bay of Safety,[1] and was at the time perhaps the furthest removed from where the King resides. Here we landed, and remained for more than a month concealed among the Highland tribes of Scotland, who are mostly Catholics. We had no want of friends, who abundantly supplied our wants, in spite of the threatening orders issued by the government against me. Indeed from the moment of our arrival the ministers were thrown into a most extraordi-

[1] In the Latin text, *Sinum Salutis*—Cromarty.

nary state of confusion and alarm ; and, as the Catholics all remarked, 20,000 Spanish troops would not have frightened them so much.

"They were afraid we should recover, or at least try to recover, from the jaws of the Devil, and restore to their true master, the prey which their lies and flatteries had not long before torn from us, or rather from Christ. Their terrors gave us renewed hopes. They obtained or extorted from the King, who had lately restored them to favour, and did everything they asked, an atrocious proclamation, forbidding anyone to receive me into his house, or give me anything to eat or drink, or show me any encouragement, under penalty of high treason, which incurs the severest punishment known to the laws of this country. The proclamation went on to say that anyone might take me prisoner, or kill me, if I would not surrender ; and a reward of a thousand gold pieces was offered to anyone who should apprehend or put me to death. But God so ordered it that, in a very short time this terrible edict came to nothing. Another was published in the beginning of July, through the interest of the Earl of Huntly, which revoked the former one, and allowed anyone who should have obtained permission from Huntly to receive me, supply my wants, and freely converse and speak with me, without either risk or loss ; but on this condition that I left Scotland before the 11th of August. Huntly had in fact bound himself under a heavy penalty that I should do so, and he sent to intimate this fact to me. I thought I ought not to refuse compliance, under the circumstances, especially as the condition only bound me to leave Scotland, and did not forbid me to return. I myself stated this clearly to the ministers, a little later, in a public conference with them, openly professing my intention to come back, to their great indignation; and, with God's favour, I mean very shortly to keep my word. Next, I reflected that by this course I should render the former cruel proclamation null and void, thus relieving the friends who had entertained and supplied me from grave embarrassment and anxiety, and lastly, I thus obtained a full month, or rather more, during which I was free to go wherever I liked, confer freely with Catholics, who were at that time extremely desolate and afflicted, and all this publicly and without risk to anyone; and I gained also the opportunity of meeting our Fathers, and consulting with them. Two of them, Fathers William[1] and Alexander,[2] came to me immediately. As Father Robert[3] was sick in a distant part of the country, I sent Father William to him with the message of your Paternity.

"Everything has been done, which was necessary at the time, for their spiritual consolation, and I shall soon make all ready, with God's help, for my return.

"I met another pious Priest, Father James Seton, who joined us from the Seminary at Pont-à-Mousson, ten years ago, and was labouring earnestly with us in our Lord's vineyard, as if he were one of us. He is desirous of being admitted to the Society, but, as he is advanced in years and somewhat infirm, we thought it best he should remain in his present condition.

"To pursue my narrative—I left my place of concealment, to the great joy and wonder of the Catholics, and with many fears on the part of the ministers and other heretics, lest their wicked corruption of God's word should lose credit thereby. Having observed the triumph of the heretics, and dejection of the Catholics, at the perversion of the three Earls, and seeing no better course to take, I offered, after consultation with my com-

[1] William Murdoch.   [2] Alexander Seaton.
[3] Robert Abercromby.

panions, a free public discussion to all the ministers in Scotland on the controverted points of religion; stipulating that it should be held in the presence of the King, of the principal nobility, and above all of the three noblemen who had lately changed their faith. This delighted all the Catholics, and raised their highest hopes. Our opponents themselves acknowledged that it was just and fair, and among them were not a few of the leaders of the party, who openly declared, and confirmed it by oath, that they would abandon the heretical sect, and embrace the Catholic religion, if the ministers refused my challenge.

"The proposal threw these last into great consternation, and as it had been made only verbally, and they had replied ambiguously, according to their wont, I committed it to writing in clear and unmistakeable terms. I then sent it all over the kingdom, to let everyone see how weak and unfounded the heretical cause must be, since its own adherents and teachers did not dare defend it publicly. I also wrote to the King, to the same effect. I now forward a copy of each of these letters to Father Crichton by the messenger who carries this, that they may be transmitted to your Paternity.

"The heretical ministers, perceiving that many of their supporters were openly offended at their conduct, and that many more were beginning to murmur, sought to gain time by replying, that they could not act otherwise, without authority from the General Assembly, which meets only once or twice in a year. This, however, will avail them nothing, for as soon as the Assembly meets, my challenge will be laid before it, and I shall then be on the spot, by God's blessing, to receive their answer. No other course than the one I have adopted seemed open to me, under the difficulty in which I then found myself. Our armour is spiritual, not carnal, and our sword is the word of God, by means of which Christ our Lord is accustomed to rout and overthrow the armies of Satan. We trust in the promises of Christ, the prayers of the whole Catholic Church, and especially of our Society.

"When the time of my embarkation drew near, and I had already reached Aberdeen, the principal town in the north of Scotland, whence the vessel was to sail, a very unexpected and providential accident occurred, which greatly encouraged the Catholics, and distressed the heretics in the same proportion. I was lodged in the house of a certain Baron, my kinsman, to which all who wished to speak to me had free access. Father William[1] was staying in the town, but secretly, and used to come to see me once a day, or oftener. I received frequent visits from the Protestant Bishop of the place, and from a whole crowd of ministers, who said they did not come to converse about religion, but simply out of respect, and on account of my relations with the Earl of Huntly, and that they might arrange for my departure. I took advantage of this opportunity, more than once, to repeat my offer of a public disputation. They put me off, as usual, by referring the matter to the General Assembly, and we proceeded to converse on other subjects. But whether from a hope of obtaining ground for calumny against me, or the desire of novelty, or a wish to try their powers in a preliminary skirmish before the general engagement, they all agreed that I should be permitted to preach to them, not in a church, but in the Baron's hall, which was large enough to accommodate the whole number, and they promised that everybody who wished to attend should be allowed to do so, without prejudice or risk. Being then asked what words

[1] William Murdoch.

of Scripture I should choose for my text, I said, 'The Church is the pillar and ground of the truth.' Upon which the Protestant Bishop interrupted me with the remark, 'You must take the theme of your discourse only from the Holy Scriptures;' for he was so ignorant of Scripture that he did not know St Paul had written those words to Timothy. I answered, these words really are in Scripture, and some of the ministers confirming my assertion, the Protestant Bishop coloured and was silent. Perceiving, however, that my choice of this text was anything but pleasing to them, I said I would undertake to preach on any text of Scripture they gave me. They fixed on the words in John x., 'My sheep hear my voice,' as appearing to them wholly at variance with our system of doctrine. They added that I was not to treat of tradition, but of the written word only. I accepted this condition willingly, and August 16th was fixed as the day for my sermon, at a particular hour. The affair was talked about everywhere, and I purposely obtained an interval of five days that it might be as widely known as possible. All thought it strange to find liberty of public preaching allowed to a Catholic priest, and he a Jesuit, after an interval of more than six and thirty years, and this by an assembled Council of the Ministers, or as it is called, the Presbytery. But when the appointed day came, and the ministers, from whom the Protestant Bishop had withdrawn, saw the great numbers gathered together, not of the common people only, but of the nobility and higher ranks, they refused at once to keep to their engagement. Not one of them would consent that any person should be admitted except the ministers themselves. Men of the highest rank, even the most determined heretics, the best known supporters and adherents of heresy, the most intimate friends of the ministers, were one and all excluded. Nay, before the ministers themselves would agree to enter the hall they sent some of their own number to search every corner of the house, the bedrooms, kitchen, larder, and every possible hiding place, lest anybody might be concealed there. Of course such proceedings gave great umbrage, not to Catholics alone, but to the leaders of the heretical party themselves, who had been asked to hear a sermon, and then found the doors shut in their faces. The very people in the streets all exclaimed that the ministers had proved the falsehood and weakness of their own cause. Every one acknowledged that it would have been better not to have given permission to preach, than to give it, and then unreasonably and insolently shut out the audience. Some of the ministers themselves declared that the General Assembly would inflict a penalty upon those who had granted me license to preach, while they laid the whole blame upon the Bishop, asserting that he had been the first to give me permission, and had then withdrawn in order to throw the fault upon them. I myself was much annoyed at the exclusion of such numbers of people who wanted to hear me, but I did not wish it to be thought that I was afraid of the ministers. Accordingly, I spoke a few words on the subject assigned me; not indeed what I should have said in the presence of the multitude, but what I thought better suited to my actual auditors.

"When I had finished, I left them space for reply, if they had anything to object. One or two spoke, but they had evidently prepared their remarks at home, and these bore in no particular way upon what I had advanced. The substance of what I said was, that the voice of Christ addressed us not in the letter alone of the written word, but rather in the true exposition of its meaning;

and that this is not to be found in private interpretation, but to be gathered from the sense and consent of the ancient Fathers and Councils. This they assented to. Then I pressed them further, asking what Fathers and Councils they recognised as trustworthy. They answered those of the first five hundred years (some said six hundred) after Christ. I then engaged to prove all our doctrines, and refute their heresies, from the writings of these Fathers and Councils, as soon as they granted us a free and public discussion. They desired me to put the substance of what I had said into writing, so that they could reply after fuller consideration. I agreed to this, on condition they would also write down what they had just said, especially their appeal to the Fathers and Councils of the first five centuries.

"I wrote out my statement the same day, and have sent a copy of it to Father Crichton, together with this letter. The ministers never sent me theirs until I had gone on board ship, when they despatched it for me, by the captain, who was the last to come on board; and were doubtless under the delusion that this would prevent my making any reply to their learned observations. In this, however, they will, by God's help, be disappointed, for I mean to answer them very soon, and to have my reply laid before them publicly.

"I embarked at Aberdeen on the 18th of August, and arrived in Norway three days later. Thence I came to the south of Denmark, where I now am. This is a most convenient place whence to return to Scotland, and I shall stay for the present, especially as we could not both safely traverse Holland together on the way to Belgium. I have no doubt of being able to go back to Scotland in eight or ten days hence, weather permitting.

"Your Paternity will see how greatly the Scottish

Mission stands in need of the sacrifices and prayers of the whole Society. Our cause was never at a lower ebb than now, but 'God is able from these stones to raise up children to Abraham.'

"I will do what I can, so long as I am able, by Christ's help; may He do all the rest as seems good to Him. I have written as best I could, when on the road and at intervals. Your Paternity will obtain further information from Father Crichton, as he can learn all particulars and every detail from my companion, whom I am sending to him.

"I earnestly commend myself to the holy sacrifices and prayers of your Paternity, and of all the Society.

"Your Paternity's unworthy servant and son in Christ,

"JAMES GORDON."

"HERSENS, in DENMARK, *September 1st*, 1597." [1]

On hearing that the state of religion in Scotland grew daily worse and worse, Father Gordon resolved to make another expedition to his native country. He had a special reason for returning. Although he more than once openly challenged the Calvinist doctors to public controversy, in the King's presence, they nevertheless boasted that Gordon was afraid to dispute with them, and that he had gone into concealment to avoid the King and his councillors, and the courts of law. This false and injurious report induced him to go back as speedily as possible, in order to try by every means to draw his opponents into discussion; and he did not despair of conducting it in the presence of the King, who knew and loved him.

He determined to visit his Majesty at once, and display before him the light of truth, whether he would

---

[1] Archives of the Society of Jesus, vol. "Scotia."

receive it or no. Indeed, he could not very easily betake himself to anybody else, even one of the highest rank, since the proclamation had made it a capital crime to receive him under any roof. How he accomplished his design, may be learnt from his own account in a letter to Fr. General.

"VERY REVEREND FATHER IN CHRIST,—I proceed to a narrative of our adventures since the date of my last letter to your Paternity from Lubeck in September last.[1] . . . There was no vessel likely to sail for Scotland, and winter was now approaching. The sea near Eukhingen is frozen over every winter, and we were therefore in danger of being detained a long time if we did not leave speedily.

"Under these circumstances our Catholic friends procured a vessel to bring us, hired the services of a captain and sailors, and fitted her out with every requisite for a long winter voyage, all at their own expense, and so after two months detention in Holland, we at length set sail for Scotland, where by God's mercy we arrived safe and sound on the fifth day, having had a favourable wind, and the weather as calm as if it were summer. My purpose was to seek publicly without delay the presence of the King, and therefore proceed at once to the capital. Many reasons suggested this step, the first being that I had openly bound myself to do so when I left Scotland. The ministers had charged me with having kept myself in concealment, not venturing to appear before the King and his Council, or demand a public discussion, such as they themselves, being private individuals, could not engage in on their own authority.

[1] A long account of Fr. Gordon's stay at Lubeck and Hamburg is here omitted.

In reply to this, I had promised that when I came back I would repair straightway to the King in the capital, and defend before him the propositions I had advanced in writing. My other reason was that two years had now gone by, and the ministers to whom my challenge to a disputation on points of controversy had been delivered did not meanwhile make any reply to it, procrastinating day after day, evidently with the hope that the whole subject would be forgotten, because they were not bold enough to accept the challenge, yet felt it would be ignominious entirely to refuse it. I thought it important to press them on the point till I got a positive answer, one way or other; and that the best plan was for me to go in person, and demand a discussion in the presence of the King and the Council, for this would surely extract some sort of reply from them however reluctantly given. I had still another reason, namely, that some persons in Scotland gave out, it was not only my religion which prevented my appearing in the King's presence, but certain political causes and civil charges against me. To prove the groundlessness of these insinuations, I resolved to go to the King before I visited a single person else in Scotland, more especially as any man of rank whom I might visit would be exposed to the danger of losing all his goods, and possibly his very life, since a royal proclamation issued just before I went away forbad any one to receive me under penalty of forfeiture of all his effects, and indeed of his head. On this account I thought my first visit was due to the King, inasmuch as it would not expose any body to danger. The other thing I had to fear was lest I should be intercepted by my adversaries before I could reach his Majesty. In order to avoid this mishap, I determined to disembark at nightfall, so as not to be recognised, and then go straight to the palace, which is only an Italian mile distant from Leith, where we were to land.

"This attempt, by the aid of Almighty God, succeeded perfectly, and averted all danger from myself or others. The very day we reached Leith, being the feast day of St Andrew, the Patron of Scotland, according to the old calendar followed by the Scots, the King had arrived at the palace, from which he had previously been for a short time absent. An hour or two after his arrival I succeeded in reaching the door of his chamber without any one knowing who I was. The second hour of the night (7 p.m.) had sounded, and the King was at that moment closeted with his ministers, holding a meeting of his Privy Council, as it is called. One of the councillors had formerly been acquainted with me, and was on terms of friendship with my kinsfolk, besides being allied to them by affinity. I sent therefore word to him by the doorkeeper of the King's chamber, that a friend of his was waiting to speak with him. On coming, he took me aside but did not recognise me, so I told him who I was, and why I had come, and requested him to repeat to the King what I had said without loss of time. He smiled, and undertook my commission, though not without an expression of wonder at my mode of proceding. He went straight to the King and informed him of what had occurred. James himself and all present were surprised, and being afraid lest the ministers, whose influence is very great, and whose audacity is still greater, might be highly incensed at my arrival, he sent me word by the same member of the Council, that I must be detained in custody within the castle not far from the palace in the same city, until they had deliberated on the course to be pursued. I said I was quite ready to obey the royal command. He left me to go and speak to the King once more, and returned along with another councillor, who had received the King's orders to convey me to the castle.

"This nobleman who conducted me was an enthusiastic friend and supporter of my cause, in part because he was himself not far from the kingdom of God, and also because his estates lay in the north, bordering on the country subject to the Earl of Huntly, my nephew. He showed me the utmost kindness all the time I was in Scotland, conveying the King's messages to me and my replies to his Majesty, who employed him for this purpose, well knowing both his friendship for me and his fidelity to his Sovereign. I had desired my companion William, for whose safety I was more anxious than for my own, to leave me before I entered the palace. I was conducted to the castle with a suitable escort, without violence, and without the knowledge of any of our opponents. The royal councillor who accompanied me was the only person that knew who I was, the servants in attendance having been told nothing as to my identity, while the darkness prevented anyone, who might happen to know me, from recognising me on the way. When we arrived at the castle the councillor spoke a few words to the officers in charge of the fortress, commended me to their care in the King's name, and desired that I might be abundantly supplied with whatever I wanted at the King's expense. The next morning I was visited by the official who had conducted me thither on the previous evening, by two ministers whom I supposed to be in the King's confidence, and by a secretary whose office it was to write down the answers given by me to the questions which the others put. I replied to everything fully, fearlessly, and faithfully; and my answers, by God's good help, were so satisfactory to the King and to his Council that they never thought it necessary to interrogate me again on any subject. The point of my reply was that I had come to keep my promise, and to obtain a decided answer, one way or the other, to the proposal of a public discussion which I had made, two years before. I added that I had not come secretly, or as though afraid, but had openly and boldly gone to the King himself, relying first, on the justice of my cause, and next, on the King's clemency and piety, well persuaded of his candour and preference of truth to error. Though he was unconsciously in error himself, I professed myself certain he would never be willing to condemn unheard and without trial, or to subject to any unjust treatment, one who only upheld the truth. If, on my trial, the ministers could show that I had advanced anything against truth and contrary to the Word of God, I would willingly undergo any punishment they could inflict. In the meanwhile the ministers were labouring earnestly, day after day, in all their addresses from the pulpit, to convince the King, the officers of State, and the populace, that I ought to be put to death, because I had led so many souls astray and consigned them to ruin ; that the laws of the realm would be outraged if I escaped capital punishment ; and that I had disobeyed the King's order, which required me not to return to Scotland under pain of death. These and many other propositions, equally bloodthirsty, they every day invented and urged.

"Within two or three days after my imprisonment in the castle, another cause of confusion arose, which at first seemed serious, but ultimately came to nothing. A certain Englishman resided in the town of Edinburgh, who was a deadly enemy to Catholics. It came to this man's knowledge that two Englishmen, whom he did not know, had recently arrived

in the town; and he suspected they had come in
the vessel which brought me, and were probably priests
of our Society, or belonged to some English seminary.
With a view to render my coming more odious, the
ministers were already spreading reports, that the Pope
had lately sent forth a number of Jesuits, or pupils of
Jesuits, to despatch all the principal sovereigns of Europe
by poison or the sword. One of these, it was said, had
been sent to France, one to Holland, a third to England,
and another to Scotland, this last being either myself, or
some one who had sailed in the same ship with me. The
King did not give the slightest credence to this extraordinary
story, nor did any of the men of influence in
the government; but many of the common people were
induced by the authority of the ministers to receive it
as unquestionably true. On this account I had been
anxiously and carefully interrogated in my examination
as to whether I knew of such a plot; whether I had had
any fellow passengers, who these were, and how many in
number. I said, according to truth, that there was no
one on board except myself, the Dutch sailors, and
William Martin, whom I had dismissed before I entered
the palace, and I knew he intended going away at once to
the west of Scotland. The Englishman above mentioned,
who was aware that I had given this answer, thought
himself now in a position to convict me of falsehood, and
of conspiring against the King. He went to the palace,
and declared that I had brought two or more English
Jesuits into Scotland, who meditated taking the Kings'
life. He had found out where they were lodged, and
asked for a body of police officers to apprehend and carry
them off to prison. Several noblemen instantly started
from the royal residence, and were joined by the guard.
They all repaired straight to the house where the two

Englishmen had been seen; and the soldiers, breaking in, arrested them both, and conveyed them forthwith through the crowded streets of the city to the public prison. A popular tumult ensued, all crying out that by the just judgment of God, and His great goodness, the Jesuit conspiracy was at length laid bare; and that I deserved death a thousand times, and in the most terrible form, for introducing these men into the kingdom to take the King's life. Everybody was astonished at what had occurred, and the friends and supporters of our cause were distressed and anxious, fearing imminent peril both to us, and to all Catholics on our account. These different circumstances were related to me, in the castle, close by where they occurred; and, though I knew myself to be innocent of the charge, I could not help seeing how difficult it would be to disprove it, in the presence of enemies so embittered, or to clear myself, as well as the two other prisoners. There remained also this danger, that the heretics might take advantage of it for some important political move, and that Catholics themselves might be scandalised and offended.

"The Englishman who was the author of all this outcry, took so much pride in what he had done, that he scrupled not to come and upbraid me, at the castle, in the presence of many witnesses, with my wickedness in bringing over, not the two Englishmen only, but several more (three or four at least as he pretended), all sworn to murder the King. Thence he set off to meet James himself, who had gone out hunting early in the morning; and, overtaking him in the open country, informed him of the signal service he had been privileged to render to his Majesty, for which he claimed due praise and reward. He explained that two English Jesuits, engaged in a plot against the King's life, had been apprehended in the capital, and were then in custody; and he begged his Majesty to enquire into the circumstances, adding that the men were companions of mine, and had sailed to Scotland with me. The King heard this with extreme surprise, for I had solemnly assured him that I had come with only one companion, and so he was somewhat put out, and began to be very angry with me. He had not previously intended returning to Edinburgh that day, being about to visit the Queen, who was expecting her confinement, and was residing four miles out of the town; but he now changed his mind, and coming back to the palace, ordered the accused to be brought before him, and questioned anew in his presence. They had already been examined twice or thrice, and the matter was considered settled, but he insisted on having the enquiry made all over again, and the witnesses, both Scotch and English, recalled; fresh evidence being also given. It appeared from the uniform and unvarying testimony of all these, and from undeniable proofs, that the two Englishmen were neither Jesuits nor priests, nor even Catholics, but were soldiers from the English garrison in the frontier town of Berwick. They had never seen me in their lives, and had come to Edinburgh for no other purpose than to drink wine with their boon companions, which they had so often done before, that they were well known to nearly every one in the town. This disturbance then, which had occasioned much alarm to many honest men, came to nothing, on the same day on which it had begun; the King, and every one else with him, having a good laugh at the expense of its English author.

"This tragedy was, however, immediately followed by another, far more serious in its consequences, but to our opponents, and not to ourselves. One of the ministers was in particularly high favour with the King and the whole Council. He was acknowledged by all to be the most learned amongst them, and had written some books in the Latin language which had been carried to Geneva, and highly lauded by Beza. He had also undertaken the care and management of the college not long before established by the Reforming ministers at Edinburgh. He had been present by the King's desire, along with others, at my examination, and seemed inclined to accept my challenge to a disputation, but insisted that it should be held privately, and not in public. In order that matter for discussion might not be wanting, he presented me with a book which he had lately written, in Latin, against the first volume of the Controversies of Cardinal Bellarmine, as a first essay towards a complete refutation of the works of that writer. I was requested to read this carefully over, and state my opinion of it, not by word of mouth only, but in writing, that so the King and the members of his Council might all know what I thought. I perceived that they preferred having controversy conducted in writing rather than verbally. I accepted the condition, lest I should seem to avoid the challenge. I drew up a refutation of the book, brief, but clear and pointed, which I finished in a few days, and showed to the Councillor of State who had conducted me to the castle, and who frequently visited me there ; I, at the same time, desired him to hand a copy of it to the King and another to the minister who was the author of the book. He willingly undertook to do this, as soon as he had read it himself.

"But the power of Almighty God, always ready to protect His own, intervened at this juncture. Within a few days, the minister was seized with a mysterious illness which occasioned him continued and intolerable anguish, both of mind and body, and at length cut short his days by a miserable death, so that he never was able to draw up any reply to what I had written. Thus the death of torment, which my enemies had so often prayed might befall me, by God's just judgment overtook their own chief and leader; and when, to the great grief of the party, he was dead and buried, none of his survivors would undertake either to answer what I had written, or engage in any controversy with me, either public or private. Some indeed openly declared that I had compassed the death of the most distinguished minister in Scotland, by magical poisons and incantations, for it had been noticed that, ever since the day of my examination (at which he had been present, and had talked much in a proud and impious strain), he had sickened and pined away. The heretics not unfrequently thus ascribe to Satan the actions of Almighty God. Meanwhile the day appointed for the hearing of my cause before the King and Council arrived. The ministers did all they could to secure my being sentenced to death, but of all the members of the Council present, one only favoured their desire, and a certain Catholic observed in jest that I possessed only one friend among them, since I longed for nothing more than to leave this miserable world and die in behalf of my religion, yet there was only one of the lords who consented to grant me this satisfaction. The King and all present, hearing this remark, laughed much at it, and his Majesty not only inveighed strongly against the opinion of my single adversary, but gave testimony to my innocence in a long and excellent speech, which he addressed to the Council. He said that, had I been one of those who interfere in politics, and endeavour to interrupt the tranquillity of the kingdom, he would punish me without hesitation. But it was evident I occupied myself only with my studies and my books, without meddling with public affairs; and even if I maintained or taught anything contrary to truth, I did so in all good faith, not with any mischievous intention, nor in opposition to my conscience. To put to death or otherwise ill-treat such a person would be unjust and cruel in the extreme; and it would be especially so for him to do this, because I had unreservedly and confidingly placed myself in his hands.[1] The King having expressed this decision at some length, all came round to the conclusion that, as I had sought the King's presence at the earliest opportunity, and had acted throughout openly and without concealment, I had not broken the laws of the kingdom. At the same time the King promised the ministers, with the view of in some degree appeasing their anger, that he would provide for my leaving Scotland as soon as it was possible for me to sail. Meanwhile I was to be kept a close prisoner in the castle, without the opportunity of conversing with any one about religion, or of leading any one astray (as they termed it); for they had often, and in many words, complained to the King that I was allowed too freely to converse with all who wished to see me, and was making many converts. Accordingly directions were given that I should not be permitted to argue with any person whatever, the ministers being absolutely opposed to all discussion.

"These proceedings in Council took place on the twentieth day from my arrival in Scotland. Shortly after this the Earl of Huntly, who had been for some time absent from Court, arrived, and obtained without difficulty my release from the castle. He would not

[1] The Register of the Privy Council of Scotland. Edinburgh, 1882, vol. v. p. 503, 504.

permit the King to pay the debts which I had incurred to persons in the castle, but discharged everything himself, though his Majesty had of his own accord, and more than once, offered to do so. I left the castle, and took up my residence at the house of a citizen of the town, one of the principal men in Edinburgh, a man excellently disposed towards me, though prejudiced against the true religion. The Catholics resorted to me in numbers, and quite freely, an act which had been of course impossible, or very difficult, while I was in the castle. But when, in the course of conversation, some of us had referred to my challenge made to the ministers, and observed that they seemed absolutely disinclined to any sort of controversy or discussion, whether public or private, my entertainer could not persuade himself that this was the case; and feeling convinced that a great point had been gained by my having mentioned a disputation in private as something I would not refuse—a public one being, he knew well, such as the other party would never agree to—he hurried off to the principal minister in Scotland, a man of note, and held in high estimation by the people, both for learning and integrity of life, reported what I had said, and then entreated and implored him to engage in controversy with me. The other replied that he could not speak to me without the King's consent, for the latter might be displeased, as I was under his protection; but if the King had no objecjection, he would willingly undertake to do what he was asked. I imagine he expected James would not give his consent, and he would thus be able to throw upon the King the responsibility of refusing the discussion. It, however, turned out otherwise. My friend had no difficulty in obtaining the royal permission, by means of one of the members of the Council; and so, returning joyfully to the arch-minister, informed him of his success, and entreated him to come at once to his house. The minister now regretted the rash pledge he had given, and tried to induce my host to forego his purpose; but the latter held him to his engagement in such a way that the minister perceived a refusal would give serious offence both to my host and to other persons who were assembled in his house. He then pretended to doubt whether the King's permission had been really given, nor could he be assured on this head until he himself went to the Councillor of State, by whom the leave had been obtained, and received an assurance from him that it was really so. At length he gave in, and promised he would come to my host's residence for the discussion; and the hour and method of proceeding were fixed upon. On the day named we waited for him, according to the hour and terms arranged, and the same on the next day, and the next; but our friend never appeared. At length he laid aside all reserve, and plainly intimated that he could not consent to any such discussion as had been proposed; that I was unreasonably obstinate in insisting upon it; that it could lead to no result; that he had not leisure for it; and that it was not right to waste time in altercations of such a nature; that as the King protected me, my host had better go to the King's preachers, and ask them to dispute with me. He proceeded to name one whom he thought most suited for the task, and suggested that the person should be sent for. My host was astonished at all this, but finding the minister determined, came away with very considerable indignation, and set out as had been suggested to invite the King's preacher. This minister likewise promised to come, reiterated his promise, yet never appeared; shortly after he also pleaded pressing business, and declined the controversy altogether. My indefatigable friend then went to a third, a man of much note among the city preachers, but he replied that he was not well enough to attend.

"It now became evident that all the ministers in Edinburgh, who had any reputation for learning, were resolved not to engage in discussion with me, even privately; and as I had been waiting for them ten days, living the whole time without concealment in an inn, my presence being thus perfectly well known to all the town, and as there was still no sort of expectation that the controversy would ever be really held, it appeared to me I might as well go. Accordingly, I left Edinburgh and repaired to the castle of a Baron not far off. I took this step by desire of the King and of the Earl of Huntly, to whose charge the King had committed me. I carried with me letters from the King, bearing not so much his commendation as his commands, and was very kindly and amicably received. The nobleman in question was Lord Seton, elder brother of Mr Alexander Seton, who had formerly made his classical studies in the German College at Rome. His house is very splendid and very agreeable, and not more than eight miles distant from Edinburgh. My removal to this place irritated the ministers to the last degree. I had shown myself the principal opponent of their faith —or rather want of faith—and yet here I was lodged in the best quarters in all Scotland, treated as a friend, and living among my kinsmen and connections, and the strongest adherents of my religion. They appointed a meeting, or, as they call it, presbytery, and drew up an admonition to the Baron, that he must turn me out of his house, under pain of excommunication. They are accustomed to act in this manner, even in opposition to the commands of the King, to which they pay no regard when it does not suit them. At the same time they sent directions to every preacher of their sect to inveigh in all their sermons, not against me only, for that they had done from the first, but against Lord Seton, for receiving me into his house, and against the King himself, who had commanded my being received there. This the ministers zealously did, referring to the subject both in their morning and afternoon discourses, since they preach twice on all solemn days, and some of them three or four times, so inexhaustible is their flow of language.

"The Baron brought this insolent act of the ministers to the notice of the King, observing that they had threatened him with excommunication, simply for complying with the commands signified to him in the King's letters. James was extremely provoked, and sent one of his councillors to the next meeting of the presbytery (which occurs at a particular time every week), with a message to the effect that if they did not desist from the excommunication of the Baron, they should all be cited to appear before the High Court. This in some degree alarmed them, and they proceeded no further with the excommunication, but made it a condition that I should leave Scotland as soon as possible. During this time they continued to declaim against me, against Lord Seton, and against the King, from all their pulpits. The minister of a neighbouring village, one of the foremost to denounce me in the most violent language, was advised by some of his friends to come and say it all to my face, as this would be more creditable than going on railing at me behind my back; to which he replied, that I was under sentence of excommunication, and it was not allowable to hold speech with an excommunicated person. The same reply was made by others. This country preacher had been in the habit of frequenting the Baron's house

R

before I came there, quite as much, I think, to indulge his appetite as for piety's sake. The day following my arrival he came suddenly into the hall, where the Baron happened to be talking with me, and was so panic-stricken at the sight of me that off he ran down the stairs, through the courtyard, across the garden, and never looked back till he found himself on the safe side of the outer fence, nor did he ever reappear while I was there. He told his friends, indeed, that he had been confined to the house the whole of that day by a violent access of fever, and had not even left his bed,— an unaccountable malady which he attributed to magical influences, and felt certain no one could safely venture into any house where I was present.

"Some weeks passed by, and people about the Court were beginning to be afraid that my affairs would lead to a serious rupture between the King and the ministers. The former insisted that I should remain at Lord Seton's house, whether the ministers liked it or not ; while they were equally resolved to excommunicate the owner of the house if I were not turned out. I thought best, under these circumstances, to find some honourable pretext for removing, and so prevent this disagreement about me from proceeding to a public quarrel. I was also informed that several vessels were in readiness to sail to different ports, and that I could be conveyed to any part of the Continent I liked. I soon received a summons to Leith, whence the ships departed, but earlier than was necessary, and hence I had to stay a month or more at Leith, waiting for favourable weather. Here I was freer than I had ever been. I found lodging in a commodious inn, not far from the capital, and still nearer to the royal residence. My friends could come to me whenever they wished, and not a few of my opponents came likewise, either openly or secretly. Among those who visited me publicly and officially, without any intention of religious controversy, were the subaltern civil officers called the Bailies of Edinburgh and Leith—for the principal magistrate of both towns is Mr Alexander Seton, before mentioned. Many others called on me, several being men of rank, though the ministers stormed at them for so doing. One of these, a magistrate of the town of Leith, had a brother a minister. This minister, while drinking with his friends, and emboldened, as is often the case, by the effect of his potations, offered to go and dispute with me on the subject of religion that very day, in presence of his brother and of the other chief men of the town, and engaged that he would unmistakably convict me of many errors. The magistrate, his brother, and the others who were present, heard this welcome intelligence with joy, and gave unbounded thanks to God that at length one minister was found who would venture to engage in controversy with me. All the bailies of Leith, with other principal people of the town, instantly set out for the house where I lodged. The minister, I know not why, turned aside on the road, saying he would follow immediately. The others came, and sat down, and we entered into conversation, they explaining to me the object of their visit, and the pledge which the minister had given. I accepted the challenge, and they sent to find the disputant. Several minutes passed, and they sent again, but the worthy man did not appear, and could not even be found, having evidently taken measures to prevent the chance of my even setting my eyes upon him. So there was an end of this disputation also, and the bailies and their friends took their departure in considerable confusion, and not without some very uncomplimentary reflections on their minister's conduct.

"At last a vessel was ready to convey me, the weather was propitious, and the Earl of Huntly provided liberally for all the expenses of my voyage. On the 10th of May I set sail from Leith, where I had arrived on the 10th of the previous December, having thus spent five months in Scotland. I crossed over to Denmark. The King of Scotland provided me with letters of protection to the States of Zealand and Holland, which letters I still have in my possession; but I thought it better to go by way of Denmark, as being more out of the way of the English and the Dutch. Having reached that country, I proceeded to Copenhagen, the capital of the kingdom, as I had very favourable letters from the Queen of Scotland to her brother, the King of Denmark. The King was absent at some distance, and I delivered the letters to the Chancellor. This functionary received me kindly, laid the letter before the Council, reported to me their reply, and asked me what assistance I required for my journey. I said I wanted nothing but a letter in the King's name, giving me and my companions (there were six of us in all) permission to travel through the country by land, because the contrary wind prevented our proceeding to Germany by sea. He sent me at once an order from the Council, not only granting me what I requested in the fullest and most ample terms, but providing much more—namely, four carriages, drawn by two horses each, to convey us, at the royal expense, through Denmark and Holstein, which last province extends to the gates of Hamburgh. Some of us reached Hamburgh, and thence Altona, with great despatch, by the help of the King's horses and carriages, and without any expense to ourselves; so much so, that even when crossing the straits, of which there are three, one of them being twenty-eight Italian miles across, not a single person asked us even for boat hire. Of course in so long a journey the horses had often to be changed, and thus between Copenhagen and Hamburgh we used about a hundred and forty of the King's horses. No one ever offered to molest or insult us, or refused us either lodging or anything else we wanted on the road. Thus we came safe to Altona, praise be to God for it, where I am now writing to your Paternity.

"Such, very Rev. Father, have been our adventures during the last few months. If our proceedings have been in any degree successful, if they satisfy you, and tend to the glory of God, we ascribe all first to the Divine mercy, and next to the pious prayers of your Paternity and our other Fathers and brethren. What has happened otherwise I ascribe to my own sins, negligence, and tepidity. This letter is rather long, but I know your Paternity will pardon that fault, because I have been obliged to write down not only what I have done, but in most cases, also, my reasons and the objects I have had in view.

"I earnestly desire to be commended to the most holy sacrifices and prayers of your Paternity.

"Your Paternity's unworthy son and
"servant in Christ,
"JAMES GORDON, S.J."

"ALTONA, near HAMBURGH, July 13, 1599."[1]

While Father Gordon waited in Denmark for better days, three Fathers continued to serve the Catholics from their hiding places. These were Robert Abercromby, William Murdoch, and Alexander MacQuhirrie. Another, George Christie, was betrayed and brought to the King,

[1] Arch. S.J., vol. "Scotia," Latin MS.

who received him kindly, but recommended him to leave the kingdom, and so he went to Belgium.

The Catholic Earls having been put down and forced to submit to the discipline of the Kirk, the ministers now looked to the ordering of the Court. They sent a deputation to the Queen, "to speak and deal with her touching her religion, her manners for favouring and acting towards the enemies of the truth—namely, the Earl of Huntly; her speaking contemptuously and reproachfully of the ministry, as also her not repairing to the word and sacraments."[1]

Anne of Denmark had not anticipated the full weight of the troubles preparing for her in the home of her adoption. She had been educated in the extremest form of Lutheranism, and a clause had been inserted in the articles of marriage, providing that the young Queen should not be molested in the exercise of the faith in which she had been educated.[2] But in Scotland to be a Lutheran was about as bad as to be a Papist. The preachers reminded James that he kept a Canaanitish woman in his household, and cherished her in his bosom. James advised her to yield. She was assailed by the preachers, by the nobility, by her own household. Young as she was, the Queen proved herself a woman of spirit; she possessed strong will and firm resolution. Help arrived at the fitting moment. The following old letter, which has recently come to light, preserves to us an episode in her life, all but forgotten, and therefore worth recording.

[1] Calderwood, v. p. 459.
[2] "Papers relative to the Marriage of James the Sixth," printed by the Bannatyne Club, p. 37. (Edin., 1828, 4to.)

The Reverend Robert Abercromby, a Scotchman, to John Stuart, Prior of the Monastery at Ratisbon.

"About the year 1600 [Queen Anne] began to think about changing her religion from Lutheranism to Catholicism, for the following reasons.

"When she came into Scotland she had brought with her a Danish minister, who was a Lutheran, and was her preacher, and she attended to her religious services after the Lutheran fashion; for an arrangement had been made, at the marriage, that she should have the free exercise of the religion in which she had been born and educated. In process of time, this same minister cast off his Lutheranism and became a Calvinist. Noticing this, the Queen declined his services any longer, and was very anxious as to what course she could take for the future, for she was most decidedly opposed to Calvinism. It recurred to her how, being in Germany while she was very young, and resident for her education in the house of a certain great princess who was a Catholic, she had seen a priest who daily celebrated Mass; the memory of whom, and the love of the princess (who, if I be not mistaken, was the grand-daughter of Charles the Fifth), suggested to her that she should embrace that religion. She consulted some friends of hers, who were Catholics, about this matter, especially a Catholic Earl, as to what should be done; and he assured her that the Catholic religion was the only true religion, and that all the rest were sects and heresies, and he recommended me by name to her as her spiritual father. After a considerable delay, I was summoned to wait upon the Queen, where, having been introduced into the palace, I remained for three days, in a certain secret chamber. Every morning, for one hour, she came to me there for the purpose of being instructed; her ladies remaining all the time in the outer chamber, while she herself went into it, as if she had some letters to write. Whenever she came out, she always carried some paper in her hand. On the third day, she heard Mass and received from me the most Holy Sacrament, and then I took my departure from her.

"My stay in Scotland did not exceed two years complete after this communion, during which time, if my memory does not cheat me, she nine times received the most Holy Sacrament, and this so early in the morning that all the rest of the household was asleep, with the exception of a few women who communicated along with her. After communion, she always gave herself up to holy conversation; sometimes she expressed her desire that her husband should be a Catholic, at other times, her son should be educated under the direction of the Sovereign Pontiff. She spoke also about the happiness of the life of a nun, among whom she felt sure she would end her days. She had a great scruple because a part of her dower arose from a monastery, and she promised that, whenever there should be a change of religion, she would restore that monastery either to its lawful owners, or at least would change it into a college of Jesuits. She would not set out for England until I had been summoned, and had provided her with the most holy viaticum, she further made me promise to come to her in England, if she should summon me.

"As a consequence of this frequent use of the sacraments, her husband noticed a great improvement in her, and suspecting that it arose from the influence of some Popish priest—noticing also that she had held her own minister in contempt—one night, when they were in bed (she herself told me the story), he spoke to her in some such terms as these:—'I cannot but see a great change in you, you are much more grave, collected, and pious. I suspect, therefore, that you have some dealings with a Catholic priest.' She admitted that it was so, and she named me, an old cripple. His only answer was this:— 'Well, wife, if you cannot live without this sort of thing, do your best to keep things as quiet as possible; for, if you don't, our crown is in danger.' After this conference between them, the King always behaved to me with greater gentleness and kindness.

"The Queen, moreover, spoke with such of the leading courtiers as had shown themselves most hostile to the priests, forcing them by the threat of her vengeance to give their word to abstain from molesting me more.

"A laughable incident happened, which gave the Queen some amusement. An action-at-law was in progress between one of the chief noblemen, who was a heretic, and a certain minister. The Queen took the part of the latter, and spoke in his favour. Upon this the nobleman said, 'Your Majesty, by the wounds of Christ, I will tell upon you, and I will accuse you before Father Robert....'"[1]

[1] Father Abercromby concludes his letter as follows:—"One of the leading ladies at the Court has written to me from Greenwich about the Queen's state of mind at this present time (September 1608). As to her religion she is just as she was when I left her; there is this difference, however, that she can no longer enjoy that free practice of her religion which she had while in Scotland. I will here record two acts of hers, which show her heroic courage.

"The first of the two occurred shortly after the arrival of the King and Queen in England, at the time of their coronation. When they reached the church, it had been decided that before they could be crowned they must receive communion in the heretical fashion. This the King did forthwith, but the Queen refused, stating distinctly that she could not communicate, and rather than receive their communion, would go without the coronation. The King and the counsellors were urgent with her, but all in vain.

When the ministers discovered that the Queen had become a Catholic, they insulted her in a manner which would have been unbearable even to a private individual. The King tried to excuse her in public by saying that she was crazy; but in private he told her that she might follow any religion she liked, provided only she was cautious about it.[1] James, however, was bitterly blamed for allowing her to be surrounded by Catholic ladies. The Countess of Huntly, a Catholic, was a great favourite at Court; Lady Livingston, a Catholic, had the charge of the Princess Elizabeth; the sister of the Laird of Bonington, a Catholic too, was one of the Queen's maids. Her brother was in high favour with

"The next instance is the following. Upon one occasion she visited the Spanish Ambassador; apparently it was a mere visit of compliment, but she heard Mass and received the Most Adorable Sacrament. When the King heard this he scolded her bitterly, and told her that she would lose the crown and the kingdom.

"What shall I say about their daughter? I knew her very intimately when she was about eight or ten years old. She was brought up in the house of a Catholic lady, who is a countess, and is a child of most excellent disposition.

"ROBERT ABERCROMBY,
"*Priest of the Society of Jesus.*"

"BRAUNSBERG, in the *Month of September*, 1608.

"To the Very Reverend Father and Lord in Christ, John Stuart, of the Order of St Benedict, Prior of the Scots at Ratisbon, his most honoured Father and friend."

A copy of this letter is preserved in the National Library in Paris, Fonds " Latin," MS. 6051, foll. 49, 50, formerly Colbert, 3236. It is printed in James Gretser's "Collected Works," vol. vii., and in the Catholic periodical *The Month*.

[1] G. Conœus, *De Duplici statu religionis apud Scotos*, pp. 147, 148, Romæ, 1628, 4to; and also a work by the same author, entitled *Prœmetiæ, sive Calumniæ Hirlandorum indicatæ*, p. 20, Bonon., 1621, 8vo.

the King, Queen, and the whole court, on account of his affability and varied accomplishments. It was noted, too, by Cecil that Elphinstone, James' principal Secretary of State, and Seton, the President of the Session, were Catholics; and that Huntly, who, notwithstanding his recent recantation, was strongly suspected of a secret attachment to his ancient faith, possessed the highest influence over the King.[1] These were sore evils in the eyes of the Kirk. The ministers made allusions to secret negotiations with the Papal Court, which occasionally caused the King to wince. There is no doubt that he had secret agents dispersed throughout the Catholic courts, to sound their inclinations towards his claims, if they were not actually authorised to make stipulations for securing their concurrence with his accession to the throne of England. In this, however, James was faithful to his old policy—stirring up hopes now in Catholics, now in Protestants; at one time tremblingly solicitous for the Pope's friendship, then as suddenly seized with the fear of incurring the hatred of the Reformers, and so allowing a fierce persecution of the most devoted of his Catholic friends. But tremble and shift as he might, James' purpose kept ever in view the one unchanging point. At all and every cost, he would be King of England.

As may be seen from the following series of letters, the deluded Catholics at last opened their eyes to the painful reality, and understood that James' only motive for not breaking entirely with them was the fear of losing their aid in raising him to the throne of England.

[1] R. O., "Memorials of the present state of Scotland," 1598, quoted by Tytler, vol. ix. p. 258.

Fr. Alexander MacQuhirrie, S.J., to Fr. Claud Aquaviva, General of the Society of Jesus.

EDINBURGH, 25*th February* 1601.

". . . What I have to say of the King must be explained more fully on another occasion, but I can venture to say this much, that he is an easy tempered prince, very desirous of peace, and, what perhaps your Paternity will be surprised to hear, is extremely well acquainted with the affairs of our mission, and with ourselves personally. He is disposed to wink at our proceedings, but he urges our friends to act with great caution, lest his ministers should compel him, by solicitation or by threats, which they do not shrink from using, to take some violent measure against us; and this he would greatly regret. Such being the case, we earnestly entreat your Paternity to confer with his Holiness very seriously about the King's position and the affairs of this mission, and to do promptly whatever is determined on, since the restoration of the faith, now utterly ruined in the country, must depend upon it. To speak plainly, what we want is some powerful agency to protect ourselves, and enable us to suppress the poisonous fomenters of heresy swarming all over the country. I am not such an ardent royalist or patriot as to desire any ill-considered or violent measure. On the contrary, I think we should proceed with great caution, since we have to deal with a prince who is still an alien from the Catholic faith, and who is struggling for the rights of his crown."[1]

DUNDEE, IN SCOTLAND, 1*st May* 1601.

"When I wrote last, I seemed to hold out to your Paternity some hopes of improvement in the condition

[1] Archives of the Society of Jesus, vol. "Scotia." Latin MS.

of our affairs; but all is now changed, and we are in
great trouble. We have lost the noble baron, whose
brother, John Wood, at this moment, is so ably guiding
our counsels. He fell nobly, a martyr to the malice and
envy of the priests of Calvin. We, the survivors, are
in constant danger of a cruel death, preceded by more
cruel torture, as if to deprive us of our hope in Christ
and our life together."

The following Memorial of the State of Scotland
during 1601, in the handwriting of Father MacQuhirrie,
is preserved in the Archives of the Society of Jesus.

THE STATE OF SCOTLAND, 1601.

"The bearer of this letter is in possession of full information as to the condition of this kingdom, during the time he resided here, derived from his own experience and observation, and we can add little to what he has to say. Heresy is everywhere triumphant, and the exercise of Catholic worship is not tolerated, as your Paternity will see from the selection of the Acts of the Parliament which the bearer carries with him.[1]

"The consequence of this is that Catholics are deprived of all protection of the laws, and so is every one who is suspected of showing them any kindness. Indeed, all these enactments and proclamations are without exception glaringly tyrannical and antichristian.

[1] Father Abercromby, writing on 1st July 1602, says:—"All are now compelled with tears to submit to the King, and to the law passed by his authority, the alternative being for the rich either exile or the loss of all their goods, which for the sake of their wives and children they will not risk; and for the poor, if they refuse obedience, to be turned adrift by their lords from the lands they cultivate, like Israel in Egypt, and to live miserably among the wild animals, a prospect from which they shrink in terror."

"The ministers have full power and authority in their hands, and the King and Council grant them everything they ask for, as long as it does not inconvenience themselves.

"The King and the members of the Council are overawed and corrupted by the power and the gold of England, they furnish her with information, and carry out her orders, receiving ample payments for doing so. The King himself accepts an annual pension, not of large amount, which I think he would be glad to refuse, if his Holiness would offer him one worthy of his rank and dignity instead of it. It is certain that nothing would tend more to the conversion of this prince; and without it, to speak freely, every other exertion to obtain that end would be quite fruitless.

The King.

"The King is not only the cause of all the evils which have afflicted the country during the greater part of his reign, but continues to support, protect, and increase them. His language consists almost entirely of blasphemy or heresy. The single object of his ambition is the crown of England, which he would gladly take, to all appearance, from the hand of the Devil himself, though Catholics and heretic ministers were all ruined alike, so great is his longing for this regal dignity.

"He hates all Catholics, except so far as he can make use of them for the purpose of furthering his design of securing the English crown. Fear of Catholic ascendency, or the hope of obtaining the favourite object of his ambition, might some day make him a hypocrite; but only a great miracle of God's power, and an extraordinary inspiration, will ever make him a Catholic in reality.

"He is a determined enemy of the Fathers of our

Society, thinking that they are unfriendly to him, and that they oppose his claim to the crown of England. He considers them also causes of discord, sedition, and civil war.

"There are two principal motives for his prejudice against us, first the recent attempt upon the life of the King of France, which he has been told was made by a disciple of ours; and secondly, a book published in England, and supposed to be written by Fr. Persons, in which the King of Scotland's right to the succession to the crown of England is denied.

"Nevertheless he cannot help seeing that, in the course of the changes which are likely to occur, and in the difficult circumstances under which he may very probably be placed, it will be in the power of our Fathers materially to hinder or to assist his plans, and he is therefore secretly desirous to get into our good graces. Mr Strachan will tell your Paternity all about this, and I hope, God willing, to write to you more fully on the subject another time.

Of our Fathers.

"All our annoyances proceed from the causes above-mentioned, and we are constantly being excommunicated, outlawed, ordered abroad, and publicly proclaimed traitors to our King and country. No one is allowed to receive us under his roof on pain of death, loss of all his goods, and outlawry. The royal order requires every one to apprehend or kill us, wherever he finds us. The laws are so strict and rigorous that we are often obliged to travel at night, and we have very great difficulty in finding shelter in the daytime. Those who receive us rarely do so except for some consideration, either a share of the pittance which God has given us, or the hope of our obtaining payment for them from his Holiness, which they consider us bound to do, because they risk their lives and property for us, which is no doubt actually the case. The remuneration of these persons we have left entirely to the wisdom of your Paternity, since we can neither perform nor promise anything without the express knowledge, advice, and direction of your Paternity, as obedient children.

"The extent of our field of labour, our mode of operation, and the results which are to be expected, will be sufficiently described by the bearer of this letter, who has passed through almost the whole district in the course of his travels, and has visited and conversed with each one of us.

"In my opinion the harvest is not so great but that the workers, at present engaged in it, are sufficient for the task; and, whatever others of our brethren may have written as to sending more labourers, I think, on the contrary, that there is no immediate hurry about sending any until the condition of public affairs becomes more peaceful, and our Lord sends us greater freedom. Whereas, if only one single additional Father landed in Scotland, we should only suffer from fresh tumults and severer persecution, and the ministers would, in their addresses from the pulpit, multiply that one into twenty. . . .

The Queen.

"Three years ago, on the feast of St. Peter *in vinculis*, the Queen sent for one of our Fathers, and secretly told him of her ardent desire to embrace the Catholic religion, and renounce every heresy. After much conversation she entreated him to stay three days, that he might instruct her fully in the Catholic doctrine and ceremonies, which he did willingly, to the great satisfaction of both. On the fourth day, full of holy joy, she made her renunciation and general confession, and having heard Mass twice, received the most holy Sacrament, with the utmost spiritual joy, in the presence of only a few persons of rank. During the three years which have elapsed since, she has received some nine or ten times, always sending for one of our Fathers for the purpose. In the first year of her reconciliation she was very desirous to render due Christian homage to his Holiness by letter, and accordingly enjoined her spiritual father to dictate a suitable letter for her to write to his Holiness, informing him of her reconciliation with the Catholic Church, and tendering her obedience and respect. She also wrote a letter, addressed to your Paternity, requesting you to act as her advocate with his Holiness. Both these letters were written out, signed and sealed, with the Queen's own hand. The person selected by her Majesty to convey these letters, James Wood of Boniton, took charge of them; but was shortly afterwards, as you have heard, taken prisoner and beheaded. He lost his life, beyond all doubt, in behalf of the Catholic religion, for, had he been a heretic, he would certainly not have exposed himself to such a death. God, for His greater glory, and the preservation of the innocent Queen, did not permit the letters to be intercepted, and Boniton had them secretly conveyed to me just before his trial. After his martyrdom, we asked the Queen what she would wish to be done with them, and whether they should be destroyed. She replied that they were not on any account to be destroyed, that she did not abandon her pious purpose of sending them, but would add three others to explain the cause of the long and unfortunate delay, and the accident which

s

had led to it. One of these was addressed to his Holiness, another to the illustrious Cardinal Aldobrandini, and the third to your Paternity; and after they had been dictated to her, she wrote them out, signed them with her own hand, and sealed them, as she had done the other two last. They were all to have been despatched to your Paternity last summer, by a nobleman who was a member of the Queen's household; but I am ashamed to own that this was prevented through want of money. I should hardly venture to write this down, only I know to whom I am writing, and in whose presence; and that your Paternity, in whom the poor Queen reposes her greatest hopes, will regard her situation with compassion. The fact is, the letters are still in the hands of the honest gentleman, who keeps them quite safe. Her Majesty has promised every day, for the last year, to send the money requisite for their despatch, but has never been able to do so. I hope, however, they will reach you early in the spring.

"I thought it best, for several reasons, to send this account to your Paternity at the present time, because I have found one who can be trusted to carry the letter."[1]

The days of Elizabeth were drawing fast to a close. Practically all doubt as to the succession had vanished, and nearly the whole of England was ready to accept James. With him both Cecil and Essex were in correspondence. Cecil recommended silence and delay, assuring the Scottish King that all parties were gradually inclining in his favour.

Queen Elizabeth on her death-bed recognised the title of her kinsman James, and when she expired, on the 24th of March 1603, the whole nation seemed ready to welcome him with joy and pleasure.

[1] Archives of the Society of Jesus. See *Notes and Illustrations*.

II.

LETTERS AND MEMORIALS OF THE STATE AND PROGRESS OF EVENTS FROM 1603 TO 1625.

CATHOLICS thought they might look for some sympathy from the son of Mary Stuart, but their hopes were speedily and rudely disappointed. James yielded to the popular clamour, and issued a proclamation, by which he strictly commanded all priests to depart the realm within less than a month, upon pain of having the laws executed against them, without the least favour or mercy.[1] In September 1604, twenty-one priests and three laymen were taken out of various prisons and placed on board a ship to be transported to perpetual banishment. Two years later, no fewer than forty-seven priests were subjected to the same treatment.[2] All the sanguinary laws enacted by Queen Elizabeth, were put into force by James, and he "revived the barbarous usage and tyranny that the rackmasters and tormentors, the inferior officers and examiners, had used in the causes of Catholics for many years."[2]

While the king inflicted such severities on his subjects in England, the persecution was continued in Scotland. Its progress is described in the following correspondence of the missionaries then labouring in various parts of the country.

[1] Feb. 22, 1605, cf. Camden's *Annals of James the First*.
[2] "Apology of T. F. in defence of himself and other Catholics," p. 4.

Fr. Alexander MacQuhirrie to Fr. Aquaviva, General of the Society.

"I will briefly relate such of the occurrences during the last year, and the commencement of the present one, as are pleasant to tell and worth recording. On the King's progress into England, to take possession of the throne, the ministers met him in considerable numbers, not with the threats and comminations they were wont to use, but with the most abject flattery, preferring at the same time three requests to him. One was, that he would not alter their form of worship, for they were much afraid of being subjected to what is called the English discipline, against their will. The next, that Bruce who had, some years ago, with the aid of a considerable body of the nobility, held the city of Edinburgh against the authority of the King and Council, should be reinstated in the post formerly held by him among the ministers of that town, and in the administration of the state, from which he had been deposed. The third was, that James would order a more strict execution of the laws against the Catholics. The King promised to reply to their questions fully and deliberately, on the following day, and appointed the place where he would meet them; but he changed his route, and hurrying on his way, left them without an answer. Since that time the ministers speak less freely in their sermons about public affairs, and in their own assemblies complain only of private injuries, and that secretly. They fear the worst, but they relax nothing of their virulence and venom against the Catholics. Some of these last have met their attacks with great courage, and many, perceiving, at length, that joining with heretics in public worship is inconsistent with the profession of the faith, have begun to stand firm. I pressed this upon them when I came back from England, urging each to provide for his own salvation, and I am in hopes that many, with whom I have earnestly conferred on the subject, will change their minds, and come to regard the matter as of more consequence than they have thought it hitherto.

"AL. MACQUHIRRIE."

"*Jan.* 21, 1604."[1]

Fr. MacQuhirrie to Fr. Aquaviva, General of the Society.

"VERY REVEREND FATHER IN CHRIST,— . . . The state of things at present may be summed up in very few words, for everything just now depends upon the proposed union of Scotland and England in one kingdom,—a project which seems to me very difficult of execution; and better judges than myself consider it impracticable. A number of our nobles, entrusted with the conduct of the negotiation, are to go to London for the purpose next October, by the King's desire. Should the union be carried out, one system of law will prevail in both countries. At present they are very different, the English laws being founded mainly on the municipal, and ours on the civil, division of the Roman code. The result to be expected is that Scottish Catholics will be liable to the English penalties for non-attendance on public worship, and will consequently be enabled to compound for a payment in money. This will at once give us a great accession in numbers, and yield quite a harvest; such composition being at present not permitted by the severity of the Scottish law, which absolutely enforces forfeiture of goods, loss of liberty, or banishment upon all who openly profess the Catholic

[1] Archives of the Society of Jesus.

faith. This is the only reason of the slender harvest we reap, and it will doubtless be richer in future, if we are allowed to live under the English law. It is impossible at present to maintain any but a very small staff of workers, because people are forbidden to receive us, under the same penalties by which they themselves are driven to the kirk, and with so cruel a restriction we labour in vain. Very few indeed will run so great a risk, and almost all, one perhaps here and there excepted, comply with the requirements of the law. They take us for fools, when we remind them of the duties on which their salvation depends; and, what is worse, they generally tell us it is easy enough for us to give such advice, because we have nothing to lose, or nothing worth regretting if we did lose it, and that were it to come to the worst, we can always go back to our college. To such a pass has heresy brought these poor people! Some of them feel deeply the misery of their position, and for those we always have great compassion. In a certain degree they reward our efforts, since every now and then they come to their senses, and for a time remain firm in their purpose.

"BURNET." [1]

"From SCOTLAND, 7th September, 1604." [2]

Fr. James Seton to Fr. C. Aquaviva, General of the Society of Jesus.

"VERY REV. FATHER IN CHRIST,—The persecution in Scotland does not cease or lessen since the departure of the King. The government is entirely in the hands of the Lord Alexander Seton, whom the King has made

---

[1] i.e., Alexander MacQuhirrie.
[2] Archives of the Society of Jesus, vol. Scotia.

Earl of Dunfermline, and who is favourably known to your Paternity. He is, or should be, abbot of that place, where there was once a famous monastery. He was formerly President of the Council, and is now Chancellor of the Kingdom. The Viceroy is the Earl of Montrose, the President of the Council the Lord James Elphinston, brother of Father George; but they are all directed by Lord Alexander Seton. He is a Catholic, as is also the Lord President and the Royal Advocate. In political wisdom, in learning, in high birth, wealth, and authority, he possesses far more influence than the rest, and his power is universally acknowledged. But he publicly professes the state religion, rendering external obedience to the King and the ministers, and goes occasionally, though rarely, to the sermons, sometimes to their heretical communion. He has also subscribed their confession of faith, without which he would not be able to retain peaceable possession of the rank, office, and estates with which he is so richly endowed. He has brought all the principal men of the kingdom round to the same view, and very few venture to differ from him, owing to his eloquence, learning, and authority. Two or three times a year he comes to Catholic confession and communion with his mother, brother, sister, and nephews, who are better Catholics than himself! Among those holding the same opinion is Mr John Colvill, an aged man, who became a Catholic after living forty years in heresy, and whom your Paternity has seen and assisted with money in Rome. This gentleman persuaded the illustrious Cardinal de Baffoli, when nuncio at Paris, that there was great hope of the conversion of the King of England, and that he ought to treat him as a friend.

"JAMES SETON."

"*Sept.* 30, 1605."[1]

[1] Archives, S. J.

Fr. Robert Abercromby to Fr. Claud Aquaviva, General of the Society of Jesus.

"Very Rev. Father,—P. C.—. . . I am now, Reverend Father, ready to be sacrificed, and the time of my dissolution is at hand. I am seventy years old, and afflicted by several maladies; my head is never at rest, except when asleep; my hands tremble, my legs swell, my feet are pained with gout, my thighs with sciatica, my whole body is racked now with fever, now with other complaints. Added to all this is the continual and cruel persecution which I suffer at the hands of the ministers of the Word (as they are called), who are so enraged at my having celebrated one Mass at Perth in the presence of some noble ladies, that they have sent after me to several places to get me apprehended and punished. The consequence is that ever since that time, which was the Holy Week of last year, I have been obliged to conceal myself in the north of Scotland, under the protection of the Marquis of Huntly, where I continue to carry on the work of our Society. I have, within a short time, brought nineteen persons into the bosom of the Church, who were never Catholics before, and I have brought back to the true sacraments some who, for forty-six years, have kept away from Catholic communion, and contented themselves with the unholy rites of the Calvinists. Your Reverence would not believe what joy they manifested while they were being instructed in the doctrine of the Catechism, and discovered the falsehoods which had been passed off on them by the ministers. The great men in this place complain that there are not more of us, and wonder no others are sent.[1]

"Robert Abercromby."

[1] Latin MS. Archives, S. J.

Fr. Crichton to Fr. Claud Aquaviva.

"VERY REVEREND FATHER IN CHRIST,—P. C.— Father James Gordon has summoned Fr. Anderson to Bordeaux, with the view of sending him to Scotland, under the impression that the persecution is coming entirely to an end, for he writes to tell me there now exists very little opposition, or none at all. This good Father is much too sanguine; it was he who believed the King himself to be a Catholic, in Pope Clement's time. Father Gordon thinks the recent disputation which the King has caused to be held between the English ministers and the Scottish puritan or Calvinist divines, will give an accession of strength to the Catholic party, as a result of the King's secession from the cause of the puritans and Calvinists to that of the English ministers. I am of a contrary opinion. His Majesty's abandonment of errors which were manifestly inexcusable, while he obstinately adheres to other errors, fewer in number and more easily tolerated, makes the ground still more difficult for the Catholics whose object is to expose the falseness of his belief; because the more obvious and intolerable error is, the more clearly and easily is it exposed. Father Cotton writes that James is proceeding to confirm the laws passed in the reign of the late Queen against the Catholics. In Scotland he has deprived the ministers of no part of their power of exercising cruelty towards Catholics, nor has their malice at all abated. The Catholics in Scotland have this much comfort, that the rulers of the kingdom, whom he has appointed, are all in favour of their cause. The Viceroy, the Earl of Montrose, though a heretic, is friendly to the Catholics, and the Lord Alexander Seton, who is favourably known to your Paternity, and who is Chancellor of the Kingdom, governs both the Viceroy and the whole country. He continues a Catholic, though he occasionally attends heretical sermons. The President of the Council, the Lord James Elphinston, brother of Father George Elphinston, is also a Catholic. But they all carry on the government in conformity with the exigencies of the times, while prudence and discretion are as much required, to avoid offending them, as zeal in the conversion of heretics. Lord Seton often said to me in Scotland, when I urged him to support the Catholic cause, 'be not eager to act before the time comes. I have to live in Scotland, and I must give way to circumstances. When the opportunity presents itself, and there is any hope of success, I shall not be sparing of my goods, my blood, or my life, for the restoration of the Catholic religion.' He is now all powerful in Scotland, but he will attempt nothing until he sees a solid foundation for hope. Meanwhile he takes his portion in this life, though at the risk of that which is eternal. In my opinion nothing is more important than caution, so as not to offend the governing powers. If our Fathers act with prudence and wariness, those in office will protect us; if not, they will persecute and drive us out, for they can do anything with Catholics, as well as with heretics. The rulers of Scotland will prevent the ministers exercising cruelty or violence, but they will not depose them from their authority. To return to Father Patrick Anderson, it would be well to send him into Scotland, and with a companion; but he should not go by way of Bordeaux, for that route is three times as long and difficult as the other. The direct way is to travel by Paris and Rouen, thence across to England, since Scotsmen have now no difficulty in traversing England, and then to Scotland by the west, which is Father Patrick's destination, and may easily be reached from England.

The English Fathers at Rome will be able to recommend him to those of our Fathers who are in England, and he will travel much more safely through that country than by sea. Scotchmen can go anywhere in England without inquiry or annoyance.

"WILLIAM CRICHTON."

"BILLOM, *July* 20, 1605."[1]

The Same to the Same.

"VERY REV. FATHER IN CHRIST, — PAX X. JESU. —Ever since the accession of the King of Scotland to the kingdoms of England and Ireland, the Catholics have awaited the liberty of conscience which he promised the Scots, before the death of the Queen of England. That hope has now failed them. At the King's last conference with his English ministers he asserted his opinion, in opposition to the Anglican doctrine that the King is the head of the English Church, as well as against the teaching of the Scottish heretics who deny that the Roman Pontiff is the successor of St Peter. Against both of these he declared that the Pontiff is the head of the Church and the true successor of St Peter, but that he is not to be obeyed, because he is outside the truth of the Faith and the doctrine of the Gospel. This is to assert the doctrine of the Lutherans. In consequence of the King's view many think that his conversion to the Catholic faith will be accomplished more easily than heretofore. I am of an opposite opinion, for the Lutherans, whose view he seems to have embraced, are much more difficult of conversion to the Catholic faith than the Calvinists, just because their errors are fewer and less intolerable than those of the latter. In the principal controversy, which is on the subject of the

[1] Archives of the Society of Jesus. Latin MS.

Holy Eucharist, they agree with the Catholics entirely, except on the single point of transubstantiation. Heretics are always convinced and converted more easily and effectually, in proportion as their errors are more numerous and more gross. It is of no advantage that the King of England acknowledges the authority of the Supreme Pontiff, while he refuses obedience to him; for this the Lutherans also do, and yet continue obstinate enemies of the Church. I have no expectation of the King of England ever being anything else, unless God and man should combine to use force, and overthrow the temporal dominion on which these laws regarding religion rest and are grounded. The three kingdoms of England, Ireland and Scotland, are all agreed in the substance of their erroneous belief, but differ in their mode of action. In England and Ireland religion is enforced by the same laws, but they carry out these laws in England in such a way as to allow Catholics, who refuse to attend the heretical worship, to pay a pecuniary fine. Those who receive a Jesuit or a priest into their houses are apprehended under charge of high treason, and condemned to death. In Ireland no fine is paid, nor is there any inquiry as to those who receive priests into their houses, the number of Catholics in that country being too great. It is done occasionally in some of the towns, but rarely, and in a gentle manner. In Scotland, on the other hand, the utmost severity is used, for the power of the heretical ministers is so great that they can compel every one to subscribe their false confession of faith, attend their sermons, and take the profane supper of the Calvinist rite, or else lose all his goods and go into banishment. Catholics are cited by the minister to render obedience to the law before a particular day, on pain of excommunication; and forty days after this excommunication, if they have not submitted, they are declared guilty of high treason, their property is confiscated to the treasury, and they are sent into exile. The Catholics are so unnerved by this severity that very few of them remain firm; but a very large number, now obedient to Satan, would raise their hands once more, were an opportunity given them of successfully asserting their liberty. Unless God quickly looks upon them, they will become so callous and obdurate in their sinful concession that it will be extremely difficult, at a later period, to recall them to Catholic practice, even if liberty of conscience were accorded them. There are very few of our Fathers left in Scotland to encourage the Catholics, and yet it would be of no use to send many more, for they would only be taken prisoners. The King has established in Scotland a squadron of cavalry specially charged to apprehend rebels, and under this title are included determined Catholics who refuse obedience to the ministers, as well as the Fathers of our Society, for whom diligent search is made everywhere. The Scottish Catholics are not so zealous as those in England, who take so much care to construct hiding places in their houses for the preservation of the priests. Some should nevertheless be sent, for Father Robert Abercromby is too much afflicted with illness to be of any use whatever. Less danger exists in the remoter parts of the country. I entreat your Paternity to intercede with his Holiness to assist in some way the Scotch seminaries in Rome and at Louvain. It is true there is no apparent hope of the conversion of these kingdoms, and still, I cannot but hope that they will all three be converted in the lifetime of the present Pope. I look for this event on account of the great number of Catholics daily groaning under the cruel yoke of heresy, and imploring the help of God, as well as because of the earnest desire which his Holiness, when Cardinal, always professed for the conversion of these countries,—a desire which I cannot but think must be increased by his accession to the supreme dignity which he holds, after Christ, on earth. There are some persons in whom the diligence of the priests is able to preserve the faith, with hope of their salvation; but for the conversion of whole kingdoms there is no hope, except that expressed in the words used in the dedication of a church, 'Stones beaten and polished, fitted in their places by the hands of the builder, to remain in the sacred edifice.' Stones are not wanting in sufficient number, but there are wanting the architect and the lime to fit and cement them in their places. May God inspire those to whom this, His work, specially belongs. It is of very great importance that such Fathers of the Society as have it in their power to afford consolation to the Scottish Catholics, should either go to Scotland, or come nearer to it, as for instance to Rouen. I would willingly offer my own services, but my age, now very far advanced, renders it impossible for me to bear the labours which the present disturbed state of the country would impose. In England the peril is very considerable, but the toil is not so great, and the means of safety are more obtainable, on account of the great charity and diligence which the English Catholics show in providing for the security of the priests. I have nothing more to add. . . . I earnestly commend myself to the most holy sacrifices and prayers of your Paternity, whom may the Lord Jesus long preserve in safety, to His Church and to us.

"WILLIAM CRICHTON."

"BILLOM, *Sept.* 30, 1605."[1]

[1] Archives of the Society of Jesus.

The increasing persecution of Catholics in England led in November 1605 to the notorious Gunpowder Plot, and upon its failure all Catholics, even those who had no share in it, suffered grievously for the guilt of a few desperate men. Although the Catholic Lord Mounteagle, who had been cautioned to keep clear of St Stephen's, revealed what he knew of the plot, and although the Catholics of England and the Continent raised a sincere cry of horror at the news, it has been termed, often maliciously so, the Popish Plot.[1] Nothing was now too bad to be believed of Catholics: to tolerate them was, in the language of Abbot Archbishop of Canterbury, to commit a deed "hateful to God;" and to prosecute them to the death was "to advance His glory." No time was lost in enacting a new penal code containing seventy fresh articles whilst the existing laws were executed with relentless severity. Eighteen priests and seven laymen suffered death for the mere exercise of their religion. One hundred and twenty-eight priests were banished; the heavy fine of twenty pounds a month was exacted with the utmost rigour from every Catholic who did not attend the service of the established church; and a new

[1] Father Garnet's trial was conducted so as to prove, cost what it might, the guilt of the Catholic priesthood, and in particular of the Jesuits. In his examination contradictory statements were recorded which he did not acknowledge as his own; the rack was freely employed to force the desired confession from him and the other accused; no heed was paid to the binding nature of the seal of confession for a Catholic Priest. What effectual measures the Jesuits could have taken to hinder the Gunpowder Plot without breaking the seal of confession, which is binding on a Catholic priest under all circumstances, has as yet never been made known. Cf. "Lingard's History of England," ix. p. 59, *seq.*; "The Condition of Catholics under James I.," and "Father Gerard's Narrative of the Gunpowder Plot," by John Morris, S.J., Lond. 1871.

oath of allegiance was framed in terms which no Catholic could subscribe without committing an act of apostasy, whilst to refuse it subjected him to all the penalties of high treason.

James had special motives for encouraging the persecution in Scotland. Being the head of the Church of England, he had naturally aspired to the same pre-eminence in his native kingdom. The maxim, "No bishop, no king," was moreover deeply impressed on his mind, and he saw danger to the throne in the growing independence of the Kirk. Hence he resolved to overthrow the fabric raised by Knox and to re-establish Episcopacy. An Act of Parliament restored the Episcopal estate, and another Act was extorted by menace and bribery from the General Assembly, appointing the Bishops moderators both of the Synods and of the presbyteries within which they officiated.[1] A commission was instituted in every diocese, consisting of the bishop and some influential laymen, invested with power to arrest and imprison any one they pleased. The Kirk was bound hand and foot and its voice stifled.

The King owed the success of the negotiation to George Home, Lord Treasurer and Earl of Dunbar. This nobleman began by intimidating the ministers, who had assembled without the royal permission at Aberdeen. Six of the most refractory were tried and condemned to banishment. The sentence frightened their colleagues, and a timely distribution of forty thousand marks did the rest.

[1] Calderwood affirms that money was given in payment of votes, though under the name of defraying travelling expenses. (History, vol. vii., 97.) Spottiswood declares that this money was given only as the payment of the stipulated salaries of the permanent moderators. (History, lib. vii., p. 513.)

To induce the refractory Ministers to yield to the wishes of the King, with respect to the superiority of bishops, he placed at their mercy the persons and property of the idolatrous papists. "This," says Balfour, "was taken as cream and oil to soften and smooth the King's mysterious designs."[1] Some of the ministers, however, had no great faith in that show of generosity. Law, Bishop of Orkney, endeavoured to reassure them. "They shall call me a false knave," said he, "and never to be believed again, if the papists be not sae handled as they never were in Scotland."[2] At last the compromise was accepted. The parliament enacted laws of recusancy; the clergy issued sentences of excommunication, and every Catholic nobleman was compelled to receive an orthodox minister into his family, and was forewarned that, unless he should conform within a given period, his obstinacy would be punished with the judgment of forfeiture. At the same time, the prisons were filled with victims of inferior quality; and so severe was the persecution, that, according to the statement of the French Ambassador, the fate of the Scottish, was still more deserving of pity than that of the English, Catholics.[3]

A loud cry for more fierce persecutions was raised by

---

[1] "The progress of persecution against the Catholics may be traced all through this period by the equal progress of the King's measures for introducing the Episcopal system into the Church. The King is so anxious to establish the English religion in that country, and get himself recognised as its head, as he is here, that in order to gain over the puritans, who are the only obstacle to his wishes, he has given them free leave to oppress the Catholics to their heart's content." ("Ambassade de Monsieur de la Boderie," vol. iv. p. 23.) Robert Chambers' *Domestic Annals of Scotland*, vol. i. p. 415.

[2] Balfour, *Annals*, ii. 18.

[3] Melville's *Diary*, p. 688.

the leaders of the Kirk, and on the 24th of June 1609, the parliament, assembled at Edinburgh, passed new penal statutes against Catholics. The Earls of Huntly, Angus, and Errol were imprisoned for returning to the Catholic Church. Huntly once more subscribed the Confession of Faith, but Errol and Angus refused to subscribe. Angus went into exile rather than forsake his faith. The laird of Gight and the laird of Newton, both Gordons, and both Catholics, were sentenced by the privy Council to perpetual banishment and never to set foot in Scotland, under pain of death, unless they professed the Protestant faith.

"I went to Scotland last June," wrote Fr. Abercromby, "and the only one of ours I found there was Fr. Anderson. The state of this poor kingdom is most lamentable. Catholics are forced to go to the churches of heretics, and very few resist. The Marquis of Huntly and the Earl of Errol are still in prison for their faith. The Earl of Dunbar, sent this summer by the King to Scotland, has roused still greater persecution. Fr. Andrew Crichton and Fr. Roger Lindsay were taken prisoners, and Fr. Anderson and myself escaped with the greatest difficulty. Fr. Anderson fled to the North, and I took refuge in England; but in a few days I propose to return to Scotland, where a great many would embrace the true Faith, were it not for fear of being thrown into prison and of losing their property. The system of persecution followed is first to excommunicate the Catholic landowner, who afterwards is either banished from the country, or sent to prison and deprived of all his goods. If the wife be a Catholic, she is excommunicated, and her husband is not allowed to keep her in the house; and, if the husband is a heretic, the ministers and the magistrates allow him to take another wife according to the present laws of the country. Should the children or the servants be Catholics, they are likewise excommunicated, and the parents are obliged to turn them out of the house. Ours have scarcely where to go, but are obliged to lie unknown in the houses of heretics, or at some inn. May our Lord give them grace and patience to bear all for Him."[1]

Father Anderson, who had now spent two years in Scotland, has left us some interesting notes of his missionary work. He was especially qualified to bear witness to the state of the Church in Scotland during the reign of James the First. His missionary excursions extended over both the Highlands and Lowlands; he was conversant with all classes, rich and poor alike, and was greatly trusted and esteemed by all.

The numerous examples of heroic defence of the faith, especially on the part of converts, which Fr. Anderson quotes in his Memorial,[2] and which took place, not only amongst the poor and uneducated, but principally amongst the Scotch nobility, show how large a proportion of noble families were firmly attached to the Catholic Religion.[3]

The only extract that we shall take from Father Anderson's Memorial is his description of a very bitter mode of persecution, to which little attention is drawn in our days.

"When one thinks of the persecution which now

---

[1] Letter of Fr. Thomas Abercromby to Fr. Claud Aquaviva, 3 October 1610, Stonyhurst Archives, Latin MS.

[2] It was printed in the Catholic periodical "The Month," 1876.

[3] The Scottish Catholics are said, in Winwood, iii. 52, to amount to twenty-seven earls and barons, and two hundred and forty knights and gentlemen. See also Spotiswood, 502, 5, 6, 9, 13.

rages in Scotland, it seems impossible that anyone could have undergone it. First, if anyone profess the Catholic religion, it is enough to make him hated by all his heretic friends, and some are so bigoted that they will not remain in the house with a Catholic, especially if he has been excommunicated. Besides, the royal statutes against Catholics are so severe, that anyone excommunicated for being a Catholic is disqualified from possessing his paternal estates, or from making a contract with anyone, and is liable to prosecution for attempting it. While I was writing these lines, a certain nobleman who had been for sixteen years excommunicated by the heretics, was summoned by them to appear before the judge. He was charged with owing a debt, for which he told me he was not responsible. He did not dare to appear, or even to send a procurator, as they term it, to plead his cause, and so lost it. Again, no Catholic lady can be married without attending the heretic churches. If, as often happens, either through cunning or by skill, they manage to evade this law, they are incredibly tormented by the importunity of the ministers. For instance, a noble lady, married to a certain baron, was much afflicted by her husband, who besought her with prayers and tears, in which his kinsfolk joined, to give up the Catholic faith. Although steadfast and fearless, she fell into such grief by reason of their pertinacity, that for a whole year she never went to bed or rose up without shedding floods of tears. She remained, however, so constant in the Catholic faith, that she used to say she would rather die than give it up, or do anything to the dishonour of the Roman Church.

I could quote many similar instances. Thus heretics avoid Catholic ladies. Hence it is difficult for the latter

to marry, and many of them wish to lead a religious life.
A Catholic heir may be disinherited by his heretic father.
If any one is suspected of being a Catholic, and does not
frequent the heretical churches, he is first cited by the
ministers to give a reason: this if he fail to do, he is
excommunicated, and if he remain a year under the
excommunication, all his goods and chattels are confiscated, and if caught he is cast into prison. Thus
it is that excommunicated Catholics are unable to
frequent the society of others, or to walk openly in the
streets. They walk at night only, and secretly, to the
great detriment of their health, and risk of their
property. The hatred of the people for any excommunicated person is marvellous. They will neither eat
nor drink with him, and if a heretic speak with an
excommunicated Catholic, the ministers either excommunicate him, or sentence him to some public and
shameful penance. The contrivances and stratagems by
which Catholics evade going to the ministers' churches
are truly wonderful, now feigning sickness, now the
intention of leaving, now imaginary actions at law.
Now they bribe the ministers to silence, now they try
one thing and now another. As an instance I will add
this amusing invention of a certain Catholic. He is so
steadfast in the Catholic faith, that when the ministers
cited him to appear before his congregation, as they call
it, he began to shuffle and sent one excuse after another.
They decreed the excommunication unless he satisfied
them. The Catholic then unfolded his plan to his
servant, and to a surgeon and public notary, who were
his friends; and these pledged their faith to stand by
him. The nobleman mounted his horse in presence of
the surgeon and of the notary. They set out on their
way, but as soon as they had reached a place safe from

observation, the nobleman jumped off his horse and cried out that his leg was broken. People ran up, for he was very well known in that neighbourhood, and friends and kinsfolk began to condole with him. The surgeon talked of the nature and danger of a broken leg, and applied some poultices and fomentations, while the notary drew out a written attestation of the accident. Thus our Catholic friend was able to evade their excommunication for a whole year. He walked about with such ingenious lameness, leaning on his stick, that any one would have believed his leg to have been really broken. His halting gait certainly deceived me, but he told me the whole truth with great delight, when I went to give him the holy Sacraments of the Church.

"It would be too long to recapitulate all the laws and statutes issued against Catholics, by which the persecution is carried on. One thing is certain; the violence shown here in Scotland is greater than in England, where Catholics (whom they name recusants) are allowed to pay a fine to the king, instead of going to the churches of the ministers. The Scotch Catholics have never been able to obtain this alternative from the King for love or money. I say nothing of the abundance of pastors, nor of Catholic books, which surely are a great help in such times. But here in Scotland there is not one of our Fathers working except myself, and only one secular priest, who is worn out with years and sickness.

"Though the severity of the persecution, to which I have briefly alluded, is so great, yet the steadfastness of the Catholics is so strong, their numbers so large, and the eagerness of their souls to approach the Divine Mysteries so keen, that they seem to have inherited the fervour of the primitive Christians. God confirms their zeal and constancy by many miracles."

Father Anderson concludes with these words: "Under a daily increasing persecution, God still preserves an immense number of Catholics, who remain steadfast in spite of ridicule, loss of goods, imprisonment, infamy, and the like; and are ready to shed their blood for the Catholic faith."[1]

Father Anderson quitted Scotland for a period towards the close of the year 1611, in obedience to the orders of his superior, Father James Gordon. This was considered an act of necessary precaution on account of the violent persecution stirred up by his zeal and success, and of the diligent search being made for him on all sides. "The ministers are searching everywhere for me, but I have many times escaped their hands by an evident miracle. One of the chief consolations of a son of the Society is that whether we die, or whether we live, we live and die to Christ Jesus, and that to us to live is the greatest consolation, and to die the greatest gain. The Catholic nobility are stricken with grief at my departure. Some of the more prudent, however, judge it necessary on account of the present persecution, and unanimously beg of your Paternity to appoint one of our Scotch Fathers to reside in Paris. The nobility of this country often go thither for amusement, and such seems to be the only way in which we can assist them."[2]

Father Anderson retired to Rouen, and remained there a few years to regain his strength. At the time of his departure there was, says Father Gordon, but one priest in all Scotland, and he very old and very infirm.[3] Two

[1] Stonyhurst Archives.

[2] MS. Letter to Father Aquaviva (Stonyhurst Archives). 25th July 1611.

[3] In this Father Gordon was mistaken; a few other priests were then concealed in Scotland.

worthy secular priests, Andrew Creighton and Roger Lindsay, had been apprehended in August 1610, and, after suffering imprisonment, had been sentenced to perpetual banishment. To supply this dearth, Father Anderson had collected nearly one hundred promising youths in Scotland, eager to serve God and the Church. "They are very fit for the seminaries," wrote Fr. Gordon, "but we have none into which we can admit them."[1]

Meanwhile, on the death of the Earl of Dunbar, who, as High Commissioner of the General Assembly, had enjoyed unbounded influence in Scotland, and had exercised great animosity against Catholics, a sudden relaxation of the persecution became manifest. Fr. Gordon deemed it advisable not to let the opportunity escape, but to send over some missionaries into Scotland. Fr. John Ogilvie[2] and Fr. James Moffat were selected.

"I entreat your reverence," wrote the Earl of Angus, "to send none but such as both desire, and are able to bear with a courageous heart, the burden and heat of the day. For by our new law it is provided that whoever receives a priest of the Society, or any other into his house, or is present at Mass, or celebrates, is held guilty of high treason." The Earl's anxiety was well founded. Notwithstanding a momentary relaxation of the persecution, the fear of Popery had not died away, and it was impossible to disabuse the minds of the people of the groundless notion that the "Episcopacy," forced by James upon the Scotch nation, was in some way connected with the old faith. The Presbyterians were accordingly looking anxiously to these new bishops

---

[1] There was a Scotch seminary at Douay, but too small and too poor.

[2] John Ogilvie was the eldest son of Walter Ogilvie of Drum, near Keith.

for some unmistakable proof of the sincerity of their hatred toward the Catholic religion, such as the hanging of a Jesuit clearly would be. The bishops were, on their part, looking out with no less anxiety for some means of conciliating the Presbyterians, and convincing them of the unfounded character of their suspicions. It was at this juncture that Father Ogilvie and Father Moffat, accompanied by Friar John Campbell, Capuchin, returned to Scotland in 1613.

The three missionaries travelled in disguise and under assumed names. Father Ogilvie took the name of Watson, Father Moffat of Halyburton, and Friar Campbell of Sinclair. The dress which Father Ogilvie wore was that of a soldier, one not unsuitable to the profession of a son of Ignatius Loyola. The wearing of some disguise was not optional, it was a matter of necessity, as it was well known that the government had spies scattered over the continent, to pick up information about the priests destined for the home missions. The information thus obtained was forwarded to the searchers of ships, who were ordered to apprehend "all Jesuits, seminary priests, and excommunicated papists."[1]

The missionaries separated on their arrival in their native land. Father Ogilvie went to the north, Friar Campbell to Edinburgh, and Father Moffat to St Andrews. For the first six months Father Moffat succeeded in gathering a rich harvest of souls, and found opportunity of celebrating Mass almost every day after his landing, when, through the contrivance of the Bishop of St Andrews, the Father was apprehended in his brother's house.[2] The Prelate's eldest

---

[1] Spotiswood, "History of the Church," p. 506.
[2] Archives of Stonyhurst College. Letter of Father James Gordon to the General, 27th January 1615. Latin MS.

son, Alexander Gladstanes, even though Archdeacon, did not consider it beneath his dignity to head the guards who had arrested the prisoner, and to escort him from St Andrews to Edinburgh, where he was shut up in the strictest confinement within the castle.

Father Ogilvie spent six weeks in the north, and then returned to Edinburgh, where he resided for nearly a year till October 1614, at the house of William Sinclair.[1] He devoted all his time to the conversion of the old and the young, of the noble and the poor. "I know," says an eye witness, "of a considerable number of persons whom he converted from heresy to the obedience of the Catholic faith during the short time he spent in Scotland outside of prison. Among them were his fellow captives, and two or three barons in Renfrew, and some other gentlemen.[2] He also visited the prisons at great risk of his life, in order to give religious consolations to the afflicted Catholics."[3]

In August 1614 Father Ogilvie ventured into Glasgow, where Archbishop John Spottiswood held supreme sway, both as prelate and magistrate.[4] Father Ogilvie's labours were at first very successful, for he received "sundrie young men" and many persons "of the better sorte."[5] This is confirmed by the Records

---

[1] Archives, S.J. "*Proceedings of the trial and mode of death of Father John Ogilvie.*" Latin MS.

[2] *Ibid.*

[3] "He, in particular, visited Sir James Macdonald, a Catholic gentleman, imprisoned in Edinburgh Castle, whom he consoled with pious counsel and encouragement. The wife of Sir James Macdonald was Lady Margaret Campbell." *Ibid.*

[4] Spottiswood held his own court and had his own officials, and divided with the crown jurisdiction in temporals.

[5] Calderwood, vol. vii. p. 193.

of the proceedings which were taken against him.[1] Treachery, however, was soon at work, for on Tuesday, the 14th of October, Father Ogilvie was seized by one of the Archbishop's men in the place of public resort. No description of what he suffered after his seizure can excel that indited by himself.[2]

"I was betrayed," he wrote, "by one of those whom I was to have reconciled with the Church. The traitor belonged to a very high family, was very rich, and had been recommended to me by many as a Catholic, and as one who, for a long time, had been seeking some opportunity of being reconciled. I intimated to him the hour which would be convenient for me to instruct him. About four o'clock in the afternoon I went out for a walk through the streets with the magistrate's eldest son; at a sign given by my betrayer, there runs up to me a servant of the Archbishop, a man of good family, and stalwart withal, and orders me off to his Lordship. Imagining that I was called to the Sheriff, the grandson of the traitor (as we had arranged), I said that I would willingly go, and accordingly turned back for the purpose. But the son of the magistrate was loath to part with me, and insisted on my first going to his house, although the other man opposed it. Whilst, however, I am amicably

---

[1] These documents show the following to have been in communication with him as a priest: the Earl of Eglinton, Lady Maxwell, Sir James Kneilland of Monkland, David Maxwell, brother of Newark, William Maxwell of Cowglen, John Wallace of Corsflat, Robert Heygate, merchant, a zealous Catholic, William Sinclair, advocate, &c.

[2] Relatio Incarcerationis et Martyrii P. Ioannis Ogilbei . . . descripta Ad Verbum ex autographo ipsius. Duaci, 1615.

In 1615, the companions of his captivity solemnly declared the authenticity and truthfulness of this memorial, and confirmed by oath their declaration. ("Proceedings of the trial and mode of death of Father John Ogilvie." Latin MS., Archives S.J.)

arranging the dispute between the two, there is a concourse of town-officers and citizens. They seize my sword, and begin pushing me and pulling me about. I inquire what harm I was doing? and whether they were quite in their right senses? I said that the others were quarrelling amongst themselves, and that I had nothing to do with it. No need for a long story. I am lifted up by the united rush of the gathering crowd, and almost borne away on their shoulders into the house of the magistrate. They snatch away my cloak. I said that I would not stir a step without my cloak, and thereupon somebody promised me his; but I wanted my own, and at last got it away from them. I protested against the inhumanity of the angry crowd, and promised them that everybody should one day know how barbarously they had treated me, when I was doing no harm to any one; and that, too, without any form of law taken out, or any cause assigned. Whilst this was going on, the Bishop, who stayed in another part of the city, was told that those whom he had sent to me had been killed, that a general slaughter was taking place, and that the city was up in arms. As soon as he heard this statement, he assembled the lairds and barons who happened to be at that time in the city, and came with them, in a body, into the street. He saw that everything was quiet there, and inquired where I was. It was night by this time. They told him that I was in the house of the magistrate that day elected. Thither he hastened with his whole company, and called me out as I was sitting between the table and the wall. I obey, and he strikes me a blow, and says: 'You were an over-insolent fellow, to say your Masses in a reformed city.' I reply: 'You do not act like a bishop, but like an executioner in striking me.' Then, as though the signal had been thus given them, they shower their blows from all sides upon me, the hair is plucked from my beard, my face is torn with their nails, until Count Fleming, by his authority and by main force, restrains those who were striking me. Then, whilst my senses had barely returned from the stunning effect of so many blows on my head, I am commanded to be stript. Some men there immediately obeyed the order, untying the strings and unfastening the buttons of my clothes; but when they are on the point of pulling off my shirt, very shame brought me back to my senses, and I cried out to know what such wanton insolence was for."[1]

Father Ogilvie was cast into prison that night. Meanwhile Spottiswood had written as follows to the King:—

"MOST SACRED AND GRACIOUS SOVEREIGN,—It has pleased God to cast into my hands a Jesuit that calls himself Ogilvie. He came to this city and said some Masses, at which we have tried eight of our burgesses to being present. He was busy in preventing some others that went too far with him, for some of them presumed to resist my servants in his apprehension. Himself will answer nothing that serves for discovering his traffic in the country, that appears to be great. . . . I will not trouble your Majesty with circumstance of his apprehension and names of his partakers here, anent whom I have written to your Highness's servant, John Murray, more particularly. Only, I will crave your Majesty's pardon to deliver my advice for the punishment of these transgressors and the trial of the Jesuit, because exemplary punishment is necessary in this case, and by the laws their lives, lands, and whole estate are in your Majesty's hands; and the condition of the per-

[1] An authentic account of the imprisonment and martyrdom of Father John Ogilvie, translated by C. J. Karslake, S.J., Glasgow, 1877.

sons offending is not equal, your Majesty would be pleased to refer the determination thereof to my Lord Treasurer, my Lord Kilsyth, my Lord Advocate, and myself, as having here jurisdiction under your Majesty.

"Commissioners would be given for this effect, and the Council commanded to depute one to the forenamed persons for putting the transgressors to the law.

"Being tried guilty and put in your Majesty's will, they would be fined according to their quality and estate. . . .

"The fine your Majesty will be graciously pleased to command the Treasurer divide with me, both in respect that all are burgesses of the city; and by the privilege your Majesty's most noble predecessors have granted to this see the escheats and forfeitures of all malefactors fall to the bishop, and that, I may have wherewith to recompense the discoverer and others that have served in the business, to whom I have particularly obliged myself. . . .

"For the Jesuit, your Majesty may be pleased to command him to be brought to Edinburgh, and examined by such of the Council as your Majesty shall please to nominate; of that number, the Secretary, Treasurer, my Lord Kilsyth, my Lord Advocate, and myself, because I have the writings (writtis), would seem fittest.

"They would be commanded to use his examination with great secrecy, and if he will not answer nor confess ingenuously, to give him the Boots or the torture. . . ."

Spottiswood is for using "the boots" and "torture." It is to be feared that nothing but Ogilvie's death will satisfy him.

On the 15th of October, Father Ogilvie had passed his first night in prison. He was faint and wearied. He writes of himself:—

"On the next day I am led out of the prison to the Episcopal palace, where there was a great concourse of preachers and barons, and whither two had been summoned from the Royal Parliament. I am brought up accordingly, ill as I am still from the blows of the previous day, and with an unusual trembling upon me. . . .

"They asked if I had said Mass in the royal dominions?

"*R.* If this is a crime it ought to be investigated, not by my oath, but by witnesses.

"We have proved it, they say, by the testimony of those who saw you.

"*R.* If the witnesses satisfy you on the point, all right; their testimony shall neither be weakened by my denial, nor strengthened by my confession, until I see fit.

"Then you are a priest, they say?

"*R.* If you have proved to demonstration that I have said Masses, by the same witnesses you will be convinced that I am a priest,

"They ask, do you acknowledge the King?

"*R.* James is, *de facto*, King of Scotland.

"Here I was a little afraid; but the stupid fellows, not understanding law terms, did not know how to examine further. . . .

"Once more I was asked if I had said any Masses in the King's dominions?

"*R.* This, by reason of the King's edicts and the Acts of Parliament, would prejudice me and my neighbour, and does not pertain to the King's forum, and therefore I am not bound to say, because I am not bound by any law to ruin myself and other innocent persons. If they were judges, I say it was their duty to inquire after crimes, not after sacrifices. And I add that thefts, treasons, homicides, poisonings, belonged to the King's forum, not the sacraments of religion. Then they asked me, what I had come to Scotland for?

"*R.* To unteach heresy.

"They inquire who had given me jurisdiction, since neither the King nor any bishop had given it.

"*R.* Neither King nor false pastor have any power over sacred things, and could not therefore confer upon others what they do not possess themselves. I have received Christ's priesthood from his lawful vicar, who alone has power in sacred things."

As Father Ogilvie insisted strongly upon this opinion, and proved that the Roman Pontiff has universal dominion in all matters belonging to religion, they inquired if he was ready to subscribe this statement with his own hand. "Yes, or with my own blood," he said. Then they brought up the old story of the Powder Treason. He repelled the calumny, and showed that Jesuits were acknowledged to be entirely free from all blame with regard to it, and reminded them of the numerous conspiracies in which they themselves had been engaged against the King in former years, a retort which reduced them to silence.

The court rose. Father Ogilvie was led down the High Street to the Tolbooth, and thus ended that day's proceedings. His narrative tells what followed.

"I am led back to prison October 15th, and two days afterwards I am shut up in a cell; after a little while I am fastened with two rings to a lump of iron of about two hundred pound in weight, shaped like a pole, so that I could only sit and lie on my back, but could do nothing else whatever, unless stand for a little while."[1]

[1] Authentic account.

It will be remembered that Spottiswood had encouraged James to order Father Ogilvie to be subjected to the torture of the boots. The hint was not lost upon the king.

"Meanwhile," wrote Father Ogilvie, "a letter comes back from London. I am ordered to be examined with the leg torture of the boots that I may betray the places and the persons of the Catholics. The commissioners from the king arrive, and condemn to death fourteen Catholics who were in prison with me, some to the gallows and some to the wheel, and whilst the king is asked about the carrying out of the sentence the condemned are shut up in different places, I am taken to Edinburgh, and whilst I am being led through the crowd of the friends and wives of the condemned I am greeted with mud, snow, and curses, the provincial judge even urging them on to it, and although it was forbidden by the servants of the bishop, the ministers looked on in silence and did not try to stop it. I ride on gaily through the streets as if I cared naught for it, so that they are surprised at my coolness. I said in a loud voice, according to the Scottish proverb, 'It's past joking when the head's off.' 'Is there anything else you may wish to do and say to me?' A certain woman cursed 'my ugly face.' To whom I replied, 'The blessing of Christ on your bonnie countenance;' thereupon she openly protested she was sorry for what she had said and would never more after that say anything bad about me. The heretics took notice that I gave back blessings for curses, and was good-humoured with those who were angry.

"To avoid being recognised at Edinburgh by my cloak, I changed it temporarily for my riding coat; but it was to no purpose. They bring in every day whomsoever they can, and question them if they had seen me before, and in whose company, and in this way they found out that many had been with me, and where I had been. Then they spread about the report that I had secretly betrayed those whom they had thus found out, or whom they had made tell and betray others from fear for their own safety. I stop at Edinburgh at the bishop's house. The boots for torturing the legs are brought forth, and I am every day threatened that they will proceed to extremities, that so I may betray the places and persons. If I would betray them they promise me liberty and rewards, and if I should be willing to turn heretic they promise me a provostship at Moffat and a grand marriage. I said laughingly that, from the similarity of the names, these ought to be offered to Father Moffat,[1] not to me, who was an Ogilvie."

The Lords Commissioners met, in virtue of James' missive, on December 12. Father Ogilvie was now again wearied with questions not unlike those which had been put to him and answered on the 15th of October. They were as follows:—

"When you came to this city where did you receive hospitality?

"*R.* I say that I am not bound to tell the persons and the places; granted they were judges it was their duty to look out for crimes, not for persons. . . .

"Your silence deepens our suspicions that you fear lest your accomplices should betray you.

---

[1] Father Moffat, who was then a close prisoner in Edinburgh Castle, was tempted with a similar offer. "They offered me," he wrote, "a bishopric, or the abbey of Coldingham, which is one of the best in the country, and still retains its leaden roof."—(Stonyhurst Archives, MS. Letter, 13th December 1615.)

"*R.* You ask me to give up the names of those who heard Mass—who were in communication with me. That I cannot and will never do. First, because by offending God, as a traitor who ruins his neighbour, I should kill my own soul. Secondly, nor would it do any good, but only harm, for the terror of you and the king's rewards might make some inconstant person feign that there was a conspiracy, to gain your favour and the king's, and thus you might have some cloak for your cruelty in taking my life, whom now, for fear of infamy, you do not punish as you would wish to do.

"The king, they said, takes no one's life on account of religion.

"*R.* And why, then, have the Glasgow prisoners been condemned to the wheel and the gibbet?

"This interchange of words ended in a threat:— 'Pray do not force us to torture you according to the king's command.'"

The judges did not much like to use the boots, because it left permanent traces of the cruelty inflicted, and they would fain have avoided the reproach of atrocious barbarity. But though they shrank from the reproach of cruelty, they did not shrink from cruelty itself. They revived an old method of torture which did not endanger the victim's life, but impaired his firmness and mental powers: this was to deprive him of sleep.

"For eight days and nine whole nights," says Father Ogilvie, "they forced me to keep awake with styles, pins, needles, and pinchings, threatening me meanwhile with extraordinary tortures and promising me great rewards,[1] so that the report of my watchings was spread

[1] Authentic account, p. 26, The Historic of King James the Sext. "This barbarous mode of extorting confession had been prevalent in cases of witchcraft. Human nature could not long stand so exquisite

through all Scotland, and many were indignant and compassionated my case. Many lords and barons had recourse to me, urging me to satisfy the King; but when they obtained nothing except reasons for reasons, the bishop grew desperate and said that he would have given a large sum of money never to have had anything to do with me."

The nine nights of watching had run out. The commissioners summoned Father Ogilvie before them. He admitted that he was quite exhausted.

"I was weak; for the watching so weakened me that I scarce knew what I said and what I did, or in what place I was, and very often I knew not in what city I was.

"They say unless you satisfy the King, there are more horrible things coming.

"*R.* Try your worst, on with your boots; with God as my guide, I will show you that in this cause I care no more for my legs than you for your leggings. I consider myself born for greater things than to be overcome by sense; but I do not trust in myself but in the grace of God."

The Royal Commission failed. Christmas was nigh, and Archbishop Spottiswood had to repair to Glasgow for its celebration. Being unwilling to leave his prisoner in Edinburgh, he ordered him to be led back to Glasgow. Hence says Ogilvie:—

"I came to Glasgow on the vigil of our Lord's nativity, and was then fastened by both feet to my iron pole; but now I am only fastened by one foot, with a

a torture. The suspected parties were often driven into a state of delirium; and in many instances they must have been glad to confess anything which may have been proposed by their examinators, to escape from a life held by such miserable torture."—(Pitcairn's *Criminal Trials*, notes, vol. iii., p. 332.)

bolt and two iron chains binding the iron, lest I should contract disease from always lying on my back."[1]

In vain were threats uttered and rewards promised. Their efforts were futile. Tortures were twice tried, and twice failed. Father Ogilvie was immoveable. It was determined at last he should be put to death. This was glad news. The martyr breathed at ease, and joyfully invited his friends to his wedding. The Catholics, however, had carefully prepared everything for his escape from the archbishop's castle the night before his death. We know from a contemporary account that "on the night which preceded the martyrdom, Mr John Brown of Lochhill,[2] father of the Rev. James Brown, S.J., whilst making a visit of charity to Father Ogilvie in prison, promised he would that night open to him a way of escape, of saving his life and recovering his liberty. The Father smiled affectionately, and embracing the distinguished gentleman with great marks of friendship, expressed his extreme gratitude for the proffered kindness, but assured him that death for so grand a cause was more acceptable than any life, and that he looked forward to it with so sincere a desire as to fear nothing so much as that by any accident he should be snatched from it."[3] The two rushed into one another's arms, and the generous martyr begged Mr Brown not to leave the city until God had completed what he had begun in him. This Mr Brown promised he would faithfully

[1] Authentic Account.

[2] Lochhill belonged to a branch of the Browns of Carsluith, &c. ... P. H. M'Kerlie, "History of the Lands and their Owners in Galloway," vol. v. p. 16.

[3] Document written and signed by Father James Brown, S.J., who was Rector of Douay College in 1688. (Presholme MSS.), published by F. Karslake. Authentic Account, &c.

observe, and undertook to keep as close to the Father's side as he could."

The rest of the night Father Ogilvie spent in prayer. He was at first much wearied by the uproar of the gaolers and others, but with the dawn there came quiet, and then he could speak as he desired to Him whom in a few moments he was to see face to face. Early in the morning, on Tuesday, March 10, a magistrate arrived with armed citizens to take him to the Town Hall.

". . . They led him out of the prison, half dressed, in a short cloak, torn under the arm, for the Archbishop's steward had appropriated his own cloak for himself. Whilst they proceed, people of all sexes and conditions come running together to the sight, and amongst them the wives and relatives of his condemned fellow-prisoners who, a few days before, had heaped reproaches upon him, and pelted him with snow balls, regarding him as they did as the cause of all their miseries. But now that the affair had been more thoroughly investigated, and his innocence, constancy, and fidelity made known, inasmuch as he had not discovered a single one of the Catholics, they were invoking every blessing on his head, and not without tears. And all the rest of the crowd, even the heretics, were doing the same." Father Ogilvie, in coming to court, was conducted to the place where criminals sat. Sir William Elphinston of Newton, read the indictment against the prisoner. The jury all in one voice found the prisoner guilty, and the dempster was summoned to read the sentence of death.

"The martyr thanked them, and imparted his blessing to the one who pronounced the sentence, and embraced him. He then thanked the rest, along with the Archbishop, and giving them his right hand, said that he forgave all from his heart, as he desired that God would forgive him his sins, and after commending himself to the prayers of Catholics, if any should be there in concealment, he turned himself to the wall and gave himself to prayer."[1]

"When the martyr was brought out from the prison on the road to the scaffold he was met by the heretical minister and gaol officials. Mr Brown and other Catholic gentlemen were also close at hand. The minister addressed the Father and expressed the extremely kind feeling he had for him. 'Oh, how much I grieve for you, my dear Ogilvie,' he said, 'who are knowingly and wilfully casting yourself into the jaws of an infamous death.' Then the Father, feigning fear, said, 'Just as if my life hung on my own free will. I am accounted guilty of high treason, and for that I am condemned.' 'Have done,' said the minister, 'with that crime of yours. Give up the Pope and Papistry and you shall be forgiven that crime, and I will reward you with gifts.' 'You mock me,' said the Father. 'I speak seriously and with certain authority,' subjoined the minister. 'My Lord Archbishop gave commission to me to promise you his daughter in marriage, and the richest prebend of the diocese as her dowry, provided I found you willing to step over from your religion to ours.' Whilst these things were being said they reached the scaffold. The minister urged the Father to be willing to live. The Father replied that he was willing, but not with disgrace. 'I have said, and repeat,' urged the minister, 'that you may live with honour.' 'Would you be willing to say that, so that the people could hear?' 'By all means,' he replied. 'Listen all present,' cried Father Ogilvie, 'to what the minister is going to say to us.' Then the

[1] Authentic Account, p. 46.

minister gave out: 'I promise to Mr Ogilvie life, the Lord Archbishop's daughter, and a very rich prebend, provided he be willing to come over to our side.' 'Do you hear this?' said the Father; 'and will you confirm it as witnesses when it shall be needed?' 'We have heard,' cried the people, 'and we will confirm it. Go down, Mr Ogilvie; go down!' Upon this the Catholics began to tremble, and the heretics to triumph. 'There is no fear, then, that I shall be held hereafter as guilty of high treason?' 'By no means!' all the people from the street cried out together. 'I stand here, therefore, a criminal on the head of religion alone?' 'Of that alone!' they cry out. 'Very well!' triumphantly exclaimed the Father; 'that is plenty. On the head of religion alone I am condemned, and for that I would willingly and joyfully pour out even a hundred lives. Snatch away that one which I have from me, and make no delay about it; but my religion you will never snatch away from me.' At this the Catholics raised their heads in triumph, whilst the heretics who had been thus taken in were in a fury, and above all the minister, who harshly received the Father as he was preparing to say more, and commanded him to be led away to the scaffold as quickly as possible."[1]

On getting upon the platform he kissed the gibbet and gave himself up to prayer. John Abercromby, his kinsman, stood near him. The minister cried out, "Ogilvie is to die for treason!" The martyr, hearing this, shook his head, showing the minister lied. He would have spoken, but was not allowed. "Don't mind their lies, John; the more wrongs the better," said Abercromby. Some one shouted, "Off with that other traitor!"

[1] Attestation of Father James Brown, S.J. Signed at Douay, Feb. 23, 1672. (Presholme MSS.)

Thereupon one of the Archbishop's servants cast Abercromby head foremost into the crowd. "Are you not," said the minister, "afraid to die?" "I fear death," answered Father Ogilvie, "as much as you do your dinner."

"They now tied his hands behind his back, so tightly that his fingers trembled, and he was commanded to ascend the ladder.[1] As he went up he was persevering in prayer, and in begging the suffrages of Catholics, if any should happen to be present. Then he invoked aloud all the heavenly court, declaring, in the hearing of all, that his hope was reposed in the merits of the blood of Christ, and that first in Latin and then in English. After the repeated command of the Sheriff to throw him off the ladder, the executioner at last reluctantly, and

---

[1] It was, very probably, just before his hands were bound that he flung his rosary beads (his farewell gift to the Catholics present) into the crowd about the scaffold. His rosary struck the breast of a young nobleman who was on his travels in these kingdoms. He was a foreigner and a Protestant—his name, Baron John of Eckersdorff. "I was on my travels through England and Scotland—as it is the custom of our nobility—being a mere stripling, and not having the faith. I happened to be in Glasgow the day Father Ogilvie was led forth to the gallows, and it is impossible for me to describe his lofty bearing in meeting death. His farewell to the Catholics was his casting into their midst, from the scaffold, his rosary beads just before he met his fate. That rosary, thrown haphazard, struck me on the breast in such wise that I could have caught it in the palm of my hand; but there was such a rush and crush of the Catholics to get hold of it that unless I wished to run the risk of being trodden down, I had to cast it from me. Religion was the last thing I was then thinking about; it was not in my mind at all; yet from that moment I had no rest. Those rosary beads had left a wound in my soul; go where I would I had no peace of mind. . . . At last conscience won the day. I became a Catholic."—(Attestation of Father Boleslaus Balbinus, S.J., Presholme MSS. See J. Schmidl, S.J., "Historia Provinciæ Bohemiæ," Pragæ, 1749, vol. ii. p. 795).

with great compassion, cast him down from the step. A deep groan broke from all the spectators; and then, as if their tongues were loosened, they proclaimed their sentiments freely enough, openly declaring their horror and detestation at the unjust sentence they had just seen executed." [1]

"It is certain," wrote an eye-witness, "that his martyrdom has been of the greatest advantage to the Catholics of Scotland, for a very large number of them have been encouraged by his example to a firmer adherence to the Catholic faith. I know this by my own experience. A similar sentence was passed against me about the same time. The Father's example and a Divine inspiration gave me so much firmness that, when in August 1615, I was brought to the foot of the gallows, with two others, named Robert Wilkie and Robert Cruikshank, in the presence of fifty thousand people, we all three, by God's grace, prepared to suffer death with the utmost firmness. Our adversaries, in deference to the murmurs of the people, obtained the King's order for the revocation of our sentence, which was received with every demonstration of joy by those present, and we were sent instead into banishment. Ever since that time the Catholics have been less molested in Scotland. Andrew Crichton, a secular priest, was apprehended by the Government, and so were Fathers Patrick Anderson and John Macbreck, priests of the Society of Jesus. They defended the authority of the Supreme Pontiff, and denied the spiritual power of the King, as Father

---

[1] "Their lamentations and expressions of compassion were so general that the same minister who accompanied him to the scaffold, Mr Robert Scott, in a sermon which he delivered on the next Sunday he appeared in public, upbraided the people for exhibiting such indications of grief for the death of a Popish priest."—(Proceedings, etc.)

Ogilvie had done, but they were all let go and sent into exile.

King James regretted the death of Father Ogilvie, and laid the blame on the importunity of the Calvinist ministers.[1]

"The death of Father Ogilvie," wrote Father Gordon,[2] "ought not much to deter us, but rather urge us to take up this mission still more earnestly, now that God has

---

[1] "After the martyr's death, George Gordon, Marquis of Huntly, had proceeded to Court, where he was high in the favour of King James. The King asked him, 'How his Scotsmen took the death of the Jesuit?' 'Very ill,' replied Huntly. 'It was not my fault,' said James; 'Spotswood hurried on the execution. I have no wish to see bloody heads round my deathbed.' Huntly was surprised at this expression, and requested the King to explain himself. James looked at him seriously, and replied, not without emotion, 'Do you not know how Queen Elizabeth died?' and proceeded to give him a relation of the miserable and dreadful end of that princess, and how she saw the spectres of the monks whom she had put to death, standing before her and gazing at her as she died. On his return to Scotland the Marquis went to see Spotswood, who was in his castle at Darse, employed as we have described, and conferred for a long time with him on the subject of what the King had said.

"After the death of King James, and on the breaking out of the civil war, Spotswood, who had been the principal cause of Father Ogilvie's death, was sent into banishment, and his eldest son Robert was killed fighting with the Presbyterians. Thus he received the reward of his iniquity. The Marquis related his conversation with the King and with Spotswood to his friend Lord Maxwell, Earl of Nithsdale, who has recorded it in his MS. History of Scotland. This history, which has never been printed, is kept in the Scottish College of the Society of Jesus at Douay, where it was seen and carefully read by a Scottish priest of our Society related to the Ogilvie family, who extracted and preserved the particulars I have related, and incorporated them in his own memoir, and told me them at Prague, when he was of very advanced age."—J. Schmidl, Historia Provinciæ Bohemiæ. Pragæ, 1749. Part II. lib. vi. p. 793.

[2] S.J., Stonyhurst Archives, MS. Letter, dated Paris, 5th May 1615.

rewarded it with the crown of martyrdom. If Father Moffat dies or is put to death, there will not be one of our Society remaining in Scotland. If we are slow in coming, our enemies will call out that we are kept away by fear of death; and what is worse, many Catholics will believe it, when they see themselves altogether deprived of the aid of our Fathers. With regard to the question of your Paternity about Father Patrick Anderson, I think he is a fit man to send, if willing to go. While he was here he was disinclined to go to Scotland, but the proposal was not then to send him alone, but accompanied by another Father, who would moderate his fervour, and was to preside over the whole Scottish Mission, in case more were sent afterwards. The fittest man for this duty would be Father John Robb; and unless this Father, who has such large experience of missions, can be sent, with power to direct and control Father Patrick and others, that they may not go beyond the bounds of prudence, I should think it better for the mission to be deferred. If Father Patrick goes alone, he will not be safe. I know by experience, when he was there alone before, that it was necessary to recal him on account of the imminent peril he ran. Will your Paternity therefore consider whether it would not be better to send Father Robb and Father Patrick into Scotland at once, lest the Catholics should be entirely deprived of the aid of our Fathers, especially now in so great affliction, or whether the mission of Father Patrick had better be deferred to another time, and until a suitable companion to him can be found. I do not think one such could be easily fixed upon, for the others are all his juniors, and not so fit."

To the great consolation of the Scotch Catholics,

Father Anderson was allowed by his superiors to return to Scotland.

After some time spent in the visitation of the Highlands, he proceeded to the south, where he was betrayed on St Patrick's day, March 17, 1620, into the hands of the magistrates of Edinburgh, by a pretended Catholic, Alexander Boyd, whose honour could not resist the bribe of £75 sterling. During his rigid confinement in the Tolbooth, the good Father, whose constitution was greatly impaired, had to stand several examinations, in which he gave evident proofs of superior learning and invincible constancy. He was subjected to the barbarous torture of the "Boots," in which the legs of the prisoner were so compressed that the blood, and sometimes the marrow, started from the compressed parts. But nothing could intimidate his generous soul, which panted for martyrdom. "Quis mihi tribuit," he says, "ut pro dulcissimo Domino Jesu moriar? O felix hora, qua comparatur æterna illa felicitas." But whilst in daily expectation of death, he was restored to liberty at the intercession, as it is thought, of the French ambassador, the Marquis D'Effiat, who chose him for his confessor.

The following narrative of his trial for heresy, which we have from his pen, forms a fitting supplement to the Notes of his Mission in Scotland in 1610. In a letter addressed to Father General Mutius Vitelleschi, and dated from Scotland, May 14, 1620, Father Anderson repeats at considerable length the Conversations, as we may call them, which took place between himself and his examiners :—

"VERY REVEREND FATHER IN CHRIST,—Pax dulcissimi Jesu,—I have been for a long time in the closest imprisonment, with nothing to expect but the sentence of death, or, at least, of imprisonment for life. I can do all things in Him who strengthens me, who is Christ Jesus, from whose love I am certain that neither life nor death, nor principalities, nor any creature, can separate me. To Him be glory, for ever and ever, Amen. Whilst in prison, I have had many conversations on the Catholic faith with its enemies, to the great joy of the Catholics. For the Lord Jesus, of His immense goodness, gave me a mouth and wisdom which His enemies could not withstand. I suffered almost daily from sickness in prison, and very severely; during which, stripped of all human aid, I always experienced Divine help. Who will grant me that I may die for my sweetest Lord Jesus? Oh, happy hour, in which never-ending happiness is gained. Oh, how many things do the heretics plot, chiefly against our Society, of which I have ever and truly borne witness, and in the strongest terms, that I have never seen anything but eminent piety and holiness. The Society, as a holy member of the Church, will have much to suffer, and we shall be hated by all men for Christ's sake. This ought to be the reason why we should be the more closely bound to each other by charity, and also to our head Christ Jesus in every virtue, especially in assiduous prayer, true humility, and perfect obedience. I kiss all my fathers and brothers in the kiss of peace, and earnestly beg their prayers. I commend to your Paternity the students of the Scotch College, for whom I compiled the lives of the Scottish saints with great trouble, knowing that this would give them no small consolation. May the Lord Jesus Christ preserve your Paternity for the good of the Church. God bless your Paternity with every heavenly blessing. God console your Paternity in so many difficulties. Amen. I have no room to say more.

"Your Paternity's most obedient son, bound for
"the Lord Jesus,
"Patrick Anderson."

"Scotland, *May* 14, 1620."

"Very Reverend Father in Christ Jesus,—Pax Christi Jesu,—Your Paternity knows well how great has been my care and trouble during these last years, and how much I have undergone for the sake of this my country, which the fierce boar of heresy has almost completely destroyed, shaken from its foundations. What labours, what perils, by land and by sea, I underwent to win these souls, redeemed by the blood of Christ to the faith of their Fathers! It at last pleased the Most High, whom I, though an unprofitable servant, serve in spirit, to receive these my labours, and by His grace to ennoble and reward them with imprisonment and other sufferings. To Him, who was with me in all my tribulations, be glory and honour, for I know that He will save me.

"I left the north of Scotland, in which I had spent the winter, and came to the south about the month of May last, on the seventeenth day of which, in Edinburgh, the capital of Scotland, by the contrivance of one Boyd, who professed himself a Catholic, I was seized by the magistrates. At the moment of my capture I greeted my betrayer most kindly, saying, 'Friend, dost thou betray the Son of Man with a salutation? God forgive thee.' Meanwhile the satellites rushed upon me, took away whatever I had, and searched everything, but in vain. A crowd assembled, and the news spread directly through the city, 'Anderson is caught; no doubt he is in all the Jesuits' secrets.' They took me to prison, and threatened the head gaoler, with the loss of his life and the confiscation of all his goods, if he let any one speak to me. The windows were nailed up, and my knife, which I used for cutting food, was taken from me. These good Evangelicals thought I had so much on my conscience, that I was likely to lay violent hands on myself. They also took away various other necessaries. The senators and other great people went away, and I was left alone. I collected myself, fell on my knees, and, overwhelmed with joy and tears, I gave thanks to my sweetest Jesus that He had granted me, not only to believe in Him, but also to suffer for His name from the enemies of the holy Catholic Church. I also humbly begged the Eternal Father, through the precious blood of Jesus, that He would grant me speech and wisdom which my enemies could not resist ; that this imprisonment might be acceptable to Him in union with the Passion of His Son Jesus, for whom to suffer is the greatest glory ; and that I might fight the good fight, and be found faithful to Him in whom I have trusted. Shut up in this narrow cell, and deprived of the fresh air, which I used to breathe through the chinks of the window, I thought of David's words, ' *Os meum aperui, et attraxi spiritum.*' I fell ill, suffering at once most acutely from colic and gravel. Vomiting succeeded, disgust of all food, and frequently utter prostration of mind. Worse than all, they would not allow the warder to give me any help. I rejoiced that my most faithful Jesus, who does not suffer His own to be tempted above their strength, did not withdraw His Divine aid when human help seemed to be out of reach. Contrary to all experience, after a few days, both my ailments decreased, the vomiting ceased, and I became soon convalescent, remaining however very weak. This is quite natural to me, since I have borne the sweet yoke of Jesus Christ in the Society. I know that strength is made perfect in infirmity, and infirmity is not a less good gift than health, but is often a better. When I was stronger one of the senators, with the principal ministers of the town, came to see me. They saluted me, and asked how I was. I replied,

"'Readily and willingly do I suffer here for Christ, for whom to suffer is the greatest glory.'

"'The cause, and not the suffering, makes the martyr, Master Anderson,' said one of the ministers.

"'I am certain that mine is the cause of Christ, and that it is that for which St Cyprian, whose words you quote, suffered.'

"'How can you be certain, Master Anderson,' said the minister, 'when it is a dogma of your faith to doubt about matters of faith.'

"'It is not so,' replied I, 'the truth is the very contrary. Our doctors distinguish two kinds of doubt. The first is intellectual, which rather embraces the manner of the thing, than the thing itself which is firmly believed; and it is evident, from your own Bible, that the holiest and most faithful men have had doubts of this kind, which are of no moment. A wilful doubt, say they, is another thing; and of such it is commonly said, "He who doubts is no longer faithful." Let it thus be far from us, Sir Minister, to harbour such doubts as these, but let us condemn them as heresy and infidelity.'

"'It is just as Master Anderson says,' said another of the ministers, whom this had much piqued; 'one can be certain of the things of faith, but one does not believe with the certainty of divine faith, for instance, that one is in the grace of God.'

"'Quite so,' said I, 'and exactly what we believe.

x

But,' added I, 'I will prove to you, my masters, that you Protestants must necessarily doubt of all the articles of your faith, if indeed faith it can be called. Pray,' said I, turning to one of the ministers, 'how do you know that Christ the Lord is the Redeemer of the world?'

"'Our Bible proves it,' replied the ministers.

"'Very well,' I retorted; 'but how do you know that your Bible is the Word of God? Is it because the Church says it? You say the true Church has erred, and consequently can err. You confess, with the King, whom may God bless, and with Calvin, that the Roman Church was the true Church during the first four hundred years, but that she afterwards erred; whence it follows that the true Church, whichever she be, can err. Let us grant that the Scotch Church be the true one, and that she approve the Scottish Bibles as the Word of God. If she do, it is in vain, for she may err in this approbation. Whence he who believes in this Church will always be in doubt concerning the things which such a Church approves, because if the true Church herself can err, how much more can one member? Let us suppose that thou art a minister of the Scotch Church, to celebrate the Lord's Supper, and preach to the people. A Protestant enters the temple to hear thee, and receive the Lord's Supper. This thought comes into his mind: the Scotch Church is indeed the true Church, but she may err; how much more this minister, who is only one of her members? How shall he preach infallibly, and with that infallibility that is required for the things of faith, and how shall he preach truth rather than fables? or how shall he have true authority to preach and administer the sacraments? Nothing here is certain; all is doubtful. The foundation of faith ought to be infallible, and if it be not, there is no Divine faith, but a vain human opinion.'

"'We will appoint an auditor,' said the ministers, 'who will examine into what we say, and compare it with the Bible itself.'

"'That would be of no use,' said I, 'for if you can err in preaching, how much more could he in this collation? You must indeed say that the Roman Church has erred, in order thus to show that you are sent from God.'

"This argument piqued the listeners not a little. They did not know which way to turn, for they knew it was an *argumentum ad hominem*, and deduced from their own principles. One of them, however, retorted, 'You Catholics and Papists have no greater infallibility in the articles of your faith.'

"'We have the very greatest,' I answered. 'We have infallibility; we tread another way, and one which leads to life. For we believe, with a firm faith, that the true Church cannot err; so all your Bibles have it, "And the gates of hell shall not prevail against her;" "I will pray the Father that thy faith may not fail;" "I am with you (all days) to the end of ages;" "the Church is the pillar and ground of truth," and any number of other things of the kind. Thus the true Church has the same infallibility which God has, who promised her His unfailing assistance. Therefore, whatsoever this Church proposes to be believed by her children, as revealed by God, must be infallible. Thus there is the greatest unity of faith with us, and no variation. What the Roman Church believed during the first four hundred years she believes still without any change. You, on the contrary, alter the Bible and the articles of faith year by year. There are as many opinions as there are heads among you, and no unity, no conformity.'

"'Surely,' interrupted a senator, 'Anderson, with his sublimities and sophistries, is corrupting the whole country.'

"Much more occurred during this discussion, which for brevity's sake I omit. The Catholic nobles, who were then in the city, heard that if I had not confuted the ministers, I had at least bothered them; and this report came from the Protestants themselves, for they never suffered any Catholic, who might tell the truth, to be present. I had at least shut them up. The report of this discussion spread abroad to the great joy and consolation of the Catholics. To Him be glory, from whom is every good and perfect gift, for ever and ever.

"But there was a circumstance which caused me the greatest pain, and made me shed many tears, so that I might have said with the Prophet, 'My tears have been my bread day and night.' I had a servant whom, for greater security, I used to send to the houses of heretics at my own expense, that he might lodge safely and quietly there. He was caught, through his own fault, by the Senate, and revealed the names of certain Catholics, or at least of those who were believed by all to be Catholics. Thus did the miserable fellow reward me. The event, by God's blessing, was fortunate, because I could deny all that he asserted, and those Catholics had not a few friends among the heretics. That servant was the brother of an excellent Catholic woman, who has been sixteen years excommunicated by the ministers for the Catholic faith. This woman, and one of our Fathers, who had shortly before reconciled her to the Church, besought me earnestly to take him for a servant, and pledged themselves for his conduct; but the event was unfortunate. He only remained five months in my service. Here, in Ireland, and in other places, our Fathers have their own servants, without whom it is impossible to live conveniently. The great inconstancy of all of them, and the venality of the majority, are the cause of frequent and daily misfortunes to their employers.

"Our Catholics are surely much to be admired for the way in which they expose themselves and all their goods to the inconstancy of these men. Their zeal for the doctrine and sacraments of the true faith is so great that they disregard everything else. Their days are passed in such purity of life, although surrounded by heretics who give the rein to every vice, that the Protestants themselves and their ministers publicly express their admiration. This, then, was the cause of my greatest trouble. But God, whose nature is goodness, and whose work is mercy, dissipated it, and I see through the plans of my enemies. Meanwhile certain senators came into the prison, and led me to the Town Hall, where four bishops awaited me. They were the Archbishop of St Andrews and Primate of Scotland, and the Bishops of Glasgow, Galloway, and Caithness; the prefect and Senators of the city, the ministers, and many others. As I was being led away, I thought of the words of Christ: 'They shall drag you before kings and governors for my sake,' . . . and 'I will give you a mouth and wisdom which all your adversaries shall not be able to resist and gainsay.' They all saluted me as I entered, and the Archbishop of St Andrews asked my name.

"'Patrick Anderson, and of the Roman Catholic religion, for which I am ready to die, and for which I am kept here; by profession a Jesuit.'

"'Your name is Master Patrick Anderson,' said the Archbishop.

"'It is now twenty-three years,' replied I, 'since I despised and made nought of all such honorary titles, esteeming them unworthy of consideration, like all else in the world, and renouncing them for Christ Jesus, for whose Name I am suffering here.'

"'We know that you have been twice in Scotland,' said the Bishop; 'thus it is the will of the King that you discover to us with whom you have been staying all this time.'

"I replied, 'It is better to obey God than man. The King commands this thing to be done, and the self-same thing is forbidden by God. Know that I am equally ready to shed my blood for this cause as for the Catholic faith itself, or for whatsoever is commanded by the Divine law.'

"'You will at least confess this, Master Anderson,' said the Bishop, 'whether you have said Mass in Scotland or not?'

"'That I have,' replied I.

"'But for whom?' asked the Bishop.

"'Alone,' I replied.

"'That is nonsense,' said the chief minister. 'Mass comes from *mitto*, because the people are dismissed.'

"'An argument founded upon etymology is worth nothing to a philosopher,' I retorted, 'and Mass does not come from the dismissal of the people, but from the Hebrew *Missach*, which signifies a voluntary oblation, or, by contraction, from the word *Messias*, for *there* indeed is the true Messias offered for the sins of the people, and art thou a master of Israel, and knowest not these things?'

"The minister was silent.

"'But Master Anderson,' said the Bishop, 'how can you prove the word "Mass" from the New Testament?'

"'Much more easily, right reverend lord, than you will find the word "sacrament" in the New Testament, or prove that the number of the sacraments is two.' (I always gave this title to bishops, and to others their proper style.) Let us open the Bible, either the Greek version of the Old Testament, or the Syriac and Hebrew versions of the New. You know I had all these Bibles, because you have just taken them away from me with everything else. Now, indeed, I can say, "For Jesus Christ I have suffered the loss of all things, and for His sake count them but as dung." We shall see whether I shall more easily prove the word "Mass," or you "Sacraments," from the Bible.'

"'You will at least confess, Master Anderson,' said the Bishop of Galloway, 'that they are Catholics whom your servant named?'

"'You are a philosopher, I know, right reverend lord, and you well know it is useless to prove from a greater what can be proved from a less. You are versed in the Scriptures, and they say, "The disciple is not above his master, nor the servant above his lord." Thus, my servant should follow my example, and not I his.' Oh, how this little breath of praise, by which I distinguished him above the others, pleased the Bishop! These sort of men are most greedy of praise.

"'How many Jesuits are there in Scotland?' asked the Archbishop of St Andrews.

"'Here am I, the last one left,' I answered.

"'I will tell you some more,' said the Bishop. 'There are two others (whom he named) and a Franciscan also.'

"'Right enough, my right reverend lord, and most mathematically. There are four of us altogether (for the archbishop had included one of the Order of St Francis of Paula); four is the number of perfection. Thus, if you, my right reverend lord, will cause us four to be hanged upon a circular gibbet, you may boast of having squared a circle, an operation which has hitherto baffled all mathematicians.'

"'I see, Master Anderson,' said the Bishop, 'that you have received many talents from God. If you would use them for the benefit of our country, you would do good service to our King, and I promise you that the King would esteem it most highly. There are ministers, very learned men, here to-day for this object. I desire that they forthwith treat of the whole of our religion. For the Lord's hand is not shortened.'

"'May God bless the King with every heavenly blessing. I will tell you plainly what I would hear of your religion, since it is the wish of your most reverend lordship. I am here before you, the chief bishops of the kingdom, the noble Lord Provost is here, and many magistrates of great weight, and here are learned ministers, and many others. I take God to witness, in whose sight I stand, and for whose name I here suffer, that I do not, and never have seen, any consistency in your religion, nor anything in conformity with the revealed will of God, nor in uniformity with even your own Bibles, or with the Fathers, antiquity, the councils, or even with natural reason. You daily compose new articles, new ceremonies, as all Scotland knows and bewails, but in vain: your Church has forsaken the fountain of living waters, and have digged to themselves cisterns in which there is no water.'

"The bishops and the rest were not a little nettled, at which certain sheriffs of the city gave orders that I should be led back to prison. When I heard this I exclaimed, 'You know, my right reverend lords, if I am not mistaken, that I am most desirous of having books.

Command, if it please you, that I may keep at least your Scottish Bible by me in prison.'

"They refused, saying that I perverted the Bible to a false sense. Thus during the various conversations which I held in prison, now with the bishops, and now with the chief ministers of the kingdom, although we often felt the want of books, neither did they bring with them a book of any kind, nor did they allow me to keep any. I left the council full of joy at being found worthy to suffer continually for the name of Jesus, and on reaching my cell I fell on my knees and returned thanks for it to the sweetest Jesus. I reiterated the exercises on the Life and Passion of our Lord Jesus Christ, and often recited the Rosary, keeping eternity and the goodness of God before my eyes. Often and often did I think of the holy lives and conversation of many of our Fathers with whom I used to be so intimate, and the example of whose virtues I quietly stored up in my memory.

"Many bishops and ministers came to the city on hearing that Anderson had been taken and was in the closest confinement, for his fame much exceeded his deserts. The Bishop of Brechin, who was renowned for his theological learning, came to the prison, with the ministers and many others, and accompanied by certain magistrates, without whom no one was allowed to enter. The bishop saluted me most politely.

"' I hope you are well, Master Anderson.'

"' I am here in bonds for Christ Jesus, and meditating over His words, "Blessed are they who suffer persecution for justice' sake, for theirs is the kingdom of heaven,"' I returned.

"' Very well,' said the bishop, ' but the Greek says for righteousness ἕνεκεν δικαιοσύνης.'

"' So I say,' replied I, ' but I pray your lordship, why

do you so manifestly corrupt the Bible in that place. In the Greek it certainly is μακάριοι οἱ δεδιωγμένοι ἕνεκεν δικαιοσύνης; but you render the word δικαιοσύνης, by righteousness, and not by justice, its equivalent, which you understand of your own supposititious justice, and ignore the true and essential justice. And why, I pray, do you translate the same word otherwise in another place. In the first chapter of St Luke we find "Ἦσαν δὲ δίκαιοι ἀμφότεροι ἐναντίον τοῦ Θεοῦ." Here you translate δίκαιοι by just instead of righteous.'

"'Have a care,' said the bishop, 'how you call our Bibles corrupt, which the royal commission have declared to be the Word of God.'

"'But,' said I, 'either the commissioners can err in this declaration, or they cannot. You surely will not say that, as men, they cannot err; and if they could err, how could they be sure of being right? I will call your King himself (whom may God bless) to witness that your Bibles are crammed with corruptions, and therefore it was that the King caused a new Scotch Bible to be printed, about the year 1616, to the best of my belief, and which is called the Royal Bible. If you compare it with yours, as I have often done, they will be found to differ totally. Take care how you condemn the errors of the Royal Bible, for it will follow that your Bibles are no more the Word of God than Tully's Epistles.'

"They all took this comparison very ill, and said I was deserving of the severest punishment for having thus openly spoken with irreverence of the Scotch Bible. I replied as modestly as I could, for it was always my care never to be a stumbling-block to them.

"This most reverend and learned bishop well knows the custom between literary disputants, to speak candidly, sincerely, and without disguise, and not to take it ill if the truth comes out during the discussion, for this is the object and end of all discussion. He also well knows that the ministers, in order to show that Catholics are wrong when they use blessings, translate the word "εὐλογήσας," which always means to bless, by to give thanks. This occurs in Matthew, twenty-sixth chapter, and, unless I mistake, twenty-sixth verse. He also knows that those ministers, in order to abolish Purgatory, or any place between paradise and hell, translate the passage in the second chapter of the Acts, 'Thou wilt not leave my soul in hell,' by 'Thou wilt not leave my soul in the grave;' whereas the Greek word ᾅδης, never, even among the profane authors, signified the grave. Those who have the most elementary acquaintance with Hebrew know that the Hebrew word which occurs in that text, signifies hell. This is clear from the twenty-seventh chapter of Genesis, where Jacob, grieving for his son Joseph, says, 'I will go down to my son into hell, mourning.' 'Hell' you have corrupted into 'the grave.' I could give any number of similar instances.

"'We may conclude from this, Master Anderson, that there are some errors in the Scotch Bibles, which I grant; but it in nowise follows that they are not in general rightly and well translated, and are not the Word of God. The guilt of the evil doer cannot be justly imputed to the innocent.'

"'I beg your pardon,' I interrupted, 'quite the contrary; if I prove the existence of one error in your Scotch Bibles, and I could prove that there are ten thousand, it would suffice to show that they are not the Word of God. If the Scotch interpreter and translator erred in one instance in his version, it would follow of necessity that in that instance he had not the infallible assistance of the Holy Spirit. Thus the reader of that Bible would ever be uncertain when he had it and when he had it not, and no rule could be given why he should have it in one instance and not in another. Whence nothing certain can be instilled into the mind of the reader or hearer of this Bible, and certainty is of the first necessity in the foundation, and in all matters of faith.'

"'It matters little,' said the bishop, 'whether the Scotch Bible be the Word of God or not (the bystanders were much irritated at this), let us go back to the fountain-head, the Hebrew, Greek, and Syriac text.'

"'I stand corrected,' replied I, 'now that we have settled that the Scotch Bible is not the Word of God. Let your reverend lordship prove, from the Greek or Syriac text of the New Testament, that there are two sacraments only, and neither more nor less; and this must be formally expressed in terms, or a necessary consequence. For, whether for better or for worse, we must leave the Bible and go to logic.'

"'All your doctors,' rejoined the Bishop, 'and especially Bellarmine, say that the sacraments confer grace *ex opere operato*—that is, by the force and nature of the sacrament, and *ex opere operantis*—that is, from the intention of him who administers the sacrament. Whence it is evident that there are only two sacraments.'

"'Bellarmine shows his wisdom in remaining in Rome and not coming to these parts,' I answered. 'If you are so severe on him when absent, what would you not do to him if you could catch him? Neither Bellarmine nor any of our doctors ever taught that the *opus operans* in the sacraments was the intention of the minister, but rather the disposition of him who received the sacrament. But all this is nothing to the purpose. I beg that this proposition, in terms, may be found in the Bible:

"There are only two sacraments of the New Law," or this: "There is no Purgatory, there is no invocation of saints, the good works of Christians do not justify or merit before God." I ask for express terms, and not for your fancies, interpretations, or inferences. If we have to refer to interpretations, who in his senses would not prefer those of the Fathers to yours, among which, especially in Scotland, there is no unanimity, as you well know. You also know that many ministers, and some very distinguished ones, have been lately expelled from their houses, deprived of the faculty of preaching, and banished to the furthest parts of Scotland because they would not administer the Lord's Supper kneeling to the people, because they would not observe five feast days, like the English, or because they would not receive other things commanded by the King, whom may the Lord bless. You, who receive these and such things, they accuse of idolatry, and declare you worthy of eternal damnation.'

"One of the magistrates, who apparently condemned the reception of the Lord's Supper kneeling, here interrupted:

"'Pray, Master Anderson, what is your opinion of this matter, which is now the subject of so much controversy? Speak freely, I beg.'

"There were so many present, and of such various opinions on this matter, that I paused for a while. I remembered the prudence with which St Paul declared himself to be a Pharisee, and not a Sadducee, by which means he escaped for that time the snares of the Jews.

"'I freely say, with the Puritans, that it savours of idolatry to kneel before bread.' The greater number approved this my opinion, in opposition to the Bishop and a few others, and said I was a good fellow. The others said I was bad, and was beguiling the whole country. Meanwhile the bishop and ministers took leave. He promised to return and confer at greater length with me. Many other.bishops and ministers made the same promise, but no one came back. These men are carnally inclined, and do not understand the things of the Spirit; they have no charity, no faith, and do all by force, instead of by reason, which with you is the noblest of powers. Meanwhile the King was daily restricting the authority of the ministers, and vesting it in such of the bishops as showed themselves ready to obey the King's slightest wish, at the expense of humiliating the ministers. Thus a great schism has broken out among the ministers, part of whom favour the bishops and are subject to the King, and others are against them. The nobility, however, at the King's behest, are with the bishops, and the people, although opposed to the bishops in feeling, do not dare to move in the matter. This diversity of opinions among the ministers is the cause why so many, noble and simple, do not know which way to turn, or what religion to embrace. The ministers, whose lives are scandalous, and the bishops, who are equally bad, have enforced the laws of the land against Catholics, and will have them punctiliously carried out in the law courts. At first they used to appeal to the Bible, and to invoke the Word of God, but now they set aside all reasoning on religious questions, and appeal only to the laws of the land.

"After some weeks I began to suffer from cholic, caused by the want of fresh air, and the other very numerous inconveniences of the prison. The Father of Mercies and God of all Consolation was with me, and He consoled me in all my tribulation. Oh, how great is the abundance of divine sweetness which He communicates to those who sincerely love Him and steadfastly suffer for Him. Later, two magistrates came into the prison. Two officers, whose duty it is to accompany the criminal, waited outside the gates. Pale and weak as I was, and hardly able to walk, they led me through the town. The people crowded round, saying, 'Here is Jesuit Anderson.' I walked cheerfully on, smiling and erect, developing St Paul's idea for the benefit of the senators as I went along, 'We are made a spectacle to God, to angels, and to men. We are fools for Christ's sake, but you are wise in Christ.' I was brought before two of the chief bishops of the kingdom, him of St Andrews, and him of Glasgow, and the Lord High Steward, a man of much prudence and judgment, and of great weight in the kingdom. These men had received a new commission from the King to subject me to a most searching examination. The High Steward read the commission granted to him and the others. He then required an oath from me, by which I should bind myself to answer all questions directly and sincerely, dilating at some length on the nature and obligation of an oath.

"'My dear Lord Steward,' said I, 'there are four heads by which I could be examined by you four distinguished men. First, concerning my religion, which is Catholic and Roman, for which I appear here, and for which I am willing to die a thousand times if I could. As the time is now come for confessing it, that Jesus Christ may confess me before the Eternal Father, I promise to reply directly and sincerely to all questions touching faith. Secondly, I could be examined on all that involves the crime of high treason against the King's person, of which I take God to witness that I am most innocent, and I pledge myself equally to reply directly and sincerely, when questioned concerning this. Thirdly,

I might be examined on things of state—to wit, whether I mixed myself up in them. I promise equally, conscious of my innocence, to reply directly and sincerely. Fourthly, I may be questioned as to what places I have visited in Scotland, and with whom I have stayed. Touching these things I am unwilling to reply directly and to your purpose, nor will I take any oath to do so. The law and commandments of Christ our Lord, for whose sake I appear here, His example, the practice of the Catholic Church during these sixteen hundred years, forbid me to reveal these things.'

"'How now, Master Anderson,' said the Bishop of Glasgow, 'you attempt to quote Christ before us; Christ, who never gave any such example?'

"'With all respect, reverend lord,' replied I, 'Christ, when brought up before Annas, the bishop and high priest, and interrogated by him touching His disciples and His teaching, and with whom He had been, replied, as St John the Evangelist says, "I have spoken nothing in secret, but have taught openly; why askest thou Me? ask those who have heard me." Upon which "one of the servants gave him a blow," as the text says. In the Greek it is, εἷς τῶν ὑπηρετῶν ἔδωκεν ῥάπισμα τῷ 'Ιησοῦ. Whence we may see how old the quarrel is between Christ and the ministers. It is no wonder if they have persecuted our King (whom may God bless) from his youth, as he himself declared in his *Basilicon Doron*, when they could first strike Christ, the King of Kings.' The Lord High Steward smiled, for, like the King, he was no great friend to the ministers.

"'What Divine law is there which forbids the revelation of accomplices? I find none such in the Bible.'

"'The law,' I answered, 'which forbids us to give scandal to our neighbour, "Woe to the man by whom scandal cometh," which is a negative precept, and binds always and for ever, as theologians teach. Their lordships the bishops well know that St Paul says, "If to eat scandalize my brother, I will not eat flesh for ever;" and, writing at some length on offerings made to idols, he inculcates this very precept upon the Corinthians.'

"'Is it therefore lawful,' asked the Lord High Steward, 'for one guilty of a capital crime, or of high treason, to conceal the names of accomplices, whom he might scandalize if he revealed them?'

"'It is certainly not lawful,' I replied. 'They have sinned against the Divine law, or against the human law, which is founded upon the Divine, whence a grave injury might ensue to their neighbour; thus their names ought to be revealed, and the law of scandal does not bind in such a case.'

"'You have sinned against our human laws, which are surely founded upon the Divine law,' said the Lord High Steward.

"'Whatever I have done while in Scotland, in virtue of my office, I will prove from your own Bibles to be in conformity with the law of God. Let us open the Bible and we shall soon see whether your human laws are equally so. This is very certain, that any man of sense would prefer the laws made by eighty Scotch Kings during a thousand and forty years, to yours made under one King only, and only sixty years ago; especially when it is well known that the most learned, holiest, and wisest men flourished under these Kings, and assisted in making these laws.'

"'Hark, Master Anderson,' said the Lord High Steward, 'if you were at Rome, and knew that a minister was preaching there in secret, and had accomplices, would you not discover him to the Pope?'

Y

"'Certainly not,' I replied, 'but I should privately admonish him, according to the precept of charity, that he might reform himself. I should not cast him into prison, nor take everything from him, nor close up the windows of his cell, nor withdraw his necessary food bought by himself, nor leave him in bed, and sick almost to death, without any help, nor expose him to the rabble under a false charge of high treason; but, like the good Samaritan, I should pour out the oil of charity upon the prisoner and let him free.'

"'Nothing will do, Master Anderson,' said the Lord High Steward, 'but violence. So we must, by the King's command, try if we cannot wring out of you on the rack what we cannot get out of you by gentleness.'

"'Come pains, torments, crosses, gibbets, and all manner of tortures, I shall count them as roses, whereby I may gain Christ, and from whose charity I am certain (with the help of His grace) that neither life, nor death, nor torments, nor racks, can separate me, and I can do all things in Him who strengthens me.'

"I was removed a little way off, and they spoke among each other for a short time. Then I was recalled.

"'What do you hold,' said the Lord High Steward, 'concerning our King and his authority?'

"'I acknowledge him as King, and often and often, during these last twenty-six years, have I prayed on my knees that God the Father would bless him in every heavenly blessing. So I was taught by my uncle, the Bishop of Ross, of holy memory, who was always most faithful to Queen Mary, the martyr, the mother of the King.'

"The Lord Steward said much in praise of the Bishop of Ross, and then asked,

"'Has the Pope, I pray, any authority over our King?'

"'The same,' I answered, 'that he was acknowledged to have by eighty Scotch Kings, from Donald I. to Mary, the martyr, and by the Catholic Church during sixteen hundred and twenty years.'

"Finally, the Bishop of Glasgow said something about St Augustine's teaching that obedience was due to Cæsar. I assented, saying that subjects were bound in conscience to obey kings.

"'I call God to witness,' I added, 'that I have never taught anything else since my arrival in Scotland than that subjects ought to love King James, whom may God bless, ought often to pray for him, and to obey him in all things not against the Word of God. Thus the Scripture teaches, "Servants obey your masters in fear and trembling."'

"This answer much pleased them all, and spared me other questions, which would not have been to edification.

"'What do you say of the Gunpowder Plot?' asked the Lord High Steward.

"'I say it was a diabolical invention, contrary to the law of God or man. I consider it is a horrible crime to *lay hands* on God's anointed, and crimes of this kind have ever been condemned by the Holy Roman Church in the Councils.'

"'You shall not escape so, Master Anderson,' said the bishop. 'I will summon a witness well known to you.'

"This was the traitor, Alexander Boyd, who had received seventy-five pounds English for betraying me to the bishops and ministers. When he appeared before the commission, the bishop asked him,

"'Have you not heard Master Anderson speaking against the King and the royal authority, especially in taking the oath of allegiance?'

"'Never,' replied he, 'but I have always heard him speak with respect of the King, and when he gave thanks to God at table, I have often heard him praying for the King.' This was quite true. The bishop was disappointed, and remained silent. My examination had lasted almost three hours, for many other things had occurred, which, for brevity's sake, I omit, especially the long speeches of my adversaries, which were full of lies, calumnies, and inconsistencies.

"The Steward saw that I was hardly able to hold out any longer, for I was too weak to eat anything that day, and very humanely ordered the Sheriffs to lead me back to prison. Many ran up to look at me, and a Catholic youth saluted me from the windows on my way into prison. A great many imitated him in his profession of faith, saluting me, and weeping for grief.

"In the prison I passed my time as before, alone with God, and meditating upon the life of Christ. I never cease to marvel at the deluge of consolations which God pours forth upon him who willingly suffers for Christ's name. When his only desire is to suffer for Christ, and when his soul is evermore steeped in consolations, what, I ask, boots the actual suffering? The very pains borne for Christ, though hard to the flesh, and to human weakness, are acceptable to reason and sweet to Divine love. He who is enduring tribulation for Christ more easily forgets the vanities of the world. Severe suffering takes possession of him, disposes him for the visits of Divine grace, and causes him to be more frequently and more deeply penetrated by its presence. Wherefore St Paul, set in the midst of tribulations, says, 'The world is crucified to me, and I to the world.'

"Fifteen days afterwards the three ministers came to the prison of the city of Edinburgh, accompanied by the

Sheriffs and many others, to hold a discussion. They saluted me most civilly, as I came to meet them in the prison. Then the chief and most learned of them spoke to me much in this way:—

"'We know that you were born and brought up in Scotland, Master Anderson, and that you studied in this renowned city and university of Edinburgh. You favoured our religion then doubtless, and openly professed it.'

"'I was born in Scotland, and brought up in Moray, as is well known,' I replied, 'and I do not deny that I studied in this your college. When I was a child I understood as a child, I spoke as a child, I thought as a child. I remember to have had good Catholic parents. If I, at that tender age, had any external connection with you, I did it in ignorance, and have thus received mercy. You know those words of Christ, for whose sake I am suffering here from you, "No man can come to Me except the Father draw him;" the Father does not draw the unwilling, but the willing; but that he will not be drawn, and that he will, is by God's mercy. It is not by him willing, or by him unwilling, but by God having mercy.'

"'Listen, I pray,' said another and the younger of the ministers. He had been preparing arguments against the Pontifical authority for many days, and could hardly contain his impatience to begin. 'When Augustine came to convert the English, do you think, Master Anderson, that the Britons who resisted him, acknowledged the Pontifical authority? Do you suppose that he brought Papal bulls with him to England. Did the English receive him as sent by the Pope?'

"I looked at the fair and rosy face, and well-brushed head of the man who had apparently so good an opinion of himself.

"'You are setting up to be a doctor here, Master Thomas, and are taking upon yourself to ask a great many questions. I will ask you three in return, which, as a Scotchman, you will find very much to the purpose. What did St Jerome mean, I pray, when thus speaking of St Pelagius? "Pelagius," says Jerome, "was a monk over full of Scotch porridge."[1] Did the Scotch porridge do Jerome no harm? Secondly, Prosper of Aquitaine, the great historian of Palladius' Mission to Scotland, about the year 440, under Pope Celestine, states that Palladius was made first bishop of the Scots. It is well known that the Scotch were converted to the faith of Christ under the Pope and martyr St Victor and King Donald I., about the year 200. This Tertullian mentions as a note in his book against the Jews. Now, pray, did all Scotland continue to exist as a Christian country, for two hundred and forty years, without bishops or priests, sacraments or preachers of the word. You will surely tell, thirdly, how it was that Augustine, of whom you just now spoke, Master Thomas, preferred the Scotch to the Britons, as Bede says; when the Scotch as well as the Britons were irregular in the celebration of Easter?'

"'Let these things pass,' said the third minister, 'let us return to religious controversy, whereby the hearers may be edified.'

"'Do let us,' I answered.

"'How can you prove Purgatory out of the Bible, Master Anderson?' asked he.

"'I can do it, and most easily, Master William, but I have no doubts as to my religion; it is for it that I am suffering here; but I have doubts about yours, and I

---

[1] This comes in his commentaries, and is quoted by Baronius in Pelagio about the year 450.

know that you are come into this prison, for which I thank you, to prove to me that it is well founded, and upon the express Word of God. Your intention so to persuade me is very good. I beg that you will tell me what text of the Bible says in so many terms that there is no Purgatory, and I will give in.'

"'It is not necessary,' replied he, 'that I should give the exact words of Scripture; it is enough that it be deduced as a necessary consequence.'

"'Enough, and more than enough,' I retorted; 'but we have first to settle how a necessary consequence is to be distinguished, and this from Aristotle's logic, and not from the Bible. We must settle what is the difference between *consequens* and *consequentem*, and how a philosopher, like you, will distinguish *consequens* from *consequentiam*. By the time we have laid down what are the rules for discerning a necessary consequence, the listeners who do not understand will be fairly weary.'

"This is the method I have always adopted in all discussions with the ministers, especially when no Catholic was present, and none was ever allowed to be there, and I have always found it the best. I begin by showing their weakness, and thus obtaining that I may call on them to prove their point, instead of being obliged to prove mine. I studied the turn of mind of the man with whom I had to do, and his capacity, which can be found out from their own words, they are so puffed up. I always spoke with modesty, checking all anger and excitement, and said little, but with energy, prudence, and to the point. It is a great thing to have the Holy Scriptures ready to be brought in on all occasions, but with brevity, even during a discussion, when there is question of any religious matter. Presence of mind and watchfulness of oneself, and of the adversary, if possible, are also necessary. The whole thing should be commended to God, who alone can touch the heart of a heretic or an infidel, and all the praise and glory should be referred to Him. Nothing so much hinders the conversion of a soul as pride; and who, indeed, can make that clean which is conceived of an unclean spirit, unless He who alone is clean.

"Eight days after, the Bishop of Moray came into my prison, with three ministers, a sheriff, and others, to speak with me. We spoke of the Church, and her works, and, although they are as clear as daylight, he took refuge in her invisibility. When entangled by my arguments, he ingenuously confessed that the Protestant Church was invisible in Scotland during fifteen hundred and fifty-nine years; that her ministers were invisible; her sacraments invisible; the temples in which they met invisible; as also the wives they married and the children they begot. Everyone laughed excessively at this. After twenty days, I was brought up for the third time before the commission of six noblemen, for the King had increased their number. The chief was the Lord High Steward, who asked much the same questions as before. This examination lasted about three hours. The only difference was that they asked me if I would take the so-called oath of allegiance. I replied that I neither would nor could with a safe conscience. This gave rise to a discussion with the bishops upon conscience and its obligations. They then brought in the stock to put me to the torture. This is a cruel mode of punishment, similar to the rack. The legs of the sufferer are squeezed so tightly that the blood and marrow sometimes come out.

"'Do your work,' I said, 'this is your hour, and the power of darkness, αλλ αὕτη ὑμῶν ἐστὶν ἡ ὥρα, καὶ ἡ ἐξουσία τοῦ σκότους. Christ, for whom I suffer, says it were better for me to go into heaven without feet or legs, which your racks can take from me, than to be cast into hell with them. Think not, because you see me weak and ill, that you can frighten me with your threats, for "my strength is made perfect in infirmity." You sent to England and Ireland to make strict inquiry whether I was guilty of high treason, or had ever mixed up in the affairs of the State. Although this was false, and would have been most unbecoming in a religious, you found me guilty of it.'

"'By no means,' said the Archbishop of St Andrews.

"'Thank God,' I answered. 'I suffer therefore for religion only, and because I am a Jesuit, and most gladly do I suffer.'

"I was led back to prison, and there continued my accustomed exercises of piety, in which, as in my bonds, and in all my sufferings for Christ, I was ever mindful of the Society, my holy mother; mindful of your Paternity; and most mindful of those in the Society whom I have known most intimately; mindful of France, most dear to me as she is in this her deplorable state; and mindful of Germany, crushed by war. Let God arise, and let our enemies be scattered, that, freed from the hands of our enemies, we may serve Him in holiness and justice. I do not know what the King, whom may God bless, will determine concerning me; may whatever is good in the eyes of my Lord and Master be done, for He hath care of us. There is a report that I am to be treated with the utmost rigour. God grant it! Oh, happy hour, but short hour, in which eternity is gained. It is said that I shall at least be imprisoned for life in the Tower of London. Therefore it is that I have written these to your Paternity in haste and by stealth, and in fear and trembling.

"I embrace all my Fathers and Brothers in the bonds of charity and in Christ Jesus, and beg for their holy prayers. May God preserve your Paternity to us. Amen.

"Your Paternity's most unworthy servant and son,
"PATRICK ANDERSON."

"By stealth and in haste. From the prison of Edinburgh, August 24, 1620.

"I beg, for the sake of Christ our Lord, that these may not be shown to externs, because there are many false brethren who will go to you in sheep's clothing, but are inwardly ravening wolves. These heretics, wiser than the children of light, have their spies everywhere.
"FELICITER." [1]

Possibly King James had heard of the merits of Father Anderson as a man of learning, and felt some sympathy for him; perhaps the French ambassador made friendly intercession in his behalf. However it was, after the Father had suffered nine months' imprisonment, the King came to the resolution to show him some mercy. At his command the Privy Council liberated the Father from prison, with a suit of good clothes and some money in his pocket, on condition that he should leave Scotland and return no more; otherwise he would be liable to capital punishment. It was enjoined upon the provost and bailies of Edinburgh that they should "try and speir out some ship bown from the port of Leith towards France or Flanders; and when the ship is ready to lowse, that they tak the said Patrick Anderson furth of their Tolbooth, carry him to the ship, and deliver him to the skipper, and see him put aboard

[1] Stonyhurst Archives.

of the ship,[1] *with intimation made to him, that if he shall return without the King's license, it shall be capital to him."* [2]

Father Anderson retired to London, where he died quietly on the 24th of September 1624.

In May 1622, Father George Mortimer was detected within the house of one Haddow, in Glasgow, and he and Haddow were both taken into custody. The King lost no time in ordering a court of justice to be held in Glasgow for the trying of Haddow and his wife for the crime of resetting Jesuits, certifying that, if found guilty, they should be banished the kingdom, as the impunity of the offence " might hearten that wicked and pernicious sort of people more bauldly to go on in perverting good subjects in religion, and withdrawing them from their dutiful obedience to us." He at the same time wrote to the principal ecclesiastical authorities, desiring them to consult about the best means of checking the present "new growth of popery," that "thereby the world may see that we strike with the sword of justice equally against the papist and puritan; that thereby no just imputation may be laid upon our proceedings as a cause of the increase of popery."

In September, we learn that Mortimer lay a prisoner at Glasgow, " so heavily diseased, as it is feared he shall hardly if ever escape." The King—" because we do not desire the lives of ony of that sort of people, if we may be secured from ony harm which they might do by the perversion of ony of our guid subjects in their duty to God and us "—was now pleased to order that he should be committed to some ship sailing to a foreign port, " with certification to him, that if at any time hereafter he shall return, it will be capital unto him."

[1] Acts of the Privy Council held at Edinburgh 13th February 1621.
[2] Original letters relating to ecclesiastical affairs, vol. ii. p. 648.

This and some other instances of levity towards Catholics in Scotland gave offence to zealous Presbyterians, and there arose murmurs to the King's prejudice. James, however, gave himself with increased energy to carry out his arrangements for the "Spanish Match." "He had resolved," he says, "to mitigate the severity of those laws which inflict on Catholics any penalty in respect of their religion. He further intended to grant pardons and dispensations to such of his subjects and Romish Catholics as within the space of five years shall apply for the same."[1] In accordance (as it would seem) with these promises, Popish recusants to the number (it is said) of four thousand were liberated from prison. The judges were directed to "make no niceness or difficulty," to extend the royal favour to all such papists as are in prison for any Church recusancy whatsoever; or for refusing the oath of supremacy, or for dispersing Popish books, or for hearing or saying Mass, or any other point of recusancy.[2]

The following letter shows how the long afflicted Catholics were induced to believe that the iron rule under which they had been living for so many years had at last past away.

Father William Leslie to Father Vitelleschi, General of the Society of Jesus.

Feb. 4, 1623.

"VERY REVEREND FATHER—P.C.,—There are only four of us in all this kingdom,—two in the north and two in the south,—and we have almost more work on our hands than we can attend to. If the marriage of our

[1] MS. Bodl. Tanner, 73, fol. 368.
[2] R. O. Dom. cxxxii. n. 84, Aug. 2, 1622.

Prince with the daughter of the Spanish King has any good effects, as is here thought likely, and if favour is shown to the Catholics, then all the Scottish priests belonging to our Society, who are fit for this mission, should be sent here. Both the nobles and the common people are now much better affected towards the Catholic faith than was the case formerly, the more so as they witness the increasing alienation between the party of the bishops and the Puritans, about which I have already written to your Paternity. We are likely, therefore, before long to want a multitude of labourers for this hitherto neglected vineyard. Would that the Holy Father, the Vicar of Christ on earth, out of his charity to God and pastoral solicitude, might duly weigh this, for if he did, he would certainly provide men to labour among this nation, so well affected as it is to the faith of its forefathers and the Apostolic See. The Catholic religion is in great peril for want of men, and it would be sad if a nation, which has flourished for so many centuries with the integrity of its faith inviolate, should fall away now under the assaults of heresy. Yet this is what will certainly happen, in my judgment, so untiring is the vigilance of the heretics, and so great their power, unless diligent and early efforts are made to supply men to work in Scotland. I do what I can, but cannot satisfy all the calls upon me. We join in greetings to our brethren, and pray the Lord of the harvest to send them hither.

"WILLIAM LESLIE."[1]

For some time it seemed as if the Spanish match would succeed, and in 1623, Charles, Prince of Wales, actually went to the Court of Spain, along with Buckingham, to prosecute his suit. Buckingham, however, having quarrelled with the leading men, and given great

[1] Latin MS., Stonyhurst Archives, vol. Scotia.

offence to the ladies of the Spanish Court, the negotiation ultimately failed. A new treaty of marriage was immediately set on foot to console James for the failure of that with Spain, and Buckingham busied himself in trafficking for a marriage between Charles and the Princess Henrietta Maria of France. She was the youngest daughter of the last King, in her fourteenth year, and distinguished by the beauty of her features, and the elegance of her figure. The Pope, Urban VIII., and Philip of Spain made several attempts to dissuade Louis XIII. from giving his consent to a marriage which caused much indignation in England, and was likely to alienate the English people more than ever from the Holy See. The King of France, yielding to the influence and the reasoning of his mother, who represented the marriage as a measure likely to prove most beneficial to France, gave his consent. Cardinal de Richelieu, aware that James had fixed his heart on the match, and that the power of Buckingham depended on the success of the treaty, required that the King of England, in a secret engagement signed by himself, his son, and a secretary of state, should promise to grant to his Catholic subjects, that all Catholics imprisoned for religion should be discharged, and that for the future they should suffer no molestation on account of the private and peaceable exercise of their worship.[1]

It was at this juncture that James instructed the Lord Chancellor Hay to put a stop to the persecution in the country.[2] This was James' last act in connection with the Catholic Church in Scotland. A few weeks later, after a short indisposition, he expired on the 27th March 1625, in the fifty-ninth year of his age.

[1] Hardwicke Papers, i. 547-561.
[2] Letters and State papers during the reign of King James VI. Edinburgh, 1838, 4to, p. 388.

NOTES AND ILLUSTRATIONS.

I.

Sir Walter Lindsay of Balgawies, younger son of David of Edzell, ninth Earl of Crawford, and a convert to Catholicism,[1] seems to have been sent on a mission to Spain even before the death of Queen Mary. A paper, entitled "*The Content of the Discourse made by Mr Walter Lindsay of Balgays, put in Spanish and in print,*" is preserved among the Cottonian MSS.[2] It is but a summary of the original Narrative, a translation of which is here appended:[3]—

ACCOUNT OF THE PRESENT STATE OF THE CATHOLIC RELIGION IN THE REALM OF SCOTLAND, IN THE YEAR OF OUR LORD ONE THOUSAND FIVE HUNDRED AND NINETY-FOUR. [By Sir Walter Lindsay of Balgawies.]

"I premise by stating that the King of Scotland is possessed of good natural abilities, and is now twenty-six years of age. He was reared in the heretical doctrine of Calvin, which he now holds, nevertheless he is mistrusted by the Scotch heretics and the Queen of England; and the Catholics, recollecting his pious mother, and trusting in his natu-

---

[1] Lord Crawford, described in 1583 as "in religion unsettled" ("Lives of the Lindsays," vol. i. p. 300), though always a favourer of the French or Catholic interest, had, between that year and 1589, been converted to the Roman Catholic faith.—("Lives of the Lindsays," i. p. 312.)

His brother, Sir James Lindsay, "exercised great authority at Court, and James VI. would have advanced him to high dignity and office, and great emoluments, but he abandoned all for conscience' sake, and preferred leaving his native country rather than give up his religion."—(Letter of Fr. Robert Abercromby, Dundee, 1st Aug. 1598. Archives, S.J.).

[2] Calig. C.IX. 477. The date 1586 is wrong. It should be 1594.

[3] A copy is preserved in Blairs College Library, Aberdeenshire.

rally good disposition, hope that he will one day open the gate to the light of truth. In general, the inhabitants of the towns and maritime districts hold heretical opinions; there reside the preachers, calling themselves ministers, who are continually seeking to fortify their positions, so as to weigh more and more on the Government, but their movements are jealously watched by the King and nobles, who are in general favourably disposed towards the Catholic faith, as are also the villagers and labourers. By the law of the land, and in virtue of their inheritance, the nobles form the King's council, in which they have a right to vote when at Court, unless found guilty of treason, and thus they have more influence, and the Crown less authority, than is the case in other kingdoms.

"The preachers meet on Fridays, and they term their assembly or congregation, church and presbytery, affirming that it is superior to the King's jurisdiction, and that it is supreme in cases of religion or ecclesiastical government, differing in that respect from their colleagues in England, who acknowledge the Queen's ecclesiastical supremacy.

"Although the King of Scotland dislikes them, he stands in awe of the ministers, in consequence of the prominent position and authority they have assumed, and because they are favoured by the Queen of England; things have come to such a pass that they excommunicate the nobles when they refuse to comply with their heretical mandates, and have actually threatened to excommunicate the King himself.

"Some years since the ministers put forth certain heretical articles, denying the principal mysteries of our holy Catholic religion, which they requested the King and his subjects to sign, in token of obedience and submission, and as a public profession of their faith and creed, in the same way as in England one might attend a sectarian place of worship, or swear that the Queen is head of the Church. In order to please the King and gratify the ministers, the articles were signed by many persons who thought that their compliance with the request was of less importance and less displeasing to God than they afterwards knew to be the case, after conferring with Father James Gordon, Father William Crichton, and other Fathers of the Society of Jesus, sent to Scotland by Gregory the Thirteenth, of blessed memory, who are now in that kingdom, and with the Bishop of Dunblane, who gave up his bishopric to become a Carthusian friar, and was sent by Sixtus the Fifth to his native land, and, after remaining there disguised for several months with much edification and spiritual advantage, ended his life at Rome in the odour of sanctity; and lastly, through the agency of certain priests of English seminaries, who, being forced to leave England in consequence of the rigorous decrees directed against them in the year 1591, and taking into account the similarity of language, took refuge in the neighbouring country of Scotland, by the special providence of God our Lord, who from the perversity of His enemies derives glory for Himself and good for His Church, as appears by the sequel. Convinced that they had given offence to God, and incurred grave sin by signing the articles, the Laird of Fintry and Lord Balgawies were the first to recant and oppose the ministers. The Laird of Fintry was beheaded in Edinburgh by command of the King, and became a glorious martyr. Refusing to submit to laws put in force by heretical judges, the other nobleman withstood the ministers for a long time with the help of an English priest, named Ingram[1] (afterwards martyred in England), who lived in his house as chaplain, said Mass, and preached sermons, which the noble lord invited heretics and others to attend, not without signal benefit, for many became converted to our holy faith.

"Seeing this, the ministers wrung from the King a deed, enabling them to apprehend the nobleman on a charge of treason, as a traitor excommunicated two or three years pre-

---

[1] John Ingram, son of —— Ingram, Esq., of Stoke, in the county of Hereford, "having employed his travel, since his mission from the Seminary, in the country of Scotland, for the restoring of souls out of heresy unto the unity of the Catholic Church, upon some urgent occasion had been in England, and returning back again had entered into a boat to pass over the river Tweed into Scotland (November 25, 1593), was stayed by the keepers of Norham Castle, apprehended, and carried to Newcastle, and put in a prison called the New Gate."—("The Troubles of our Catholic Forefathers related by Themselves." Third Series. Edited by John Morris, S.J., p. 200.) John Ingram was executed at Gateside-head, on the 26th of July 1594.

viously; and he gave them a blank warrant, authorising them to arrest the nobleman, on condition of their finding a person to execute it. We should here remark that the Scotch, especially the nobles, are accustomed to act in concert, so that every one sides with his family, consequently an offence given to a member of a family is resented by the whole of his house; and in cases of bloodshed, vengeance is not confined to the guilty person, but involves the whole family and lineage of the transgressor. That law and custom, invented by Satan to shed innocent blood, entered Scotland with heresy, which is wont to produce such fruit, and diffused itself over the whole country. But as the wisdom and goodness of the Almighty are infinite, God has deigned to convert the poison into a remedy, and to use the adversary's device to introduce the Catholic religion.

"In consequence of this custom, Lord Walter Lindsay, Baron Balgawies, being son of the Earl of Crawford of the royal family, and nearly related to two or three earls and many other Scotch noblemen, not only did no one dare to exhibit the warrant or to take him into custody, but when the ministers, after having excommunicated certain persons, and threatened them with severe punishment for having dined with an excommunicated recusant, were assembled for the purpose of having him arrested, Lord Balgawies, accompanied by a numerous escort of friends and relations, came into the room where the preachers were plotting, and after making them beg his pardon and promise that they would molest no one on his account, he insisted on their partaking of a sumptuous banquet prepared for them. He had come for the purpose of making short work with them, but, in deference to the representations of his friends and kinsfolk, he contented himself with this proof of their submission, and did them no harm.

"Encouraged by this example, the Earls of Huntly, Errol, and Angus, and many other noblemen and gentlemen, openly professed themselves Catholics. The ministers had recourse to the Queen of England, the Catholics appealed to the Pope and to the King of Spain, and sent Mr George Carr to Spain;

but the English ambassador at Madrid, having got wind of his departure, caused the ship and despatches to be seized; and the ministers, after inserting the letters to the King of Spain, and many others, previously addressed to the Duke of Parma and others, in a pamphlet of theirs, entitled "Treason of the Scotch Papists revealed," prevailed on the King to have them proclaimed traitors; and, by the advice of Cecil, Treasurer of England, a law was passed, declaring guilty of high treason any one who should celebrate Mass or harbour a priest. But, as the Crown is less powerful in Scotland than in England, the law proved beneficial to the country, inasmuch as it stirred up numbers to profess their creed and unite in defence of their faith.

"The ministers have excommunicated the Earls of Huntly, Errol, and Angus, and many other noblemen, and the King in Parliament has pronounced them rebels, and has ordered their goods and chattels to be confiscated; but they hold their own by the strong arm, they make head against the heretics, and they have entered towns, and have had some obnoxious ministers beaten with ropes, in consequence of which the others have thought fit to decamp, and in the hurry-scurry and confusion of a nocturnal flitting, some have disappeared, and their place has known them no more.

"The King threatens the allied nobles, but does not act against them; the ministers hold their peace in fear and trembling, and regret having pushed matters so far, for every day the league receives fresh accessions; the heretics put their faith in the Queen of England, and hope she will send them troops.

"A few months since, his Holiness Pope Clement the Eighth, moved by the zeal and compassion which, as Pontiff, he feels for the whole Church, wrote to the King of Scotland, to exhort him to embrace the Catholic faith, and sent him forty thousand ducats, promising him a monthly allowance of ten thousand ducats, on condition of his protecting the Catholics, and allowing them to remain unmolested in the exercise of their faith. When the vessel from Flanders arrived at Aberdeen with the Pope's Nuncio, bearing the letters and money, accompanied by Father Gordon, of the Society of Jesus, on his return from Rome, where he had gone to inform his Holiness of the state of affairs in Scotland, with several other Scotchmen and three English priests, the heretics were afraid to seize Father Gordon, uncle of the Earl of Huntly, nor did they interfere with the Scotchmen, but they seized the Nuncio, money and letters, and detained the English priests, on the strength of a decree of the King, that no English subject should enter or leave Scotland without a passport from the English Government or embassy.

"When the Earls of Errol and Angus heard that the Nuncio and priests had been imprisoned, they immediately took measures to deliver the captives, for fear lest they should be removed to another place, and being joined within three days by the Earl of Huntly at the head of a large force, they attacked the town and set fire to it in four places, in consequence of which the heretics were only too glad to escape destruction on condition of releasing their captives, and promising to assist the Catholics. Seeing how little dependance they can place on the King, the nobles in league have used the money, their soldiers keep the field and hold possession of the northern half of Scotland, not to mention a great number of Catholics who live peaceably in the other districts.

"Many remarkable events have occurred here, tending to encourage the adherents of the true faith, and many signal visitations of providence have befallen persons who have submitted to the ministers, which has caused many conversions and has encouraged timid dissemblers to avow their creed openly. It is customary with the Scotch Catholics to draw lots on St Valentine's day in order to determine who shall be their guardian saint and the object of their especial care during the following year. After the Earl of Huntly had prepared himself by devout confession and communion for celebrating the festival of St Lawrence, who was to be his patron that year, the Earl was listening to the sermon when he was informed that his enemy the Earl of Argyll, taking advantage of the censure of the ministers and royal proclamation, had marched six or seven leagues into his dominions, pillaging and burning villages and farms, harrying cattle and spoiling the land. As soon as he had finished his devotions, the Earl and thirty-six followers rode off in pursuit of the enemy over the mountain pass by which they were retiring, and having come up with them near some lakes, the Earl, being afraid lest the troopers driving the cattle should reach a morass where the horses might be in danger of sinking, assailed the enemy's rearguard single handed, slaying right and left, until the arrival of his followers, who discomfited their adversaries miraculously, for they were only thirty-six, and the hostile force more than fifteen hundred ; they put more than five hundred to death, and recovered the whole of the spoil, having only one man hurt, though all the horses were killed. The heretics were much dismayed by this success, and the King caused the details of the affair to be related to him several times, and would not believe them until they were confirmed by some of the vanquished invaders. The Earl said that he never felt so courageous in all his life; it seemed as if nothing could resist him ; while his followers declared the same. This victory, which led to many conversions, encouraged the Earl to fight for God's cause, and many of his vassals who had rebelled against him, in consequence of the censure of the ministers and the royal proclamation, returned to his service.

"Great alarm was caused by a no less marvellous event which befell the Earl of Morton, who, although a Catholic, was persuaded by his kinsfolk and relations to treat with the ministers and sign the articles contrary to our holy faith. While he was in this frame of mind, sitting alone in his room about twelve o'clock, he had a vision of an angel in the form of a young man, who warned him : Earl, do not comply with the advice of your relations, for if you sign the articles you will lose your right hand and perish miserably. Moved by these words, the Earl again fastened round his neck a gold crucifix and Agnus Dei which he used to wear and had laid aside when he gave up his resolution of serving God as a good Catholic, and said to his chief advisers that they had led him astray. He told them of the angel's visit and of his repentance, and in order that God's great mercy might be ever known and thankfully acknowledged by his lineage, he caused an angel to be represented in his ancestral coat-of-arms, declared himself opposed to the ministers, and refused to sign the articles. Subsequently, however, owing to the long continued and persevering representations of his relations, after the King had made him great offers and had appointed him his lieutenant-general, the unhappy noble again consented to sign the articles, but he did not live long to exercise his new office, for some time afterwards, being commissioned by the King to arrest Baron Johnston, with five thousand soldiers, he met with the end foretold him by the angel, as we shall presently relate.

"On the approach of the Earl of Morton, the Baron took advantage of his position, and arranged his band of six hundred horsemen in three separate companies, in the form of a triangle, so as to allow the vanguard of the Earl's forces to penetrate the centre of his troops, on which the Baron attacked the Earl's squadron in flank so violently that, breaking through the pikemen and musketeers, with one blow he cut off his right hand, and with another he broke his leg and unhorsed him, after which he was killed, on which the assailing forces took to flight, the Baron gained the day, and it became evident to all that the Earl had perished by the judgment of God.

"Lord Claud Hamilton, youngest son of the Duke of Chatellerault, signed the articles, aware that he was doing wrong, but yielding to the persuasion of the ministers and of his wife and her relations, being desirous moreover to gain favour with the King. Being seated one day at dinner, while the Gospel was being read, as is the custom in Scotland, when the reader repeated the words, 'Whosoever denieth Me before men, I will deny him before my Father,' Lord Claud rose from his seat and tried to cut his wife's throat, saying that it was in consequence of her and her brothers' persuasions that he had renounced his faith and lost his soul. For many days afterwards he remained raving mad, so that it was necessary to bind him with cords, and even now he has to be watched, and has not entirely recovered his reason.[1]

"The example of the house of Hamilton is an awful warning to men to look to themselves and to their families, bidding them fear the just judgments and chastisements of God, which, though they may delay, are sure to fall on the guilty. The Duke of Chatellerault, head of the family, one of the noblest and bravest knights that Scotland has produced for many years, was esteemed and prospered in Scotland and in France, as long as he served God and the Catholic faith. But when the Queen of England had deluded him into believing that she was willing to marry his son the Earl of Arran; when the Duke and Earl came to Scotland with their adherents, and by the help of the English dethroned the Queen Regent Dowager, widow of James the Fifth, sister of the Duke of Guise, and mother of Queen Mary, who about this time suffered martyrdom in England; and when the Duke of Chatellerault made himself Regent of Scotland, and turned out the French garrisons, laying hands, he and his accomplices, on the revenues and possessions of the Church, and demolishing churches and monasteries; in the midst of his seeming prosperity he began to feel the weight of God's judgments on himself and his family. Pierced with poignant grief and sorrow upon seeing how he had been deceived by the Queen, who had craftily induced him to offend God and ruin his native land, the Earl went out of his mind, and at the present time is living in a state of idiocy. The Duke himself, being of the blood royal, thought by changing his religion, and by arranging the marriage which he desired, to make himself lord of Scotland and England, but he too saw himself deposed, all his family possessions confiscated, and his whole kindred proclaimed traitors by those very men who for his sake had turned heretics; to which punishments God

---

[1] Lord Claud Hamilton had been received into the Church by Fr. James Tyrie in 1580. His son, James Hamilton, Earl of Abercorn, was a Roman Catholic. His grandson, James Hamilton, second Earl of Abercorn, was, in 1649, excommunicated by the General Assembly of the Church of Scotland, and ordered out of the kingdom. He died about 1670.

our Lord added that he lived to see all his sons lose their reason, with the exception of Lord Claud Hamilton, who has become insane since, and thus overwhelmed by anguish and affliction, he ended his wretched life in dishonour, after incurring, as is to be feared, the Divine displeasure, that he might be a warning, not only to his own countrymen, but to powerful noblemen in other lands.

"To conclude this sketch of the present religious condition of the realm of Scotland as far as it concerns our holy faith, I may add that whereas there has existed in times past amongst English and Scotch a national enmity and hatred, which has led to the most cruel wars, and has been productive of infinite bloodshed, by the grace of God our Lord there is now such mutual love and union between the Catholics of England and Scotland, that in persecutions and afflictions they assist one another with the greatest charity and goodwill. I have thought it right to note this, in order to show how much the grace of God can effect when it is received in earnest; and as, in the days of the primitive Church, it caused all the faithful to be animated by one heart and one soul (*cor unum et anima una*), so the present unanimity between the Catholics of both countries may well lead us to hope that great good may result therefrom in regard to the glory of God, the welfare of souls, and the prosperity of our holy Catholic faith in those lands."

II.

THE PRESENT STATE OF THE NOBILITY IN SCOTLAND, 1st July 1592.

(State-Paper Office. "Scotland Eliz.," vol. xliii. No. 53, indorsed: "Of the Nobility in Scotland." Burghley had studied the paper, and marked the names of the Papists. Quoted by Tytler, vol. ix. p. 376.)

LIST OF THE CATHOLIC NOBILITY.

EARLS.

"HUNTLY (GORDON). *Of thirty-three years. His mother, daughter to the Duke Hamilton. Married the now Duke of Lennox's sister. His house, Strathbogy.*

"CRAWFORD (LINDSAY). *Of thirty-five years. His mother, daughter to the Earl Marshall. Married first the Lord Drummond's daughter, and now the Earl of Athol's sister. His house, Finhaven.*

See above, p. 351, footnote 1.

"ERROL (HAY). *Of thirty-one years. His mother, Keith, daughter to the Earl Marshall. Married first the Regent Murray's daughter, next Athol's sister, and now hath to wife Morton's daughter. His house, Slanes.*"

The Earl of Errol, as a "recusant Papist," was only enabled to remain in his country on a condition that he should not pass beyond a small circle around his own castle in Aberdeenshire. Being embarrassed by debt, and troubled by his creditors, he found himself constrained to take some legal steps " for the provision of his mony young children, and settling of some good course for the estate of his house." He therefore got a formal licence (Nov. 9, 1615), " to repair to Edinburgh, and there to remain in some lodging, not kything ony way in *daylight upon the heich street*, for ten days after the 20th of November."—(P. C. R.).

Deprived of his possession, the Earl was compelled to eat the bread of exile. Nor was he more secure abroad than at home. Shortly after his arrival in Holland, where he was carried by contrary winds, as he was about to make his way into Flanders, disguised as a menial, suspicions were excited by his appearance and manner, and he fell into the hands of the emissaries of Queen Elizabeth, to whom he was delivered contrary to the law of nations, and he would assuredly have been put to death if, the day before the sailing of the vessel on which he was to embark, the Earl had not invited his captors to a sumptuous banquet, during which, throwing himself on his bed, as though he had taken too much wine, he contrived to intoxicate his guardians so completely that he managed to escape unperceived by a back door, leaving his servants to complete the work he had begun, and prevent his escape from being discovered by the retinue of the English officials. He then went on board a Scotch vessel which happened to be in waiting, and was restored to his family and friends.

After James' accession to the throne of England, at the instigation of the crafty Cecil, a fearful storm of religious persecution burst forth against Catholics. Errol was imprisoned in the castle of Edinburgh, acquiring great merit, and bequeathing to others a bright example of constancy in confessing the true faith. He was still alive in 1628.—(Conn. De Duplici Statu Religionis apud Scotos, p. 153.)

" MONTROSE (GRAHAM). *Of forty-nine years. His mother, daughter of the Lord Fleming. Married the Lord Drummond's sister. Auld Montrose, in Angus.*

LORDS.

" SETON. *Of forty years. His mother, daughter to Sir Wm. Hamilton (of Sanquhar). His wife is Montgomery, the Earl's aunt. His house, Seaton.*"

George, fifth Lord Seton, a man whose diplomatic talents

and unshaken loyalty had recommended him, in the first instance, to Mary, and afterwards to James VI., was employed during the greater part of his life in important embassies to the different Courts of Europe.

Hay, in his MS. collections, has preserved a curious anecdote of George, fifth Lord Seton. "After the battle of Langsyde," says he, "the said George, Lord Seton, was forced to fly to Flanders, and was there in exile two years, and drove a waggon of four horses for his livelihood. His picture, in that condition, I have seen vividly painted upon the north end of the long gallery at Seton, now overlaid with timber."—("Hay's Coll.," vol. iii. p. 261, Advocate's Library. Cf. Tytler's "Life of Craig," p. 230.)

Alexander Seton, fourth son of George Lord Seton, and Isabel Hamilton, had resided long at Rome, where he was much esteemed for his virtue and piety, and on his return to Scotland he was held in high honour, no less on account of his illustrious origin than for his prudence. He was much loved by the King, from whom he received valuable grants of land.[1] After having been appointed President of the High Court of Justice, he subsequently became Chancellor of Scotland, in which high office he acquired such a wide-spread reputation for justice and integrity that, on the occasion of his funeral, all classes vied with one another in exhibiting every mark of respect and sorrow for the loss the nation had sustained. Four years before his death, in presence of a numerous assembly of Catholics, attended by the ringleaders of the Puritan faction and many other Protestants, after affirming that he had never ceased to hold the doctrine of the orthodox Church, he declared that nothing gave him greater pain than to recollect how he had shown himself lukewarm and remiss in his profession of faith, in order to ingratiate himself with his Sovereign. When he had thus spoken with tears in his eyes, he called the assembly to witness that he would die in the profession of the Roman Catholic faith.—(Conn. De Duplici Statu Religionis apud Scotos, p. 154.)

[1] Queen Mary stood godmother to him at the font; on which occasion she presented to him as "one godbairne gift the lands of Pluscarty, in Moray."

"LIVINGSTON (*surname*, LEVINGSTON). *Of sixty-one years. His mother, daughter of umquhile Earl of Morton. His wife, the Lord Fleming's sister. Calendar.*"

Alexander, seventh Lord Livingstone. He married Dame Eleanor Hay, only daughter of Andrew, seventh Earl of Errol. The charge of the young Princess Elizabeth was entrusted to the care of Lady Livingstone. Among the causes assigned, in the General Assembly in May 1601, "of the defection from the puritie of true religion," one was, "the educatioun of his Majesties childrein in the companie of profest and obstinat Papists, such as, the Ladie Livingstoun."

"MAXWELL (*surname*, MAXWELL). *Of forty-one years. His mother, daughter of the Earl of Morton that preceded the Regent. His wife, Douglas, sister to the Earl of Angus.*"

"HARRIS (*surname*, MAXWELL). *Of thirty-seven years. His mother, Harris, by whom he had the lordship. His wife is the sister of Newbottle. His house, Terragles.*"

"SANQUHAR (*surname*, CHRICHTON). *Of twenty-four years. His mother, daughter of Drumlanrig. Unmarried. His house, Sanquhar.*"

"GRAY. *Of fifty-four years. His mother, the Lord Ogilvy's daughter. His wife, the Lord Ruthven's sister. Fowlis.*"

Andrew, eighth Lord Gray, was lieutenant of the Gens-d'armes Ecossais in France, under Lord Gordon, 1624, and was much engaged in the wars there.

He was banished the kingdom by parliament, never to return on pain of death, for being with Montrose, 6th October 1645; but this does not appear to have been carried into effect. He was excommunicated by commission of the General Assembly, 1649, on account of his being a Roman Catholic, and had a fine of £1500 imposed on him by Cromwell's act of grace and pardon, 1654. . . .

His son Patrick, Master of Gray, was killed at the siege of a town in France.—("Wood's Peerage," p. 672).

"OGILVY. *Of fifty-one years. His mother, Campbell of Caddell. His wife, the Lord Forbes' daughter. No castle, but the B. of Brichen's house.*

"FLEMING. *Of twenty-five years. His mother, daughter of the Master of Ross. His wife, the Earl of Montrose's daughter. Bigger.*

"URQUHART (*surname*, SEATON). *Of thirty-five years. The Lord Seaton's brother. His wife, the Lord Drummond's daughter. Founded on the Priory of Pluscardy.*"

To Burghley's list should be added the following names of Catholic noblemen.

EARL OF ANGUS.

The Earl of Angus, one of the three Catholic lords whose correspondence with Spain caused so much trouble in 1592, had since lived at home in quietness and obedience. In 1608 we find his lordship pleading that, to avoid imprisonment for his religion, he might be allowed to go into exile. In a letter to the King, August 10, 1608, adverting to the fact of the General Assembly having given forth an act for his immediate excommunication, he says: "What grief and sorrow this brings to my heart, God knows; because my greatest care has ever been, and sall be, that I might end my days (whilk, I am persuaded, will not be many) at peace with God, and in your Majesty's obedience. . . . The permission whilk of grace only I crave (gif it please not your hieness to ease me with a better), is either to depart this country . . . with surety not to return, or else that it wold please your majesty to confine me in ane of mine awn houses, and so many miles about the same, where I am glad to live as ane private subject, and never to meddle me with public affairs, but by your majesty's direction."

Compelled to leave his country, Angus took refuge in France, and established himself in Paris, where he ended his days in the exercise of solid piety.

"He was so fond of prayer," wrote an eye-witness, "that he assisted every day at the Canonical Hours in the Abbey Church of St Germain des Prés. The church doors being shut at Matins, he rose and recited the office at midnight by himself, and often spent two hours at a time in meditation. He observed the fasts and commandments of the Church with such exactitude that he would rather have died than transgressed in these respects without great necessity. Such a holy life won for him the esteem and respect of every one, and it was in these dispositions that he died in the fifty-seventh year of his age."[1]

EARL OF ARGYLL.

Archibald, seventh Earl of Argyll, succeeded his father, 1584, being then under age. His lordship's first public appearance was in 1594, when the Catholic Earls of Huntly and Errol, who had been convicted of high treason, and their estates forfeited, raised a rebellion against King James VI. The Earl of Argyll, then a gallant young man of eighteen, was appointed the King's lieutenant to go against the rebels. They encountered at Glenlivat, on the 3d of October 1594.[2]

After the conflict at Glenlivat, the Earl of Argyll remained some time in Rome, and became a Catholic. On his return to Scotland, he was reconciled with Huntly, and their friendship was cemented by the betrothment of Argyll's daughter to Huntly's son.

The Earl concealed for a long time his change of religion,

---

[1] (T. du Breul, *Théatre des Antiquités de Paris.* Paris, 1639, 4to, p. 261). Cf. "*Discours funebre sur la mort de feu M. Le Comte d'Anguys, seigneur écossais, décédé à Paris, où il estuit réfugié pour y avoir libre exercice de la religion Catholique,*" Paris, 1611.

[2] "Wood's Peerage," vol. i. p. 93. Cf. A faithful narrative of the great and miraculous victory obtained by George Gordon, Earl of Huntly, and Francis Hay, Earl of Errol, Catholic noblemen, over Archibald Campbell, Earl of Argyll, lieutenant, at Strathaven, 3d October 1594. "Scottish Poems of the 16th century," edited by Dalyell, i. 136. Edinburgh, 1801.

but King James having discovered it, he obliged Argyll to make over all his estates to his son, reserving only such a provision for himself as might support him.

In 1618 he left Scotland, and entered the service of the King of Spain, and distinguished himself in the war against Holland.

On the death of his first wife, the Earl had married again at St Botolph's, Bishopsgate, London, in 1610, Anne Cornwallis,[1] a Roman Catholic. Three of the Earl's daughters, "*Victoria de Campbell d'Argyle,*" the *Honourable Lady Barbara Campbell,* and Dame Melchiora Campbell, became Benedictine nuns in Bruxelles.

LORD ROBERT SEMPLE, COLONEL SEMPLE, &c.

In September 1560, "was the Castell of Sempill[2] besieged and tane, because the Lord thairof disobeyed the lawes and ordinances of the Counsall in many thingis and especiallie in that, that he wold manteane the idolatrie of the Messe."

The Earl of Arran having taken possession of Castle Semple, Lord Semple took refuge in France.[3] On the 6th of May 1573, "Robert, Lord Semple, was denounced and put to the horne, for intruding Sir Johnne Hamilton, a Papist priest, in the vicarage of Eastwood."[4]

On the 20th Aug. 1588, order was issued by the Privy

---

[1] She was the daughter of Sir William Cornwallis, of Brome, ancestor of the Earl of Cornwallis. She published, in 1622, a Spanish translation of the Confessions of St Augustin: "El Alma del Incomparable S. Augustin, sacada del cuerpo de sus Confessiones." Antverpiæ, 1622, 4to. (Archives of Lille. Cf. "Historia Sacra . . . Archiepiscopatus Mechliniensis Cornelii van Gestel," 2 vols. fol. Hagæ, 1725.)

[2] The castle surrendered about the 21st of October 1561. "R. O. Scotland Eliz.," vol. v. No. 39.

Castle Semple is in the parish of Lochwinnoch, and county of Renfrew, and stood at the northern end of the lake called Lochwinnoch, from which the parish derived its name; it was demolished in the year 1735, and replaced by a modern mansion.—(D. Laing, "Works of Knox," vol. ii. p. 130.)

[3] "Diurnal of Occurrents," pp. 62, 63. "R. O. Scotland Elizabeth," vol. vii. No. 40.

[4] "Register of the Privy Council," vol. ii. p. 229.

Council against resetting Captain Semple, who had recently come on a " pretended" mission from the Prince of Parma, and had been trafficking treasonably with his Majesty's subjects " for alienating thair myndis frome his Hienes obedience, and overthraw of the trew religioun."[1]

Captain William Semple was the son of the third Earl of Semple. He was born in 1546, and resided for some years in the Court of Mary Stuart. When that unfortunate Princess fled into England from her rebellious subjects, he also forsook his native country, and passing into Belgium, served for some time under the Prince of Orange, deceived, it would seem, by the professions of loyalty with which that Prince at first strove to conceal his rebellion. In 1573, Mary Stuart, from her prison in England, was enabled, through the agency of John Seaton, son of the Earl of Winton, to undeceive him, and to notify her pleasure that he should pass to the service of the King of Spain. He immediately obeyed the command of his Sovereign. Through his influence three regiments of Scottish infantry and three companies of cavalry, together with the fortresses of Guelders, Bruges, and Lierre, embraced the Spanish cause. In recompense of these services, and of his heroic defence of Lierre against the French, commanded by the Duke of Alençon in person, the Duke of Parma offered him 70,000 ducats, but he would accept of nothing.

In 1582 Colonel Semple passed into Spain. Philip II. availed himself of him, to send to Scotland the succours of money which he gave to the Catholic missionaries in that kingdom; he also employed him in several confidential missions, and especially in the secret correspondence with the Catholic nobility of Scotland. In 1588, the Duke of Parma sent him on a secret mission to James, King of Scotland, to induce him, by the offer of aid in men and money, to declare war against Elizabeth of England. The King appeared to favour the design until the miscarriage of the Armada; but he then ordered the Colonel to be apprehended, and appointed for his prison the uppermost apartment of a house seven storeys high, in Edinburgh. That the Catholics might not be

[1] " Register of the Privy Council," vol. ii. p. 229.

able to liberate him, the King placed a guard of 400 men around the house, and ordered that four sentinels should always remain in the Colonel's room, and not lose sight of him by day or night. Notwithstanding these precautions, God delivered him from the death which his enemies had prepared for him. The Countess of Ross, a sister of the Colonel, sent him, by a trusty servant, what appeared to be three large pies, forewarning him that only two were in reality pies, that the third was a silken cord covered with paste. She informed him that he was condemned to die on the following day, after having suffered the torture of the boot, to make him denounce his accomplices; that in consequence, if he wished to save his life, it was necessary that he should make his escape by the window of his prison that night, and that he would find horses ready at the South Gate. The Colonel knew how to avail himself of the means of escape thus offered to him. At night-fall he divided the two pies among the soldiers, and for this kindness they consented to leave him alone while he said his accustomed prayers; he immediately fastened his door, placed his bedstead at the window, and having tied the cord to it, and put on his gloves, he began to descend. On account of his corpulence and the extreme thinness of the cord, his flesh was cut with the most acute pain, and he was on the point of abandoning the cord and letting himself fall to the ground, when his foot struck upon a balcony. After resting for a short time upon it, he reached the ground in safety. He now found himself in a garden, the wall of which, on account of the inequality of the ground, was low inside and high without. Before him was a square (the Grass Market), guarded by soldiers. In this difficulty, with great presence of mind and assisted by the darkness of the night, he resolved to act the drunkard, and throwing himself into a pool which adjoined the enclosure, he purposely besmeared his clothes and face, and bespattered the soldiers with mud; they believed him to be really drunk, and after a few kicks suffered him to pass. Having thus regained his liberty, he had interviews with the Marquis of Hamilton and the Earls of Huntly and Errol, with whom he arranged that the secret correspondence should be continued by Sir David Graham, Baron of Fintry, and Robert Bruce. He thereupon returned to Flanders, and the Duke of Parma gave him a letter of recommendation to the King of Spain, setting forth his great services, and praying his Catholic Majesty to reward him as he deserved. He was consulted on several occasions by the King regarding the manner in which Spain might most efficaciously interfere in the affairs of Scotland and England. The King assigned him considerable sums of money as pensions and salaries, which he in part accepted, as he was now deprived of his patrimony; but these pensions were so irregularly paid that he was often reduced to great want. He married, in 1593, Dona Maria de Ledesma, widow of Don Juan Perez de Alizaga, and daughter of Don Juan de Ledesma, member of the "Council of the Indies." By her he had two daughters, one of whom married, the other entered into religion.

As the salaries of the Colonel were not paid, his arrears amounted to a very considerable sum, and seeing no other way of obtaining payment, he asked His Catholic Majesty to grant him, as an equivalent, the house known by the name of Jacomotrezo. It had belonged to the celebrated Milanese artist Jacomo or Jacobo de Trezo—the same who erected the beautiful tabernacle in the Church of the Escurial—and his heirs had sold it to the King. On the 13th of December 1613, the house of Jacomotrezo together with its title-deeds, &c., were delivered over to the Colonel, as payment for 175,256 reals, at which the house was legally valued. The site was 25,348 square feet in extent, and the measurements of the frontage in the streets of *Chinchilla, Jacomotrezo*, and *La Salud*, were respectively 139,159, and 165 feet. The house was in a ruinous condition, and, in order to repair it, the Colonel had to contract a debt of 200,000 reals.

Grieved at the state to which he saw the Catholic religion reduced in his native country, the Colonel at this time formed the design of founding a College for the education of missionaries, to perpetuate the true faith in the Kingdom of Scotland. At his entreaty the King of Spain, Philip IV., wrote in 1625, to Pope Urban VIII., praying him to grant an annual rent of 38,000 reals from ecclesiastical benefices, to assist in founding and endowing a College for that object. The foundation was to be made in Madrid, in the house of the Colonel. The Holy Father thought it more convenient that the foundation should be made in Rome; but the Colonel proved in his answer, by reasons founded on experience, that it would be more useful in Madrid, and besought His Holiness to accede to the desires of His Catholic Majesty. On the 10th of May 1627, was executed the deed of foundation, an authentic copy of which exists in the Archives of the College, in Valladolid. On the 17th of June of the same year, the Pope addressed a brief to the Colonel, in which he gave him his apostolic benediction, congratulated him on the foundation of the College, and on the good fortune which he had had, of being brought up in the Court of Mary Stuart; and he prayed Almighty God to reward with eternal happiness his great virtues and merits, of which he had been fully informed by George Conn.

The foundation of the College closed the active life of the Colonel. His health was then very delicate, and in the following years it gradually declined until he was confined to bed, and deprived of the use of his hands and feet. On the 20th of February 1633, he made his last will, in which he confirmed the foundation and endowment of the College. He ordered that it should never contain more than twelve students, and that they should be drawn from the nobility of Scotland, with a preference for his own family.[1]

Philip II. in his letter to Don B. de Mendoca observes that in spite of the zeal in his service manifested by the Colonel, "he is nevertheless extremely Scotch."[2] He died in his

[1] Cf. Catholic Directory, 1873. Conn, De Duplici Statu Religionis apud Scotos, p. 144, 145. Valladolid MSS., Blairs College, Aberdeenshire. During the lifetime of the Colonel some Scottish youths had come to Spain, with the intention of preparing themselves for the missions of their native country. These he maintained at his own expense. In 1639 the foundation of the College was approved by the King in Cortes, but some years passed before any students arrived.

[2] Teulet, vol. viii. p. 582.

house of Jacomotrezo on the 1st of March 1633, at the age of eighty-seven.[1]

A brother of Colonel Semple, Gilbert, lost his life in the wars in Flanders. His sister Helen sought refuge in Belgium, being reduced to a state of great poverty. She is thus described in a letter addressed by F. M'Quhirrie, to Father General, 6th October 1601.

"The bearer of this letter to your Paternity has always been among the most zealous of our friends, and, for years past, she has rendered us constant assistance and encouragement. She has adhered to the Catholic faith so constantly and resolutely that this, and the good offices which she has rendered to us, have exposed her to great injuries and sufferings, to imprisonment and danger of death, and at last being obliged to seek safety in exile from her native land, she is taking refuge with your Paternity." [2]

F. Hugh Semple, S.J., a relative of Colonel Semple, was born in 1596, entered the Society at Toledo in 1615, and was esteemed an eminent linguist and profound mathematician. He died rector of the Scotch College, Madrid, September 29, 1654, at 58.[3]

The Semples remained Catholics till 1680, when Francis Lord Sempill made profession of the reformed religion and took his seat in Parliament, where none of his ancestors had sat since the reign of Queen Mary.

HAMILTON.

Lord Claud Hamilton, the youngest son of the Duke of Chatellerault, was received into the Church by Fr. James Tyrie, S.J., in 1580. (See above, p. 359 and 360.)

James Hamilton, styled "Master of Paisley," son and heir apparent of Claud (Hamilton) 1st Lord Paisley, by Margaret,

---

[1] Teulet., Papiers d'Etat, vol iii. p. 582.

[2] Archives of the Society of Jesus, Latin MSS.

[3] For his writings see Father de Backer's Biblioth. des Ecrivains, S.J. He is also briefly referred to in a letter of Father Christopher Mendoza, dated from Madrid, 1675, as residing in that city. (See F. Richard Cardwell's Collection of Transcripts from MSS., S.J., Brussels Archives, vol. iii. p. 649, Stonyhurst, MSS.; also Oliver.)

daughter of George (Seton) 6th Lord Seton, being P.C. and Gent. of the Bedchamber to James VI., obtained in 1600 the office of sheriff of Co. Linlithgow to him and his heirs male, and in 1601, a grant of the *lands* of Abercorn, &c., in that Co., subsequently erected into a free Barony. In 1604 he was on the Commission which treated of a proposed union of Scotland with England. On 10th July 1606 he was created Lord Paisley, Hamilton, &c., and Earl of Abercorn (Co. Linlithgow), to him and his heirs male whatever. He married Marion, first da. of Thomas (Boyd), 5th Lord Boyd, by Margaret, da. of Sir Mathew Campbell of Loudoun. He died at Monkton, 23d March, and was buried 29th April 1618, in the Abbey Church, Paisley, aged 43. His widow died in the Canongate, Edinburgh, 26th August 1632, and was buried 13th September, with her husband.

James Hamilton, Earl of Abercorn, succeeded to his father's peerage in Scotland in 1618, and in 1621 he succeeded his grandfather as *Lord of Paisley*. Being a Roman Catholic, he was excommunicated by the General Assembly of the Church of Scotland and ordered out of the kingdom. He died about 1670. ("The Genealogist," Jan. 1884.)

JOHN LORD HUME.

In September 1565 the following letter was addressed to Lord Hume by Pope Pius IV.

"To our beloved son, the noble Lord John Hume.

"Beloved son and nobleman, health, &c. — We were delighted at the information brought by our Venerable Brother the Bishop of Dunblane, sent as ambassador to us by your most Serene Queen, who told us about many of the noblemen of your country, and regarding yourself in particular, described your resolution and perseverance in God's service, and in the defence of the Catholic religion, and your loyalty to the Queen. This disposition towards our holy religion, and fidelity to those who bear rule, are due alike from all men, but are particularly conspicuous in men of high rank. We congratulate you on the praise and honour you have thus won in the opinion of men, and you may look for much greater rewards from God; and since, by God's blessing, there is every hope of improvement in the condition of that valued kingdom, we entreat your Lordship to persevere in your efforts in the service of the Catholic religion and of the State. By so doing you will earn our deep gratitude, and our prayers to God for the furtherance of all your wishes.[1]

"Given at Rome, at St Mark's, under the Fisherman's Ring, Sept. 25, 1565; in the sixth year of our Pontificate." [2]

LORD JAMES ELPHINSTON.

Described in Burghley's list as "Neutral," became a Catholic before 1605. (See above, pp. 279, 282.)

LORD EGLINTON was also a Catholic.

Sir Charles Cornwallis in his letter to the Privy Council, 10th June 1609, refers to a list of Scottish Catholics "containing 27 Earles and Barones, and 240 Knights and Gentlemen, Lords of Signories and Tenants that are of that Affection." (Sir Ralph Winwood's Memorials, vol. iii. p. 52; cf. Registers of Privy Council of Scotland, vol. vi.; Spotiswood, 502-13.)

---

[1] In 1603. Lord Hume (il baron di Hume) is described as a zealous Catholic by the Nuntio in Paris. (Archiv. Vatic. Francia, vol. xlviii. p. 31.)

[2] Rome, Barberini MSS., xxxi. 10.

ALPHABETICAL INDEX.

Abercromby, John, 312, 313
Abercromby, Fr. Robert, 226, 236, 261, 265, 269, 280, 285, 290
Ady, 198
Albany, Regent, 3
Allen, Cardinal, 174
Anderson, Fr. Patrick, 281, 290-296, 314, 316, 317-347
Angus, Archibald, sixth Earl of, 4, 18
Angus, David, seventh Earl of, 184, 189, 210
Angus, William, tenth Earl of, 220, 223, 228, 229, 231, 290, 296, 357
Anne of Denmark, Queen, 218, 262-267, 272
Argyll, Archibald, fourth Earl of, 20
Argyll, Archibald, fifth Earl of, 34, 39, 50, 53, 55, 61, 101, 105, 106, 113
Argyll, Colin, sixth Earl of, 120, 124, 134, 154, 177, 189
Argyll, seventh Earl of, 224, 356
Argyll, Countess of, 108, 116
Arran, *see* Hamilton
Athole, John, fourth Earl of, 50, 101, 134-137
Aubigny, Duke of Lennox, Esme Stuart, 136-138, 160, 163, 171, 177, 179-183, 186

Balfour, James, 103
Balfour, Robert, 196
Balnaves, Henry, 26, 27, 41
Barlow, Dr, 9
Beaton, David, Cardinal Archbishop of St Andrews, 11, 12, 16, 17, 19, 20, 21
Beaton, James, Archbishop of St Andrews, 4
Beaton, James, Archbishop of Glasgow, 7
Beaton, John
Bedford, Duke of, 116
Bellenden, Sir John, 101
Boniton, Wood, Laird of, 228, 266, 269, 273
Bothwell, James, fourth Earl, 104, 113, 114, 117, 119-125

Borthwick, Lord, 50
Bothwell, Francis Stewart, Earl of, 216
Bothwell, Lady, 121-124
Bowes or Bovis, 183, 227
Boyd, Lord, 189
Boyd, Alexander, 317
Brown, John, Laird of Lochhill, 309, 311
Brunston, Laird of, 23, 24, 25
Buccleugh, Laird of, 20
Buchan, Earl of, 154
Buchanan, George, 130
Burgoigne or Bourgoing, 214

Caithness, George, third Earl of, 50, 171, 177
Campbell, Friar John, 297
Cassillis, Earl of, 24, 25, 50
Castelli, Julius Cæsar, 180
Cecil, Sir William, 44, 49, 56, 274
Chalmer, 196
Chalmers, David, 106, 113
Cheyne, Dr James, 197
Chisholm, Sir James, 223
Chisholm, William, Bishop of Dunblane, 70, 71, 75, 94, 104, 114, 124
Christie, Fr. George, 261
Clement VIII., Pope, 355
Coldingham, John, Prior of, 87, 90
Colville, John, 279
Crawford, David, Earl of, 189, 193, 216, 217, 351
Crawfurd, Thomas, of Kilburnie, 120
Crichton, Fr. Andrew, 290, 296, 314
Crichton, Robert, Bishop of Dunkeld, 70, 71, 75, 82, 200
Crichton, Fr. William, 78, 79, 181-183, 197, 198, 222, 226, 241, 281, 283
Croft, Sir James, 41, 43

Darnley, Henry, King of Scotland, 99. 100-107, 117 *et seq.*
Davison, 212
Douglas, George, 126
Dunglas, Patrick, 196
Dury, Fr. John, 204, 205.

INDEX

Eckersdorff, Baron, John of, 313
Elizabeth, Queen of England, 39, 41, 42, 47, 56, 58, 92, 93, 100, 105, 107, 120, 129, 133, 187, 189, 198, 206, 209, 211-217
Elphinston, Fr. George, 279, 282
Elphinston, Lord James, 267, 279, 282
Elphinston, Sir William, 310
Errol, George Hay, Earl of, 64, 107, 147, 204, 216, 217, 220, 223-225, 229-233, 274, 290, 354, 357, 361
Erskine, Alexander, 113
Erskine, of Dun, 32
Evers, Sir Ralph, 22

Fintry, Graham of, 185, 190, 198, 199, 200, 220, 353, 370
Fleming, Count, 301
Fleming, Prior Malcolm, 94

Galway, Andrew, 196
Gladstanes, Alexander, 298
Glammis, Lord, 189
Glencairn, Earl of, 18, 32, 34, 53
Gordon, Lord Adam, 104
Gordon, George, fourth Earl of Huntly, 14, 17, 19, 53, 60, 83-90
Gordon, George, fifth Earl of Huntly, 86, 91, 113, 115, 117, 120, 124, 139, 189, 193, 216, 217, 218, 220, 221, 224, 225, 229, 231-233, 238, 256, 260, 262, 267, 290, 354
Gordon, Fr. James, of Huntly, 197-206, 222, 224, 225, 228, 232-260, 281, 296
Gordon, John, 84-86, 104
Gordon, Sir Patrick, 223, 224
Gouda, Fr. Nicolas de, 63 *et seq.*
Gowrie, Earl of Ruthven, 183-186
Gray, Lord, 171
Gray, Master of, 185, 186, 189, 190, 192, 193, 209-210

Hamilton, Alexander, 196
Hamilton, Archibald, 196
Hamilton, Lord Claud, 208, 358, 360
Hamilton, Gavin, Commendator of Kilwinning, 106
Hamilton, James, Earl of Abercorn, 359, 373]
Hamilton, James, Earl of Arran, 15, 20, 21, 32, 42, 50, 53, 91, 95, 101, 102, 103-107, 359, 373
Hamilton, John, Archbishop of St Andrews, 31, 34, 49, 50, 71, 82, 107, 116, 123, 129
Hay, Fr. Edmund, 64, 65, 66, 69, 72, 78, 115, 198, 206
Hay, Fr. John, 141

Henry VIII. King of England, 9, 10, 11, 12
Hertford, Lord, 21, 23
Holt, Fr. William, 166, 188, 193, 194, 201, 206.
Home, George Home, Earl of Dunbar, 189, 288, 296
Howard, Lord William, 9, 10, 11
Hume, Lord, 177, 230

Ingram, Fr. John, 353

James V. King of Scotland, 4, 9, 10, 11, 12
James VI., 116-129, 130, 133 *et seq.*

Kennedy, Hew, 92
Kent, Earl of, 213
Keir, Master Thomas, 86
Ker, Lord George, 220
Kerr or Keir, Alexander, 87
Kerr of Cessfurd, 168
Kerr of Ferniehurst, 171
Killigrew, 120, 212
Kirkaldy of Grange, 23, 55, 125, 131
Knox, John, 26, 32, 33-39, 41, 43, 49, 51, 60, 61, 65

Lang, James, 196
Law, Bishop of Orkney, 289
Lennox, Lord d'Aubigny, Duke of, 136, 138, 160, 163, 171, 177, 179, 180-183, 186
Lennox, Countess of, 100, 133
Lennox, Matthew, fourth Earl of, 20, 30, 95, 100, 126, 129, 130
Leslie, John, Bishop of Ross, 7, 54, 85 *et seq.*, 103, 113-115, 117, 123, 134, 210
Leslie, William, 349
Lethington, *see* Maitland
Lindsay, Patrick, Lord, 60, 104, 112, 113, 117, 123, 124
Lindsay, Fr. Roger, 290, 296
Lindsay, Sir Walter, of Balgawies, 351

Macbreck, Fr. John, 314
MacQuhirrie, Fr. Alexander, 228, 261, 268, 269, 276, 277
Maitland, William, of Lethington, 29, 43, 55, 92, 100, 101, 124, 131, 193
Mar, Earl of, 130, 184, 189
Mary of Guise, 10, 31, 33, 39, 45, 47
Mary Stuart, Queen of Scotland, 33, 47, 52, 54-56, 60, 62-95, 104, 105, 106, 113, 114, 118 *et seq.*, 210 *et seq.*, 214
Maxwell, John, seventh Lord, Earl of Morton, 168, 204, 216, 230

INDEX. 377

Maxwell, Sir John, Lord Herries, 105, 117, 189, 216, 230
Melville, Andrew, 225
Melville, Sir James, 196
Mondovi, Bishop of, 114
Montgomery, Hugh, Earl of Eglinton, 123, 171, 177, 299, 374
Montrose, William, Earl of, 279, 281
Moray, James Stuart, Earl of, 39, 49, 53, 54, 60-67, 81-102, 104, 113, 115, 116, 118, 120, 125, 129 *et seq.*
Moret, Count, 93
Mortimer, Fr. George, 226
Morton, James Douglas, Earl of, 34, 117, 123, 124, 131, 132, 135, 139, 154, 165, 166
Morton, Fr. John, 226
Murdoch, Fr. William, 226, 236, 261

Norfolk, Duke of, 14, 43, 46

Ogilvie, Fr. John, 296, 297, 298
Ogilvie, James, Lord, 84, 171
Ogilvie, Fr. William, 226, 228
Oysel, H. Cloutin, Sieur d', 43, 44, 46, 55

Panter, David, Bishop of Ross, 6
Paulet, Sir Amias, 212
Persons, Fr. Robert, 182
Philip II., King of Spain, 77, 97, 182, 195, 215
Pius V., Pope, 114

Randolphe, Thomas, 58, 61, 62
Reid, Robert, Bishop of Orkney, 6, 17
Rinaldus, John, 66
Rizzio, David, 93
Robb, Fr. John, 316

Rothes, Master of, 23
Ruthven, Patrick, Lord, 112

Sadler, Sir Ralph, 11-13, 24, 41, 43
Sampiretti, George, 222
Sandiland, Sir James, 52
Semple, Lord Robert, 367
Semple, Colonel, 367-368
Seton, Lord Alexander, 177-229, 259, 267, 278, 281, 363
Seton, George, fifth Lord, 123, 125, 171, 172, 177-181, 186, 256, 257, 362
Seton, Fr. James, 236, 278, 279, 282
Seymour, Lord, 30
Sinclair, Henry, Bishop of Ross, 7, 67, 70, 71, 94
Sinclair, John, Bishop of Brechin, 104
Smeton, Thomas, 139
Somerset, Duke of, 27, 29, 30
Spottiswood, John, Archbishop of Glasgow, 298, 301 *et seq.*
Strachan, Mr, 271
Stuart, *see* Mary, Darnley
Stuart, John, Captain of the Queen's Guard, 86, 189
Stuart, Captain Robert, 135

Throckmorton, Sir Nicolas, 47, 56, 101, 102, 103
Tullibardine, the Laird of, 124, 133, 134
Tyrie, Fr. James, 57, 182, 206, 207

Watts, William, 166, 174
Wharton, Thomas, Lord, 30
Wilson, Stephen, 65, 66, 114
Winter, Admiral, 44, 45
Wyndham, Admiral, 29

www.ingramcontent.com/pod-product-compliance
Lightning Source LLC
Chambersburg PA
CBHW032033220426
43664CB00006B/455